IMAGES
of America

HOPE

I0806481

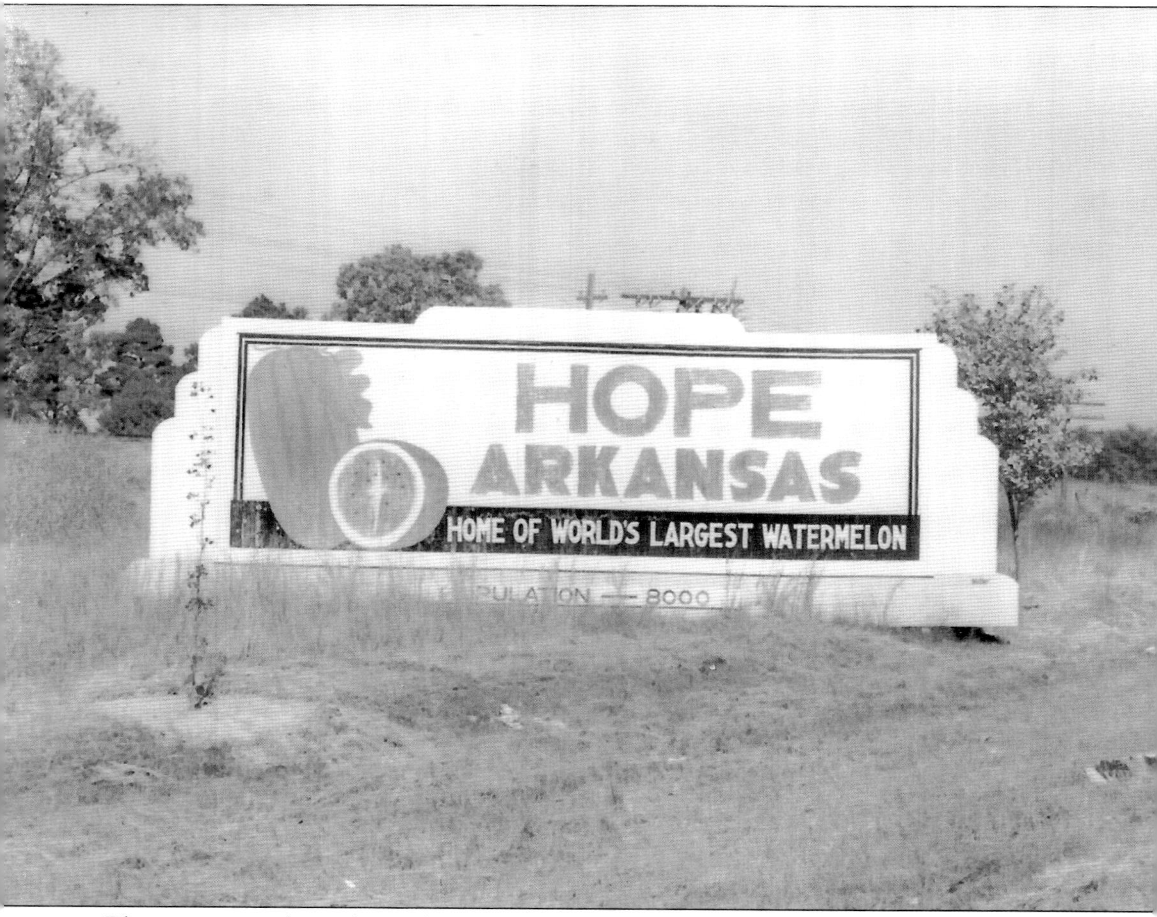

This sign greeted people on the "Broadway of America," U.S. Highway 67, coming into Hope, Arkansas, in the 1940s. By that time, the population of Hope had increased to 8,000 people, and it was the largest town in Hempstead County. From its beginnings in the 1870s, Hope had gained the reputation of being the home of large watermelons. In 1935, a 195-pound melon grown by Oscar D. Middlebrooks and his sons, Arnold and Melvin, received recognition as the world's largest watermelon. The recognition lasted for 45 years. (Courtesy of AHC.)

On the Cover: On August 31, 1945, Arkansas governor Ben Laney visited Hope with world famous sportsman Jack Lamb to view the watermelons grown in Hempstead County. After speaking to the Rotary Club, which met at the Barlow Hotel in downtown Hope, and while holding a large Black Diamond watermelon, Governor Laney poses with the watermelon queens representing the different townships of Hempstead County. (Courtesy of SARA.)

IMAGES
of America

HOPE

Joshua Williams

ARCADIA
PUBLISHING

ISBN 978-0-7385-8596-3

Published by Arcadia Publishing
Charleston, South Carolina

Printed in the United States of America

Library of Congress Control Number: 2009943082

For all general information contact Arcadia Publishing at:
Telephone 843-853-2070
Fax 843-853-0044
E-mail sales@arcadiapublishing.com
For customer service and orders:
Toll-Free 1-888-313-2665

Visit us on the Internet at www.arcadiapublishing.com

To my mom and dad for their ever loving care and support in my efforts in creating this book

Contents

ACKNOWLEDGMENTS

There are many people I would like to thank for their support in this project. I would like to thank the residents and citizens of Hope who have contributed so much to the work that was put into this book. Several took the time to go through their collections of photographs and share them with me along with the stories that went with each image. It was through this process that you truly see the meaning of a local community and how each person and his or her family plays a pivotal role in the formation and maintenance of the community.

I would like to thank the staff at the Southwest Arkansas Regional Archives for helping and supporting me in this endeavor. Thank you, Peggy Lloyd for providing me the time and space to work through the different collections housed at the archives. I particularly would like to thank Gail Martin for her continued patience and service in scanning several different photographs that were too large for my personal scanner and in helping me locate different items within the collection. Also, thanks go to Dr. Wendy Richter, director of the Arkansas History Commission, for allowing me to scan photographs in the collection at SARA in exchange for duplicate scans to be placed on the commission's digital database to help make more people aware of the amazing collections in the state archives and its branches.

Specifically, I would like to thank Mary Nell Turner and Mark Keith for their continued interest in preserving the local history of Hope and Hempstead County. Through their endeavors and support in many different ways, they have helped make this book possible. Also, thanks to my Arcadia editor, Amy Perryman, for her continued diligence and guidance in helping make the publishing process as smooth as possible for this book.

Above all, I would like to thank my parents, Keenan and Peggy Williams, for their continued support and encouragement throughout the whole process. They have instilled in me a love for local history and a sense of passing it on to the next generation.

The images in this volume appear courtesy of friends and families of Hope as noted; the Southwest Arkansas Regional Archives (SARA), a branch of the Arkansas History Commission; the Arkansas History Commission (AHC); and the Hope Visitor Center and Museum (HVCM).

INTRODUCTION

Of all the towns in the United States, one can say the name and someone automatically picks up on the line, "I still believe in a place called Hope." Those words, stated by Bill Clinton in his acceptance speech for the Democratic nomination for president in 1992, brought the town of Hope to the forefront of history. Despite political preferences, the line rings true to the nature and story of Hope, the town. Throughout its history, Hope has always been a place where people have come from all over to make a new life for themselves and to have hope in making a future.

The town began with the Cairo and Fulton Railroad, which established the location where the town was to be located on Prairie De Roan. On February 1, 1872, the first passenger train pulled by the steam engine *Roswell Beebe* pulled into the location of the station being built by railroad employees. James. M. Loughborough was the land commissioner for the Cairo and Fulton and decided that the established stop would be named after his daughter, Hope. A plat of the new town of Hope was then designed, and the first lots were sold on August 28, 1873. One of the first owners of land in the new town was a Civil War veteran from Michigan named Walter Shiver. He built the first house in town near the depot in 1873. On April 8, 1875, the town of Hope was officially incorporated, and the first city officials were elected on May 14.

Hope was truly a major rail hub in the late 19th and early 20th centuries. In 1874, the Cairo and Fulton Railroad was reorganized and the main line became known as the St. Louis, Iron Mountain, and Southern Railroad. By 1902, three other railroad branches intersected in Hope with the St. Louis and San Francisco Line (Frisco) coming into Hope from Oklahoma, the Louisiana and Arkansas Line connecting Hope to Shreveport, Louisiana, and the Arkansas and Louisiana Line, also known as the Nashville branch, connecting the town to Nashville, Arkansas. In 1917, the St. Louis, Iron Mountain, and Southern Railroad, after bankruptcy, was reorganized and changed officially to the Missouri Pacific Railroad Company.

With the formation of this new town came many different gentlemen and families to make new lives. After retiring from the steamboat business in 1876, Capt. Judson T. West moved to Hope. He helped form a bank and lumberyard and later pushed for ways for the community to produce electricity, resulting in a municipally owned utility plant. Nathaniel P. O'Neal moved to Hope around 1908 and helped establish one of the most respected brickyards in the region, using the clay soil in the land south of town. Henry C. Yerger arrived in 1886 and became one of the leading African American educators west of the Mississippi. Each of these men came from a different background yet embodied the dream that the town of Hope inspired.

Reflecting on growing up in Hope in the 1890s, Tom McMath described it as a town unique in every way. Even though it was in the South, it had a western feeling to it since everyone who lived in Hope was originally from some other town across the United States. McMath went on to describe that there were no antebellum traditions in Hope. The town was altogether new, and everyone who lived there was like a pioneer, working hard to build and make a new life. This was the character and dream of Hope.

People from all different walks of life came together and formed churches, civic clubs, and community events. Industries of all types and sizes were established, making Hope a potential place to settle. After several decades of debate, Hope was made the seat of Hempstead County in 1939, and a new courthouse was erected. In 1941, before the beginning of World War II, the federal government purchased large tracts of land north of Hope for the testing of air and ground munitions. Residents on this site had to leave their homes. This brought Hope new residents who were looking for a place to live and jobs for people already there.

Over its history, Hope has been reliant on an agricultural economy. One of the things it is best known for is its large watermelons. In 1935, Oscar D. Middlebrooks and his sons grew the world's largest watermelon at 195 pounds—a record lasting 45 years. The record for growing large watermelons continues to this day with Lloyd Bright growing a watermelon reaching 268.8 pounds in 2005.

Over the past years, different famous people who have impacted the United States have had roots in Hope. With each of these individuals, the dream of the New South town of Hope—that you can become whatever you wish to be despite your background—is reflected in their lives. That has been the nature of the town of Hope. From its beginning as a railroad town, people were coming here to excel in a new enterprise. That thought continues in much of the town today.

In this collection of photographs, I hope to give just a glimpse of the diversity of the town of Hope and its history. The photographs have been divided into chapters focusing on people, community, commerce, celebrations, and celebrities that came out of the community. The town is a product of a New South mentality that embraces much of the industrialism of the North that brought people together from all over the country. At the same time, the municipality displays the charm of a southern town in the Bible Belt, with a friendly atmosphere of everyone knowing his neighbor and people looking out for one another. Above all, it embodies the American Dream: that, whatever their backgrounds, people have the freedom to make new lives and fortunes for themselves.

One

PEOPLE

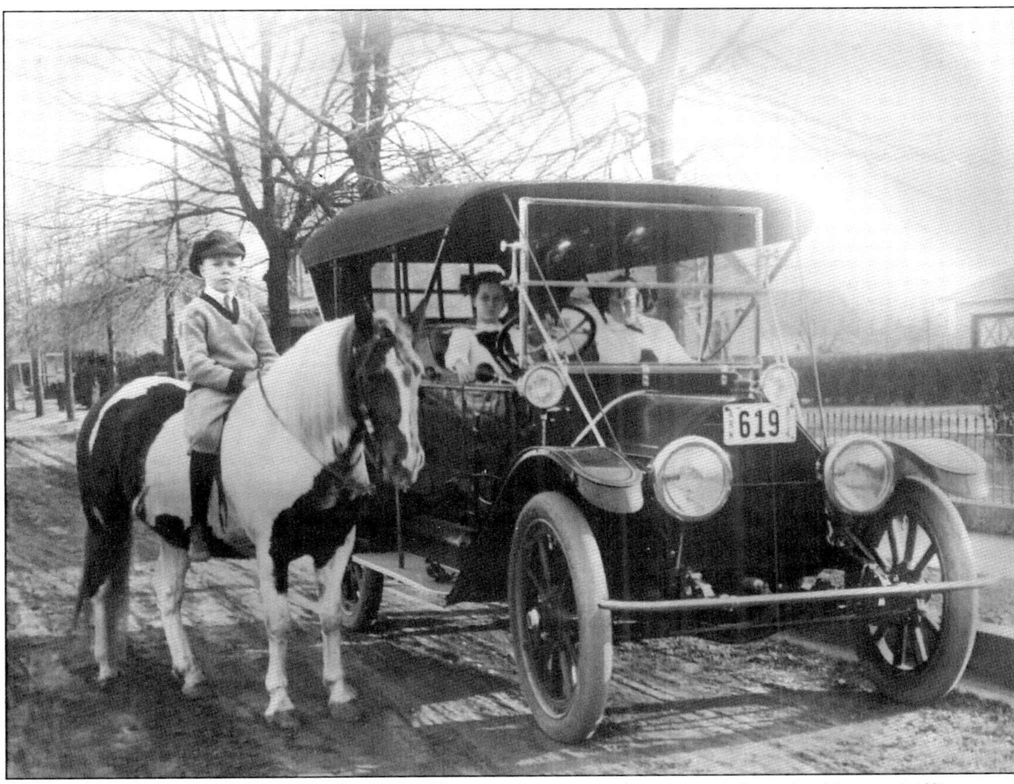

In 1914, Robert M. LaGrone Jr. poses on his pony, next to his sister Marie LaGrone Gilliam and Mary Black Johnson in the automobile. LaGrone said he was probably the only person ever arrested in Hope for speeding on a horse. He was charged a $5 fine and $3.65 in court costs. His father, Robert M. LaGrone Sr., established Citizens National Bank of Hope in 1912. Robert LaGrone Jr. succeeded his father in managing the bank. (Courtesy of SARA.)

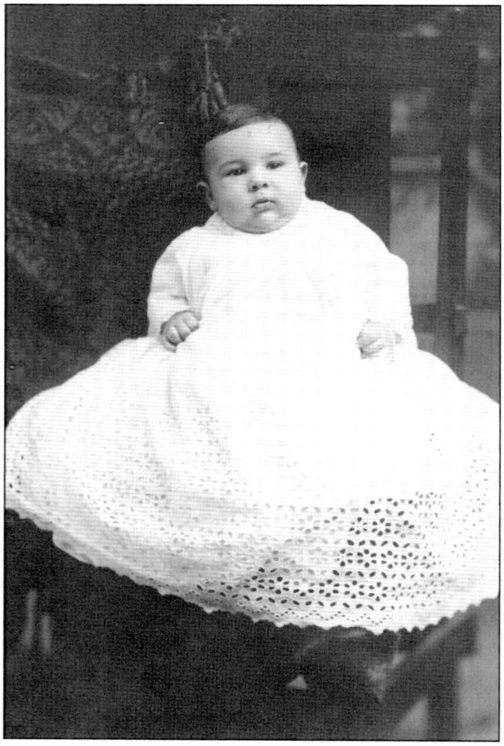

Several families moved to Hope over the course of time. According to the U.S. Census, the population increased from 1,644 residents in 1900 to 3,639 in 1910. This was the largest increase Hope had seen since it was chartered in 1875. With the new families, of course, came their children. Shown in the *c.* 1910 photograph to the left is newborn Newt Bundy, son of Jett and Leon Bundy. He is wearing a child's gown common at the time. Below is a photograph of one of the sons of Rev. William Augustus "Gus" Freeman. Freeman was the pastor of First Baptist Church in Hope from 1902 to 1903. The Freeman family lived in a house on Elm Street near Hatch's blacksmith shop, located at the corner of Elm and Third Streets. (Courtesy of Janice Harrison and First Baptist Church of Hope.)

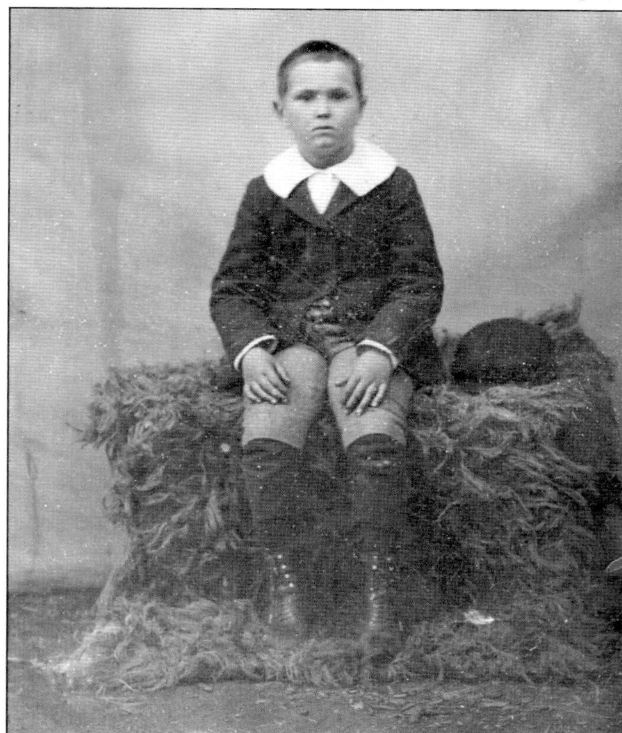

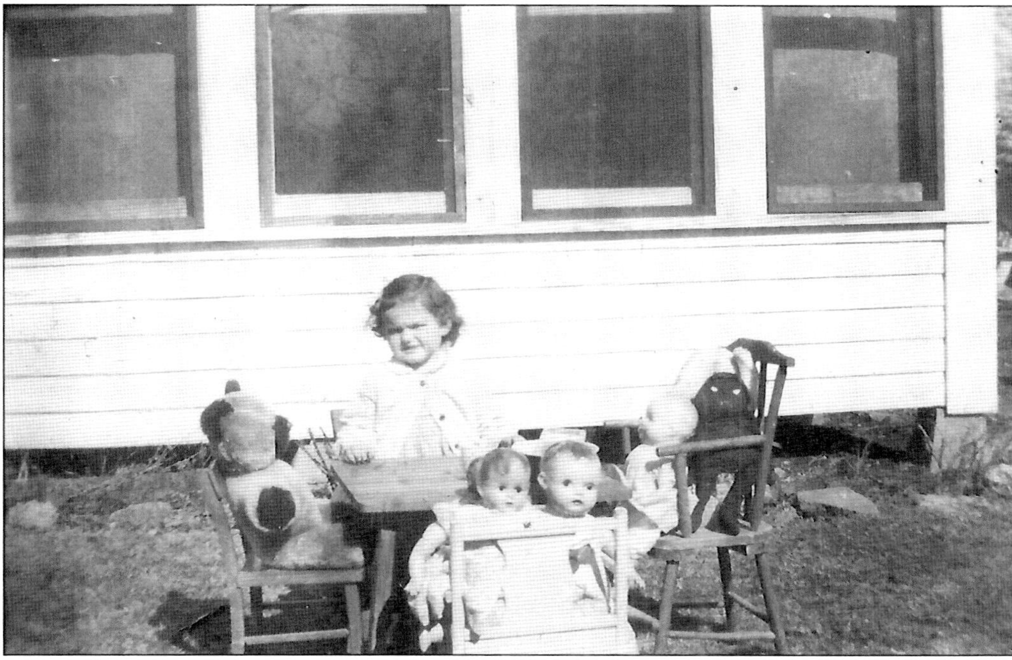

In 1941, several families moved from central Hempstead County to Hope due to the Southwest Proving Ground. The David P. Watkins family purchased property just outside Hope and rebuilt their old home on the new site. Peggy Lloyd was born on April 23, 1943. In 1946, at age three, she enjoys a cup of tea with her friends at her grandparents' rebuilt home. (Courtesy of Peggy Lloyd.)

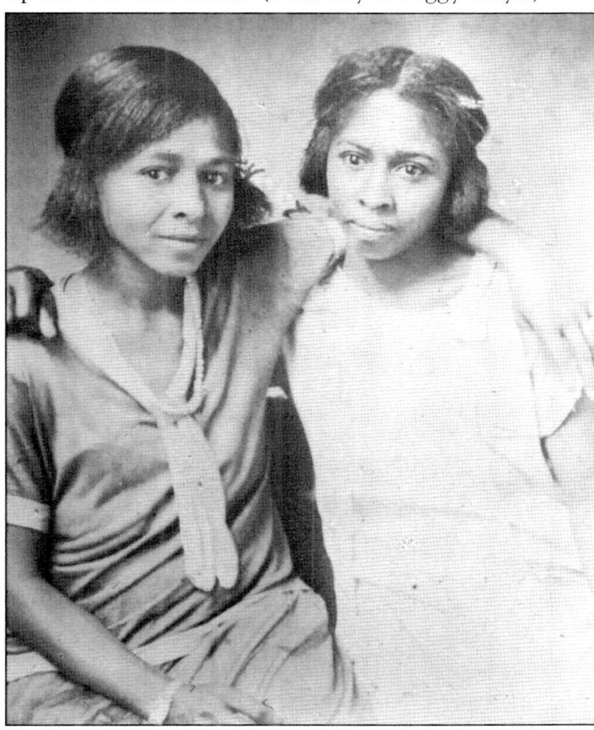

Photographers in Hope would take pictures of different residents. Here are two unidentified young girls posing for the camera around 1925. (Courtesy of Mark Keith.)

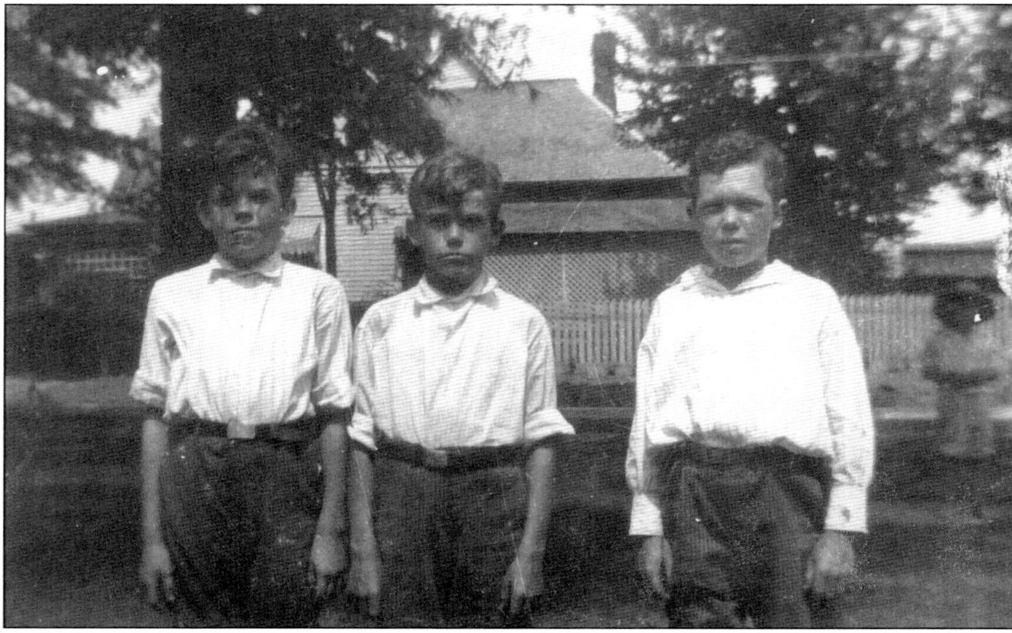

Leon S. Williams moved to Hope from Spring Hill and lived on South Pine Street, a block south of the LaGrone family residence. He had four sons. Shown here in this *c.* 1925 photograph are the three younger Williams boys—Dale (left), Ferrell (center), and Ross. Dale's middle name was LaGrone, after his father's good friend, R. M. LaGrone. (Courtesy of Keenan and Peggy Williams.)

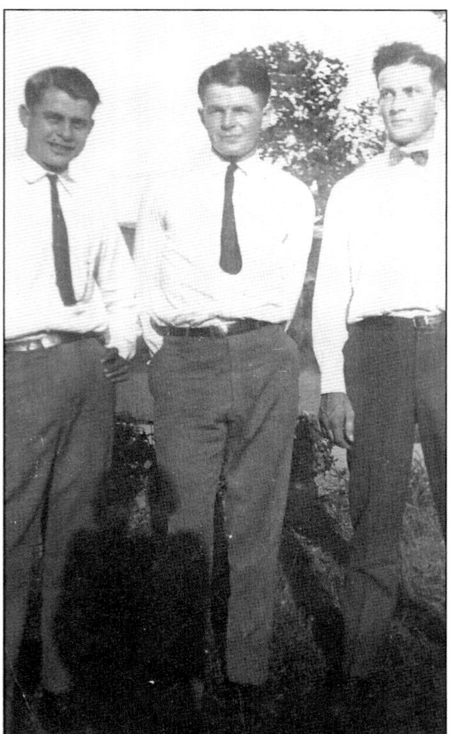

The Shiver family resided in Hope from the town's beginning. John C. Shiver's sons pose in this *c.* 1925 photograph. They are, from left to right, Harry, Ernest, and Jack. John C. Shiver and his son Harry ran a longtime plumbing business for the town. (Courtesy of SARA.)

Rev. Horace Jewell was an early resident of Hope and a Methodist minister. Born in 1832, he died tragically in 1917 after being hit by a train. He joined the Confederate army during the Civil War and served as a chaplain in Grindstead's Regiment from Arkansas. He was once called the most beloved man in Hope. (Courtesy of SARA.)

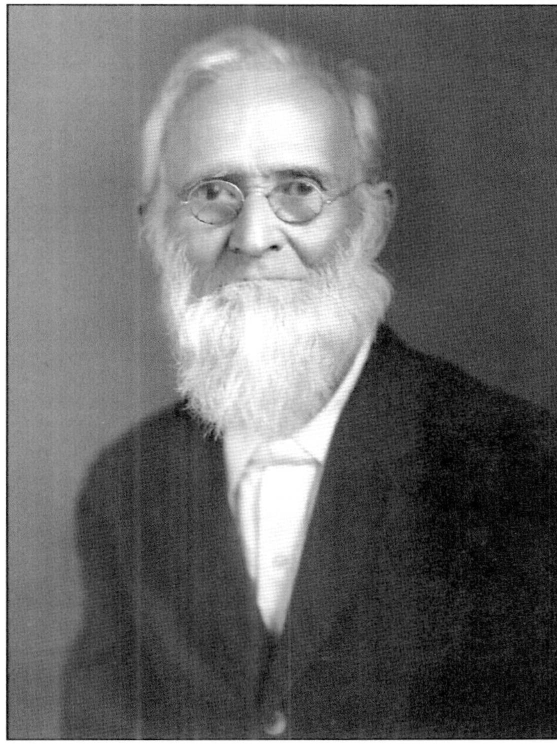

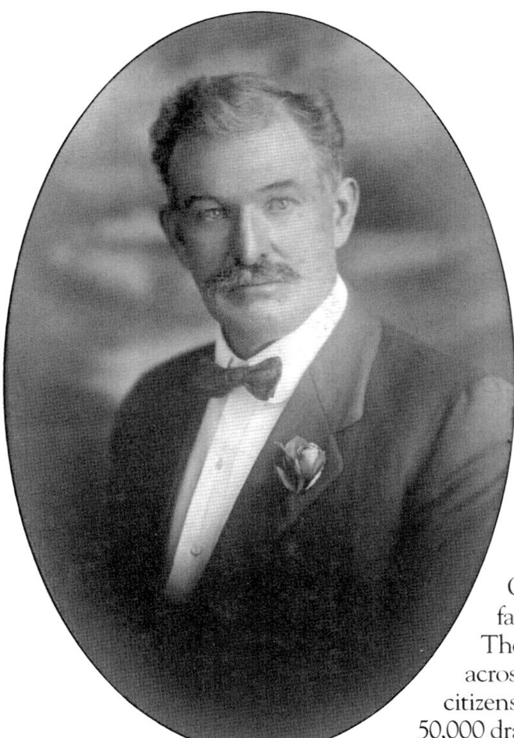

Born in 1870, Nathaniel Paul O'Neal came to Hope from Gurdon, Arkansas, around 1908, when the Gurdon Brick Company was dissolved. He continued a family tradition by establishing the Hope Brick Works. The machine-made bricks from Hope became famous across the region, and the company employed several citizens. By 1920, it was producing 5.5 million bricks and 50,000 drain tiles annually. (Courtesy ofLloyd Paul Powell.)

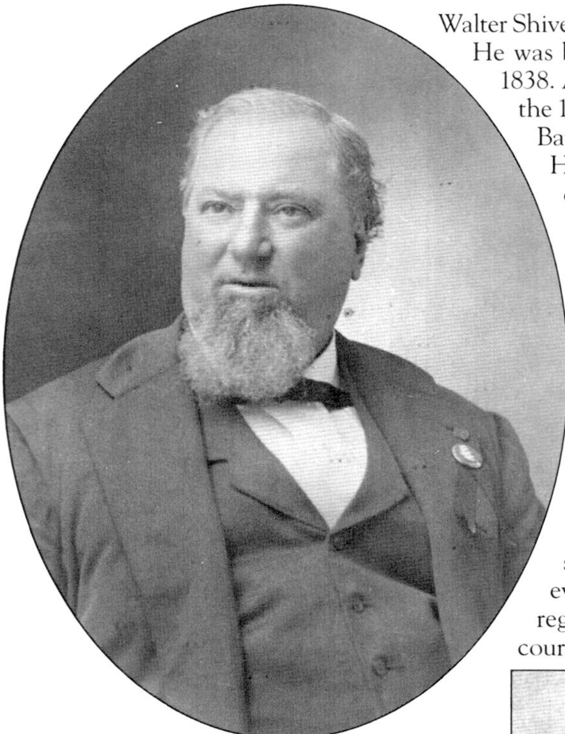

Walter Shiver, above, was one of the Hope's first residents. He was born in Niagara-on-the-Lake, Ontario, in 1838. At the time of the Civil War, he enlisted in the 12th Michigan Infantry and saw service at the Battle of Shiloh and in campaigns in Arkansas. His unit was the first Northern regiment to enter Washington, Arkansas, the Hempstead County seat and the Confederate capital of Arkansas at the end of the war. Shiver returned to Michigan but moved back to Arkansas around 1873 and built the first house in Hope. The photograph to the left was taken while he was attending the national Republican convention for the nomination of William McKinley for president in 1896. One Hope resident, Tom McMath, stated that Shiver was one "of the personalities that gave Hope its flavor in its earliest days." Seen below, Shiver's son John was active in several community events. In the photograph, he is dressed in full regalia of the Knights Templar Order. (Both courtesy of SARA.)

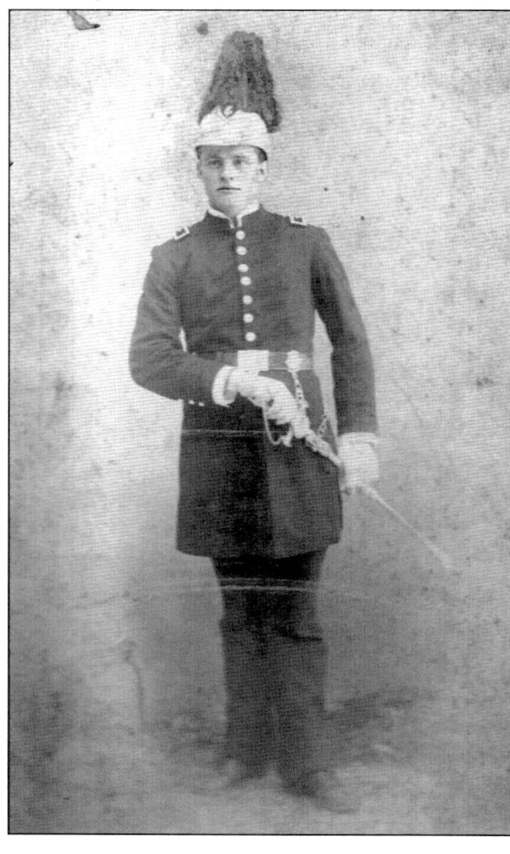

Dale LaGrone Williams was raised in Hope, at his home on South Pine Street. He worked throughout his life in the hardware business, first at Hope Hardware and later at his own hardware, named LaGrone Williams Hardware. His store complemented the various merchants and goods that were sold in the area. This photograph was taken around 1941 for his wedding to Polly Ann Brock. (Courtesy of Keenan and Peggy Williams.)

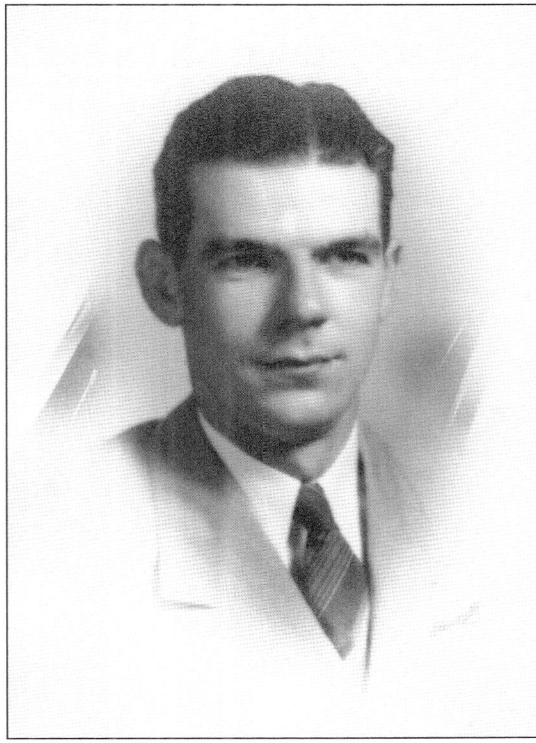

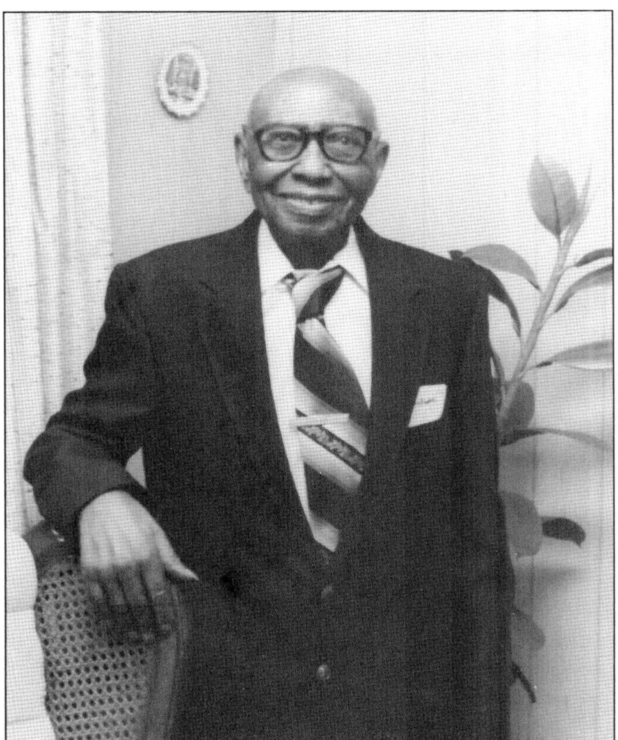

Moses Yerger was born on November 17, 1888, and was a longtime Hope resident. Growing up, he helped his father, who was a sharecropper. Yerger served in World War I and was later an employee at the Hope Water and Light Company. His belief that trust was important to life caused him to be respected throughout the town. Yerger died in 1989 at age 100. (Courtesy of HVCM.)

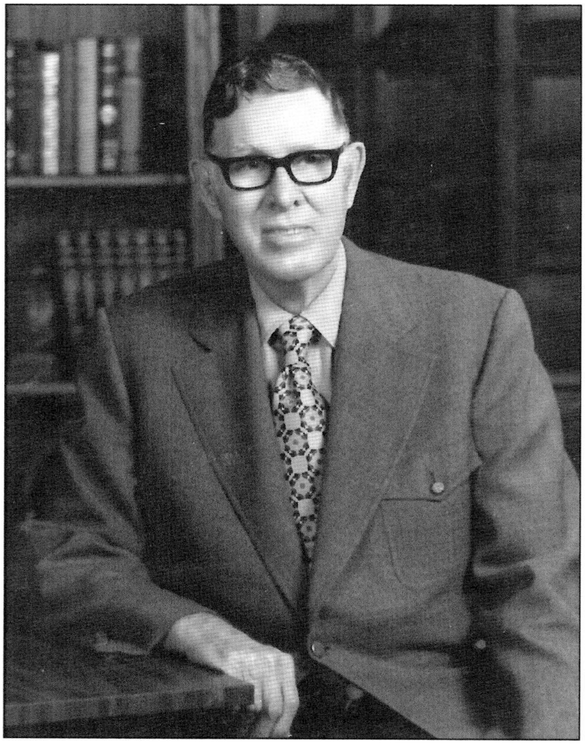

Earl O'Neal was the son of N. P. O'Neal, who founded the Hope Brick Works. Like in many father-son relations, Earl assumed the leadership of his father's business. Earl grew up in Hope and was involved in several athletic ventures at the high school. In 1920, as part of the track team, he broke the state pole vault record of 10 feet 8 inches. (Courtesy of SARA.)

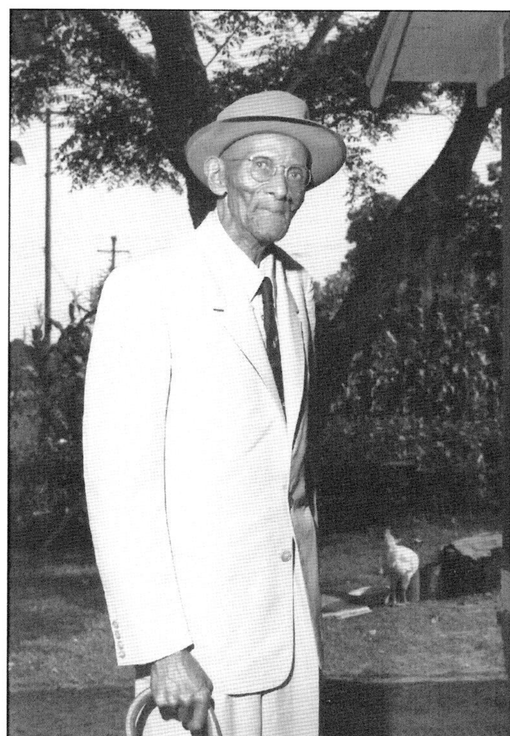

Another long-lived Hope gentleman, Henry Criner was born March 21, 1866, to Levi and Martha Criner. Henry worked around southwest Arkansas until 1921, when he began employment at the Hope Lumber Company. He married Mary Randall of Camden, Arkansas, in 1906, and attended Lonoke Baptist Church. In this 1974 photograph, Henry is 108 years old. (Courtesy of SARA.)

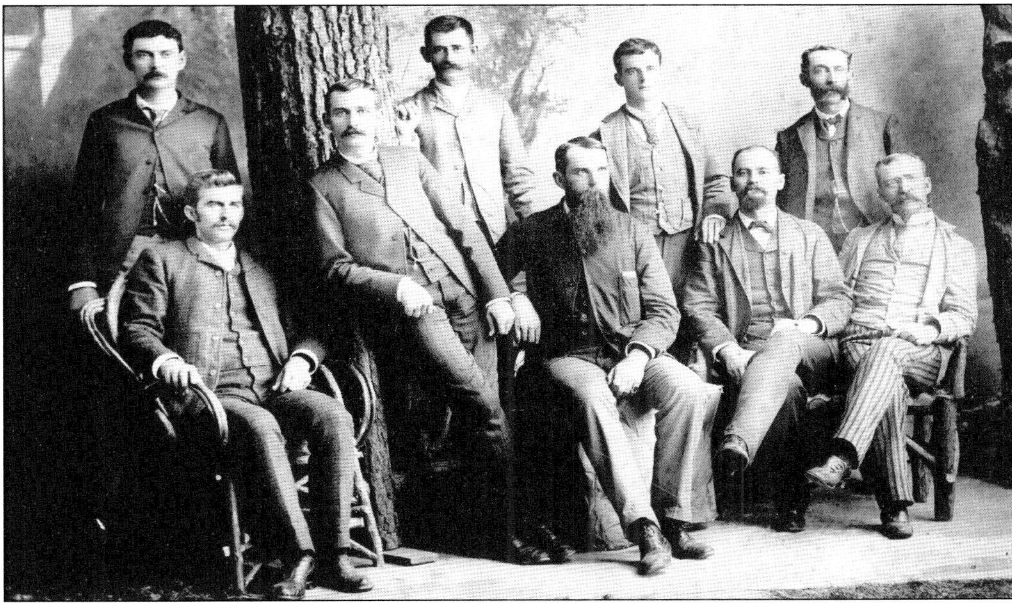

Fraternal societies, like the Freemasons, were popular in the late 19th century. Shown here is an unidentified gentlemen's group in Hope on July 18, 1889, with two officers identified. From left to right are M. V. Shelton, E. W. Davis, J. S. Crim, Tom Elliot, S. K. Young (division superintendent), John C. Shiver, M. B. Copiar (general superintendent), E. F. Hamilton, and L. E. Kittrell. (Courtesy of SARA.)

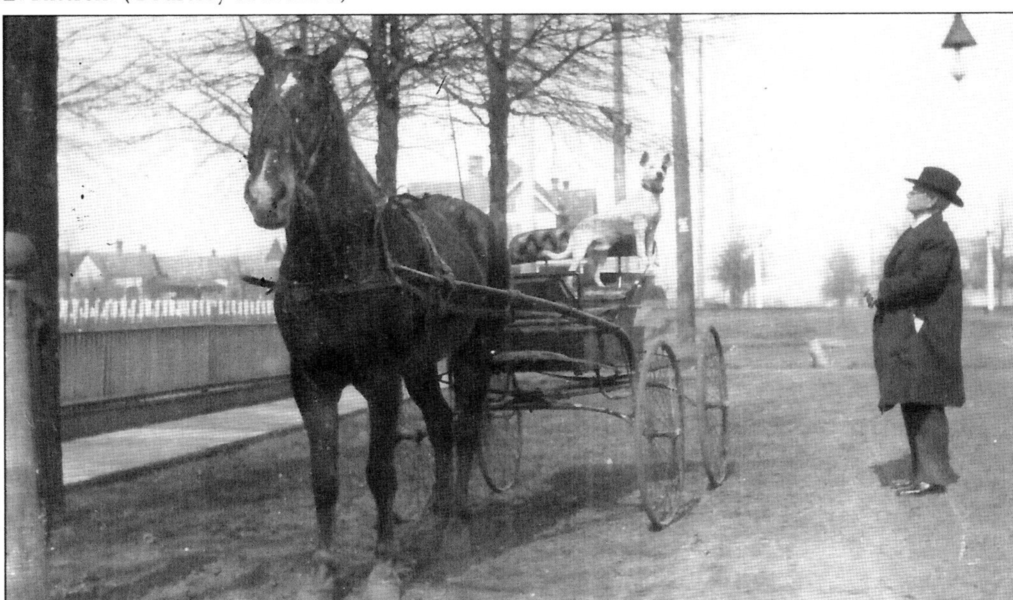

Capt. Judson. T. West was a steamboat captain before moving to Hope in 1876. He organized the Hope Lumber Company, which helped supply lumber to several northern states, and was the president of the town's first bank, the Bank of Hope, established January 2, 1893. He is seen here with his dog at the intersection of South Pine and West Division Streets around 1905. (Courtesy of SARA.)

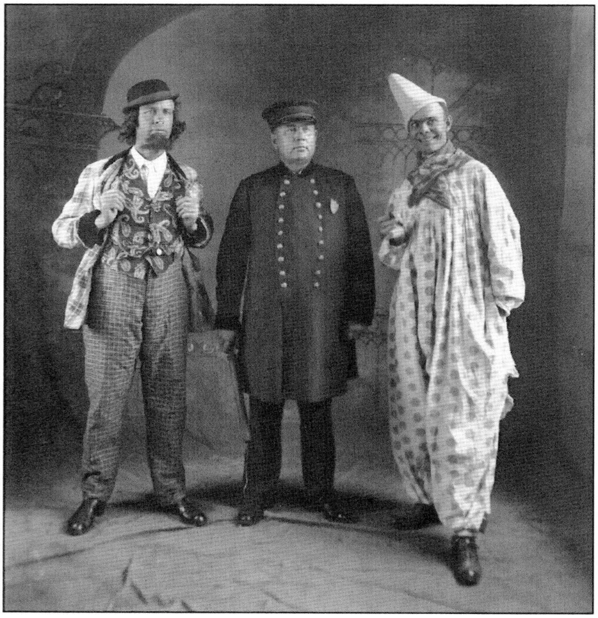

Shipley Studios was one of the major photography studios in Hope from the second decade of the 20th century up through the 1950s. Citizens of Hope and Hempstead County came to the studio to have pictures made. Around 1925, residents, from left to right, Dr. E. Y. Cloud, Ed Stewart, and Reverend Newton pose in costumes for a particular event. (Courtesy of SARA.)

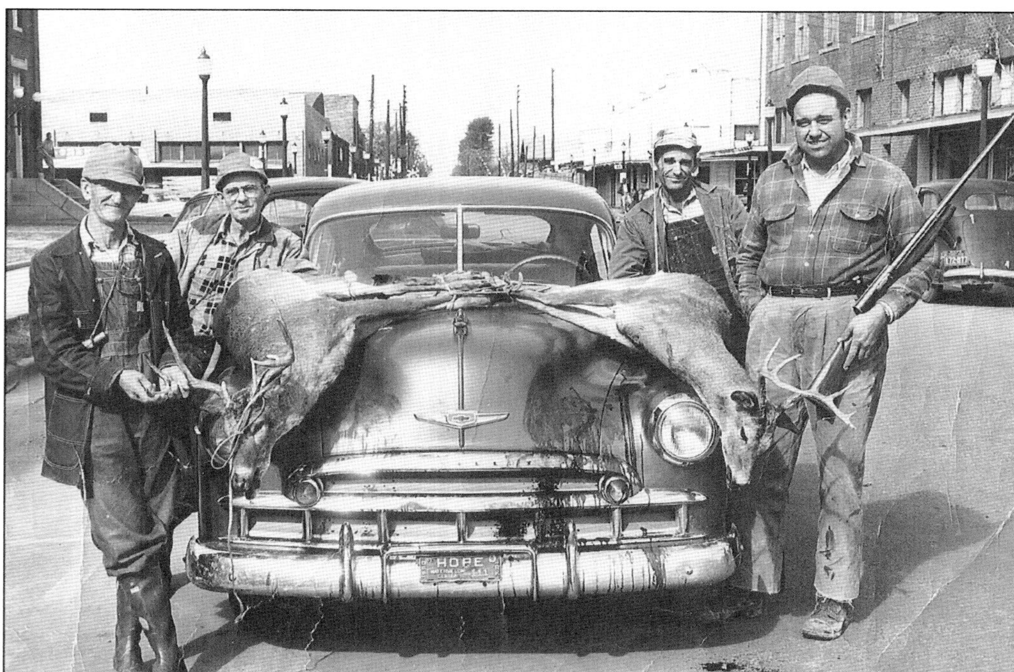

In southwest Arkansas and Hempstead County, hunting has always been a popular pastime for gentlemen. Before World War II, recreational hunting was not as widespread due to farming schedules and larger open fields in a predominantly agricultural economy. In this 1950 photograph in downtown Hope, hunters, from left to right, Frank Turner, Sid Sinyard, Hugh Garner, and Ralph Smith show off their kill of the day. It was Ralph Smith's first deer hunt and Frank Turner's first kill in over 16 years. (Courtesy of Mary Nell Turner.)

With the railroad, Hope was on the corridor of progress, and even the latest fashions could be found in town. Grace Briant Jewell poses in her wedding dress on March 7, 1911. The dress with the large hat is typical of the Edwardian style. Grace married Nicholas Jewell, one of the sons of Rev. Horace Jewell. (Courtesy of SARA.)

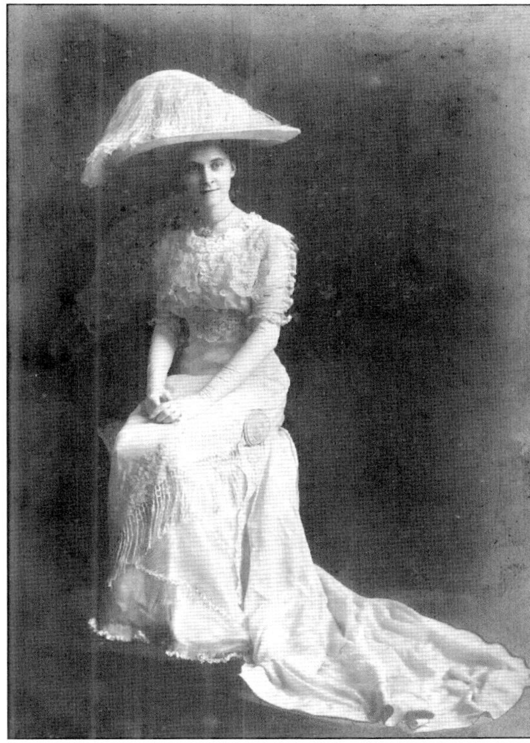

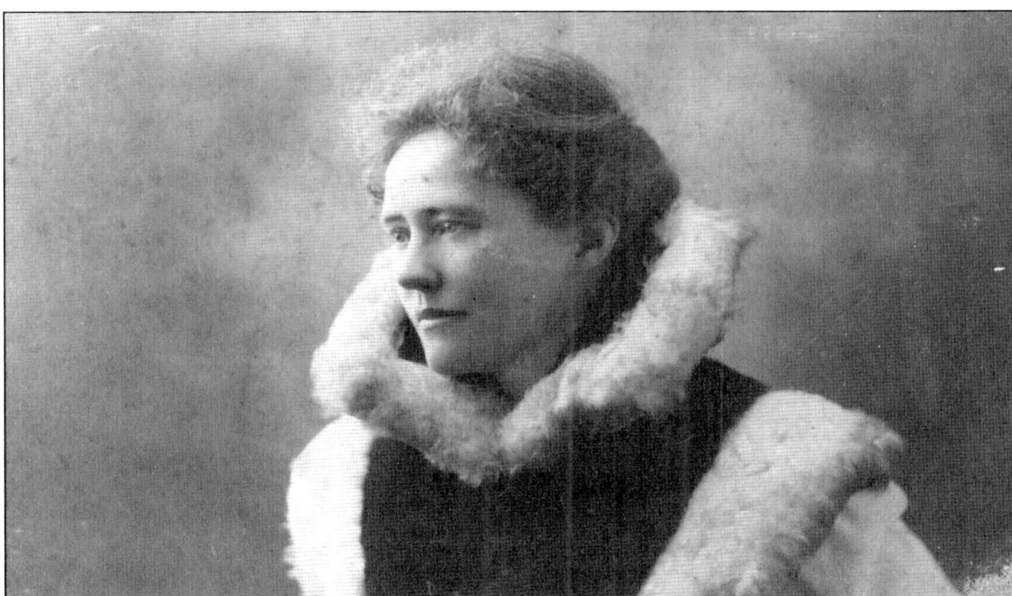

Rosa Bell Barton was the wife of Rev. Levi E. Barton, pastor at First Baptist Church from 1899 to 1900. During his term, Barton went to Virginia and met a "well educated and highly cultured young Virginia woman." Rosa Bell returned with him to Hope, where she became a favorite of the church family and "delighted the people with almost mesmeric spell." (Courtesy of First Baptist Church of Hope)

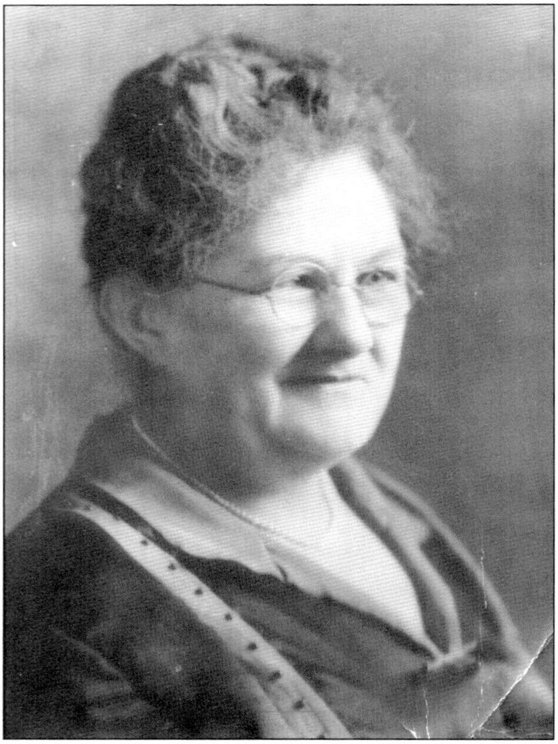

This portrait of Mollie Williams Bundy was taken around 1920. Like many women in Hope and across the United States at that time, she did not have a job outside of the home, but worked full-time taking care of her family and household. (Courtesy of Janice Harrison.)

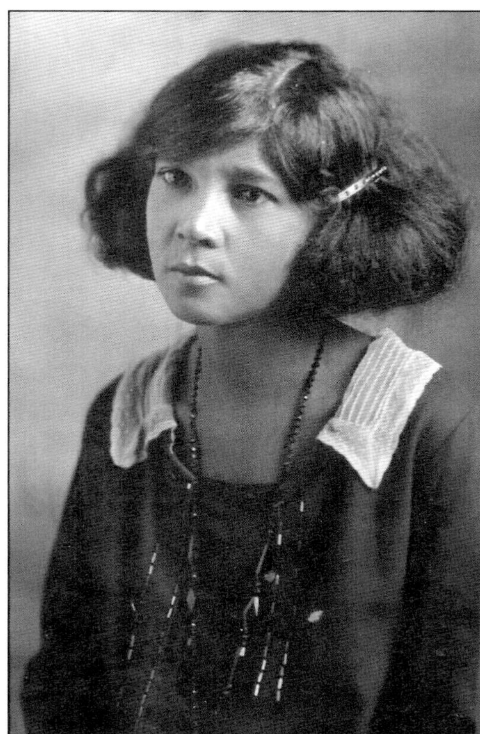

The 1920s brought different fashions to Hope. In this photograph, the young unidentified lady is dressed in the latest design of clothing from that era. Hair for ladies began to be worn short and cut to shoulder length as seen in this photograph. (Courtesy of Mark Keith.)

After World War II, many women in the Hope area began to work at jobs outside of the home. Jett Bundy helped her husband for several years running a bakery in town. Later in life, in the 1950s, she would put together community baskets, known as the Contact Greeting Service, which included donations from local merchants that would be given to new residents of Hope to promote local businesses. (Courtesy of Janice Harrison.)

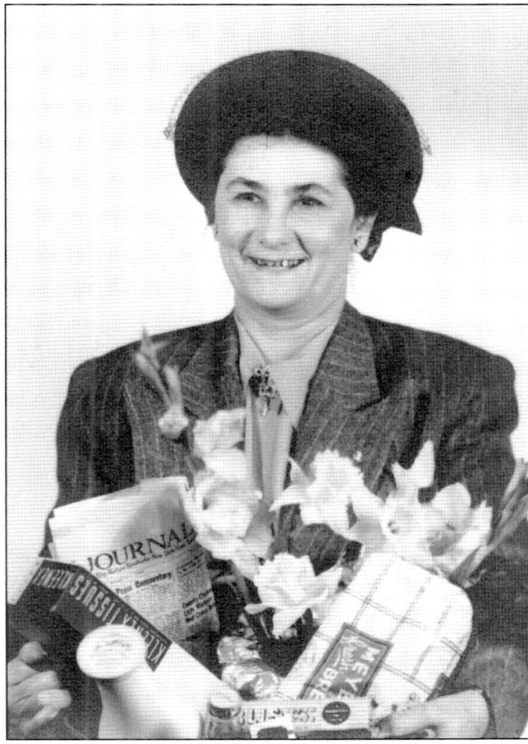

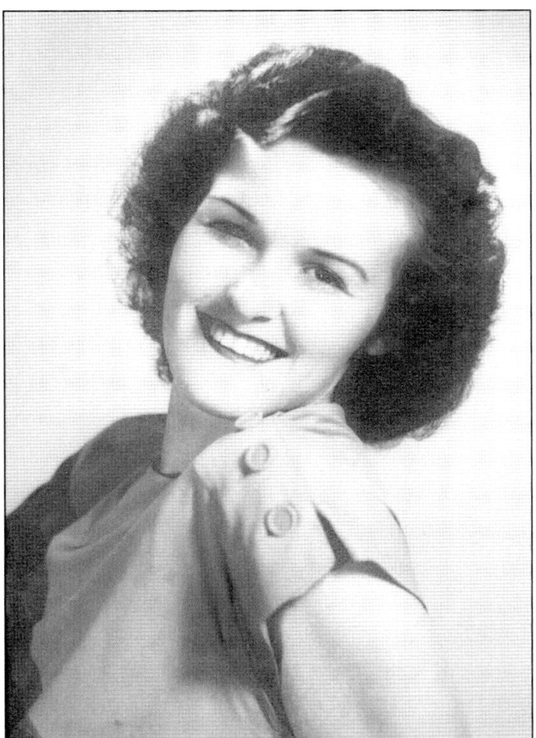

Several young ladies from around Hempstead County came to town during the 1940s. Willie Mae Griffin moved to Hope with the rest of her sisters from their family farm in Columbus, Arkansas. She took a job at Scott's Department Store on Second Street and met her future husband, Arthur "Buddy" McIver, who commented that he "found a million-dollar baby in a five-and-ten-cent store." (Courtesy of Keenan and Peggy Williams.)

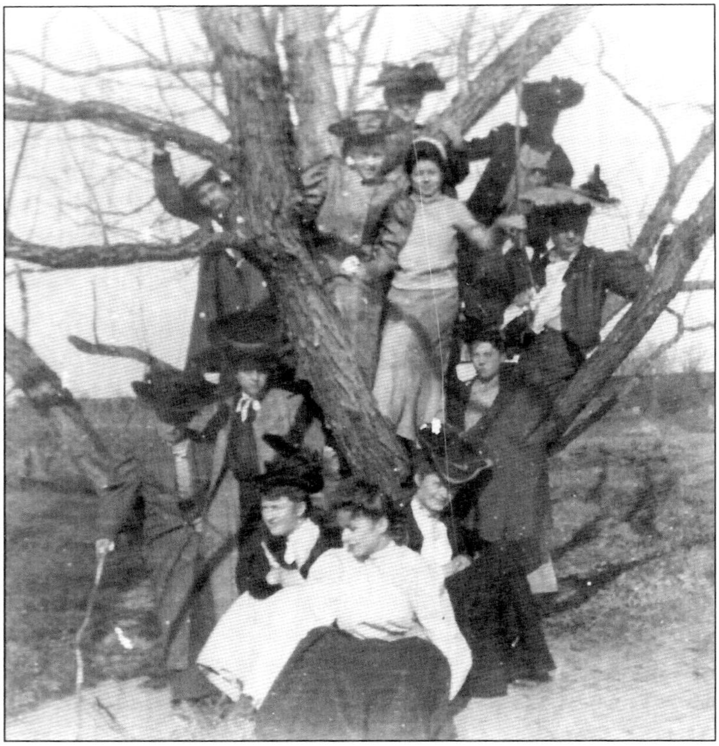

The early 20th century was a growing and prosperous time for Hope. Residents had time for many different leisure activities. In the image to the left, several young ladies from Hope pose in a tree in 1904. Five are identified as Grace Briant Jewell, Vera Murphy Anderson, Mary Yates, Nina Knighton, and Edith Knighton McRae. Other activities gained interest in the century's second decade. Different tableaux were presented such as the one seen below. Several unidentified young ladies dressed in costumes form the shape of a chariot. (Left, courtesy of SARA; below, courtesy Earl Waggoner.)

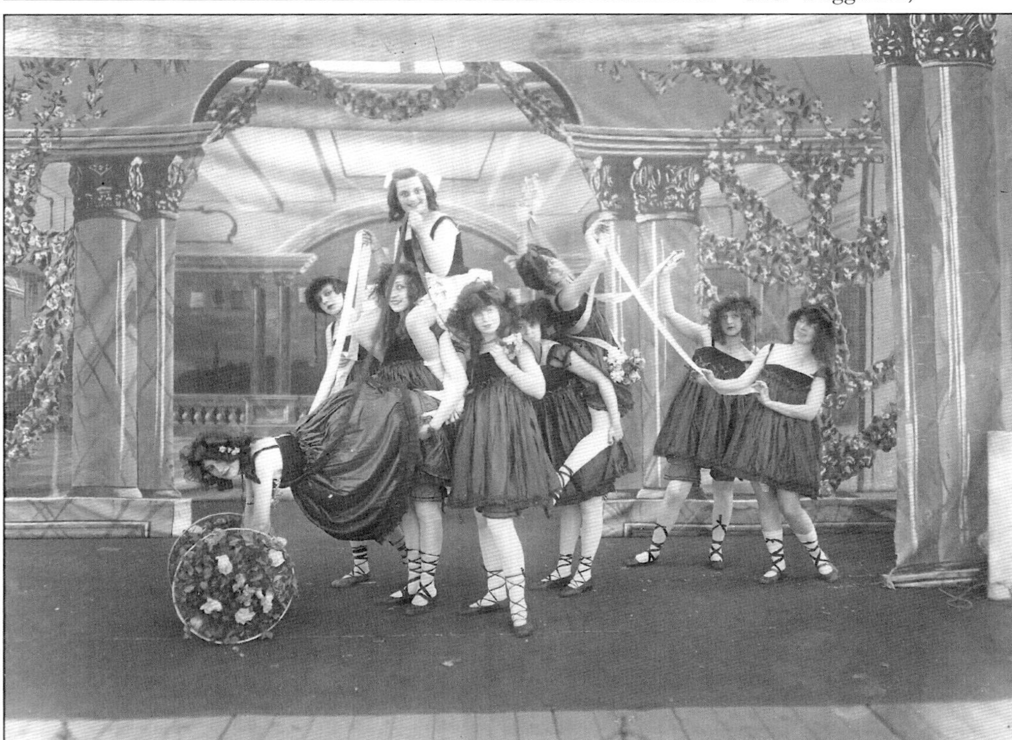

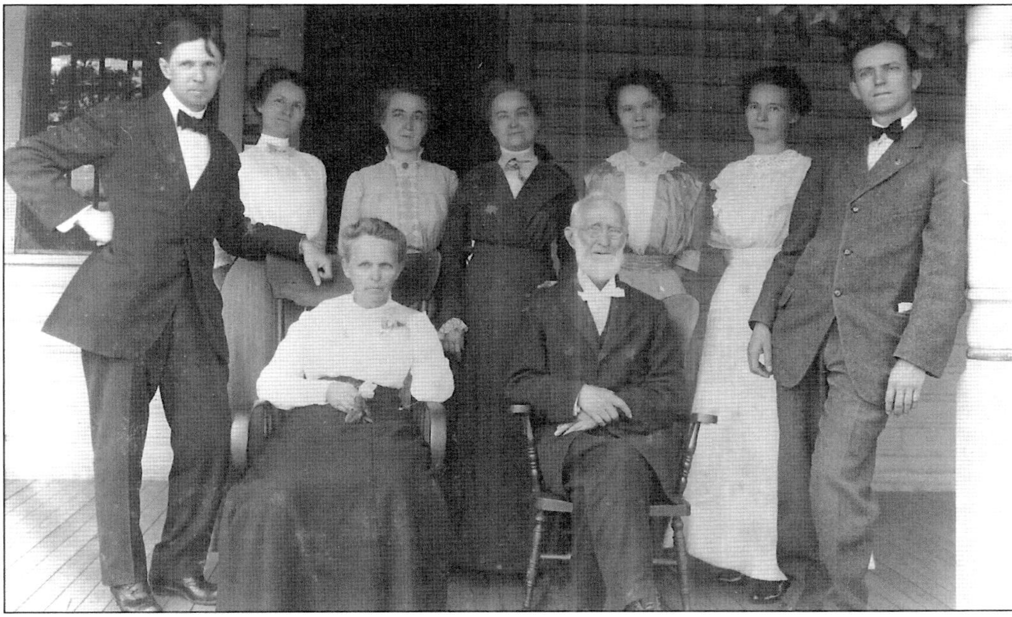

Horace Jewell was married twice during his life. His first marriage was in 1861 to Mattie Powell, from Camden, Arkansas. They had five children, three of whom died in infancy. Horace outlived Mattie and later married Martha Duncan on December 27, 1877, who is sitting next to him at their home in Hope, around 1910. They had five children together. (Courtesy of SARA.)

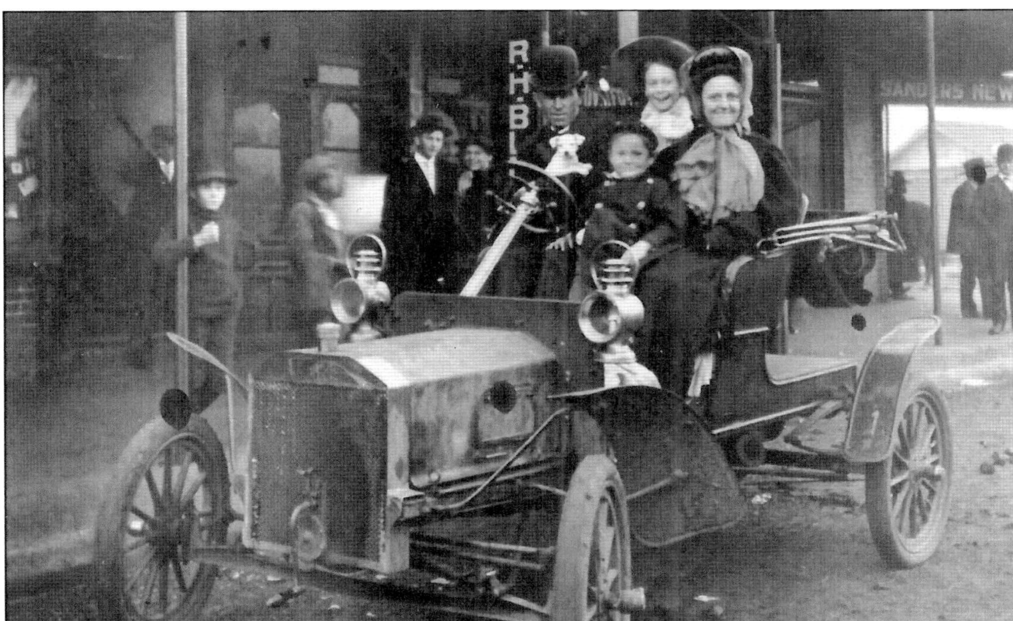

The Thomas R. King family was the first family in town to own one of the horseless carriages that were coming out in the early 1900s. In 1905, the Kings drove around town and parked in front of a café at 104 South Main Street. In the automobile are, from left to right, Thomas (with their dog), Harold, Lucille (standing), and Dora King. (Courtesy of SARA.)

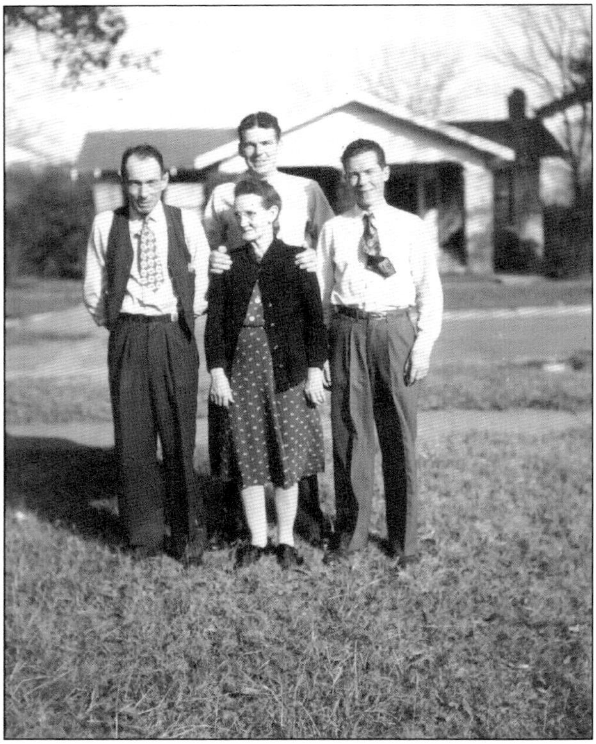

Viola Elizabeth Williams is seen with three of her four sons outside her home on South Pine Street around 1945. Standing behind her are Snow (left), Dale (center), and Ferrell. After her husband, Leon S. Williams, died in 1923, she would only wear dark or black dresses when she went to town to shop. She died in 1958. (Courtesy of Keenan and Peggy Williams.)

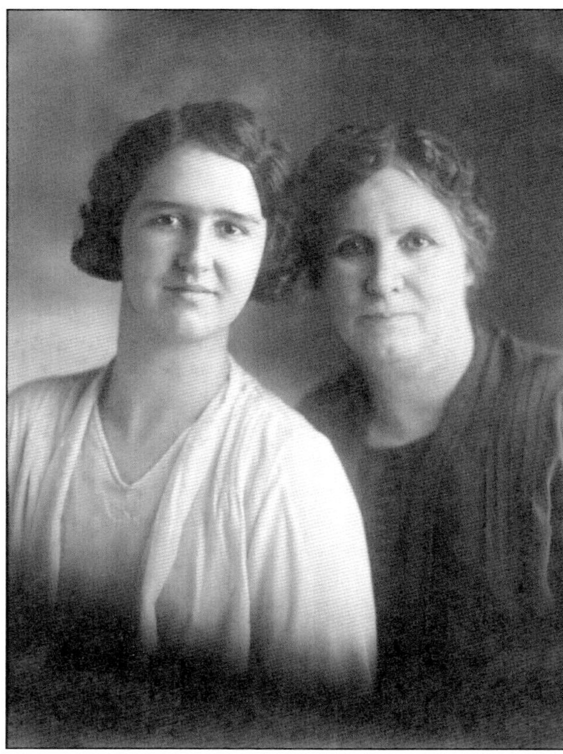

Nathaniel Paul O'Neal, who managed the Hope Brick Works, and his wife, Blanche, had one daughter, Joy, seen here with her mother around 1925. Joy later married Basil W. Edwards, a local building contractor who helped construct the Hempstead County Courthouse in Hope in 1939. (Courtesy of Lloyd Paul Powell.)

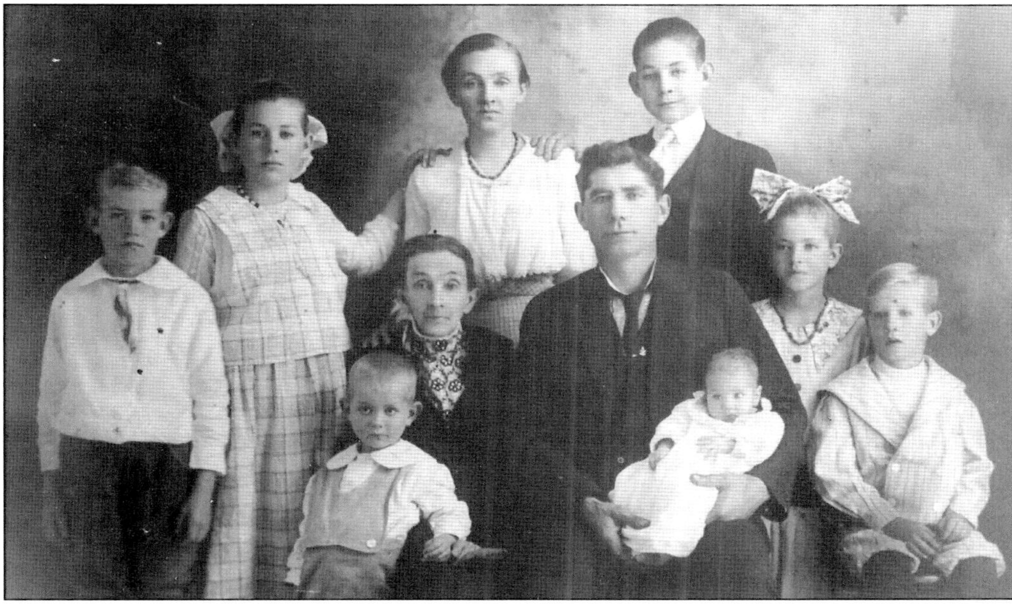

In 1919, the Schulte family decided to get a photograph taken. They had moved to Hope from the community of Spring Hill in the southern part of the county. Standing, from left to right, are Otto Schulte, Lucille Schulte, Birdie Schulte, Carl Schulte, and Lois Schulte. Sitting, from left to right, are Harold Schulte, Louisa Schulte, Henry Schulte holding baby Ruth, and Claude H. Schulte. (Courtesy of Vivian Wilson.)

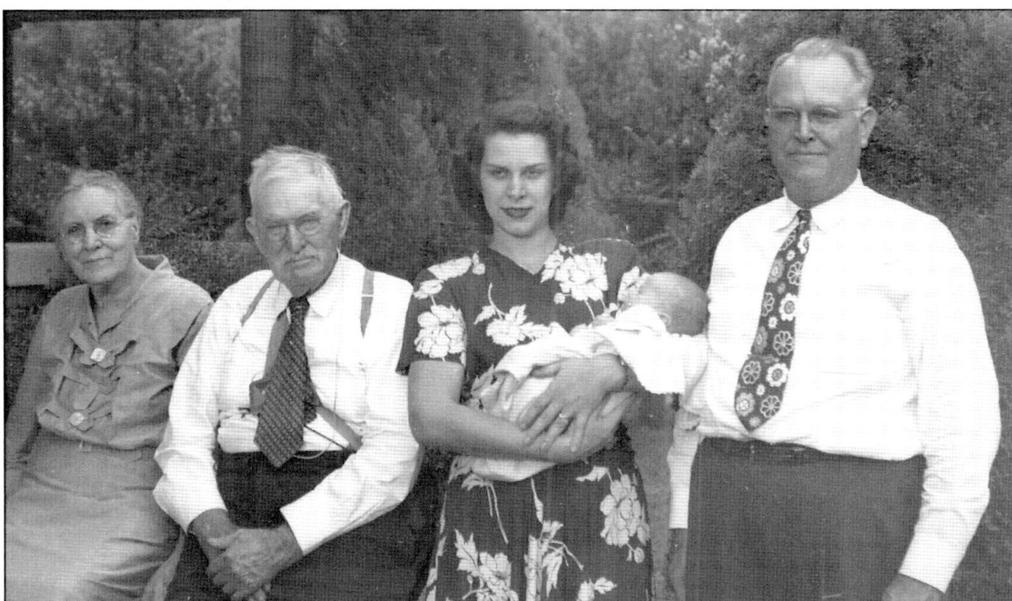

The O'Neal family established generational roots in Hope when N. P. and Blanche O'Neal moved there. After World War II, the family took this photograph that shows four generations. From left to right are Blanche and N. P.; granddaughter Margie Powell, holding great-grandson Lloyd Paul Powell; and son, Ernest Paul O'Neal. (Courtesy of Lloyd Paul Powell.)

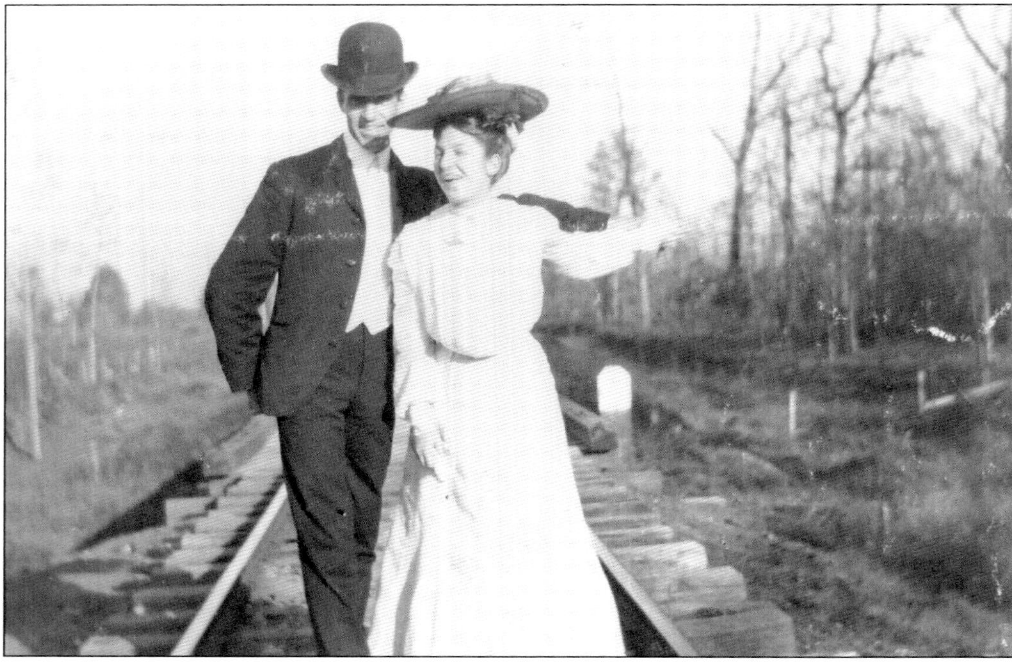

Throughout history, romance continues to be a part of any town, including Hope, Arkansas. Around 1910, Dr. Edward and Lucille Richards enjoy a nice stroll along the railroad tracks near Hope. They were married in 1906. (Courtesy of HVCM.)

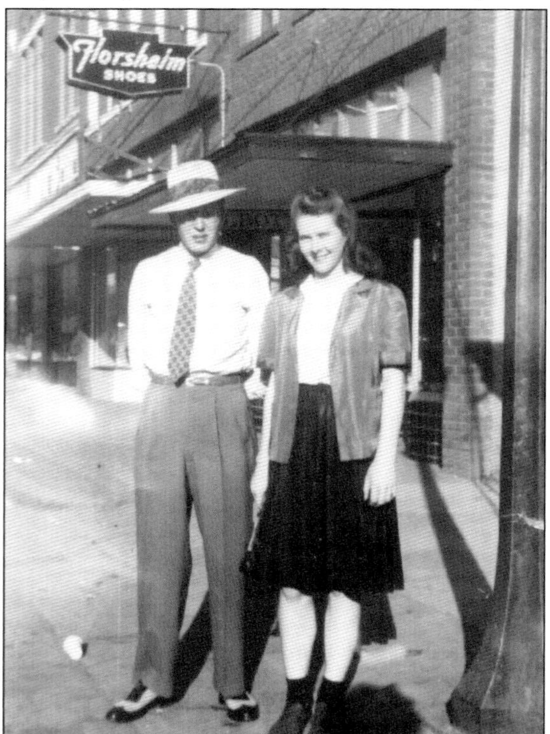

Raymond Jordan and Hazel Griffin stand in front of the George W. Robinson and Company store after work in the early 1940s. Both worked at the store in downtown Hope, at 119 West Second Street. Raymond Jordan was a store manager. The couple later married. (Courtesy of Hazel Jordan.)

Two

Community

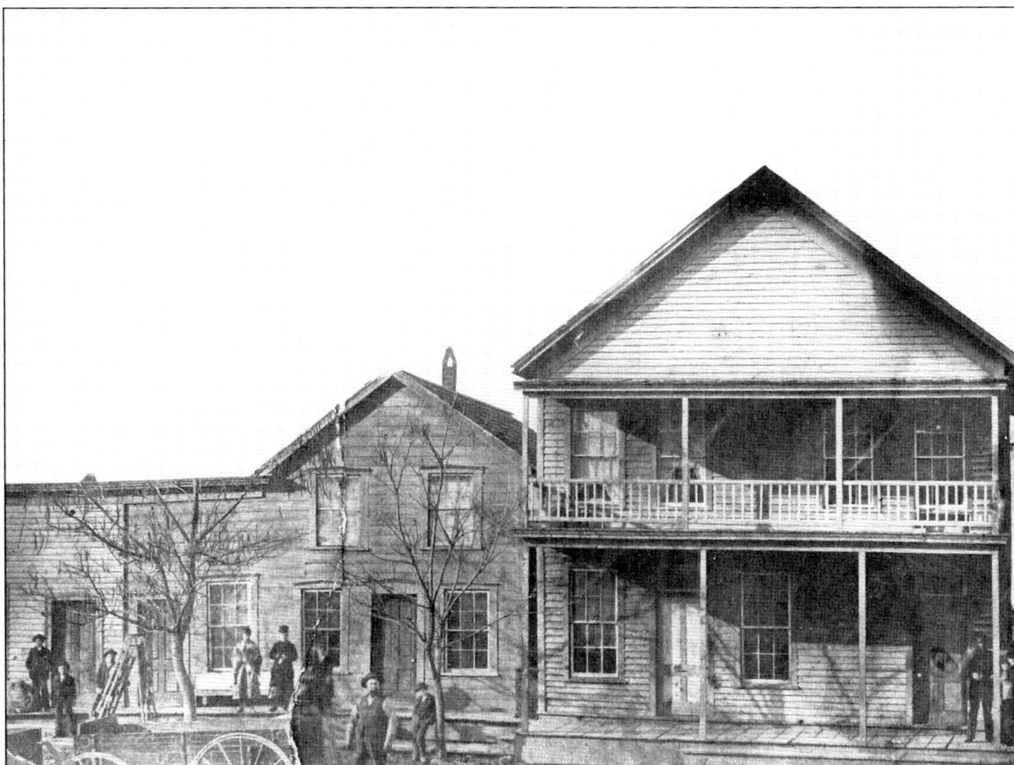

In 1873, the Cairo and Fulton Railroad Company laid out the town plat for Hope and sold lots. After returning to Arkansas from Michigan, Walter Shiver bought some of the lots and built the town's first house at the corner of West Avenue A and North Main Street. He is standing to the right of the wagon with his son, John C. Shiver, leaning up against the tree. (Courtesy of SARA.)

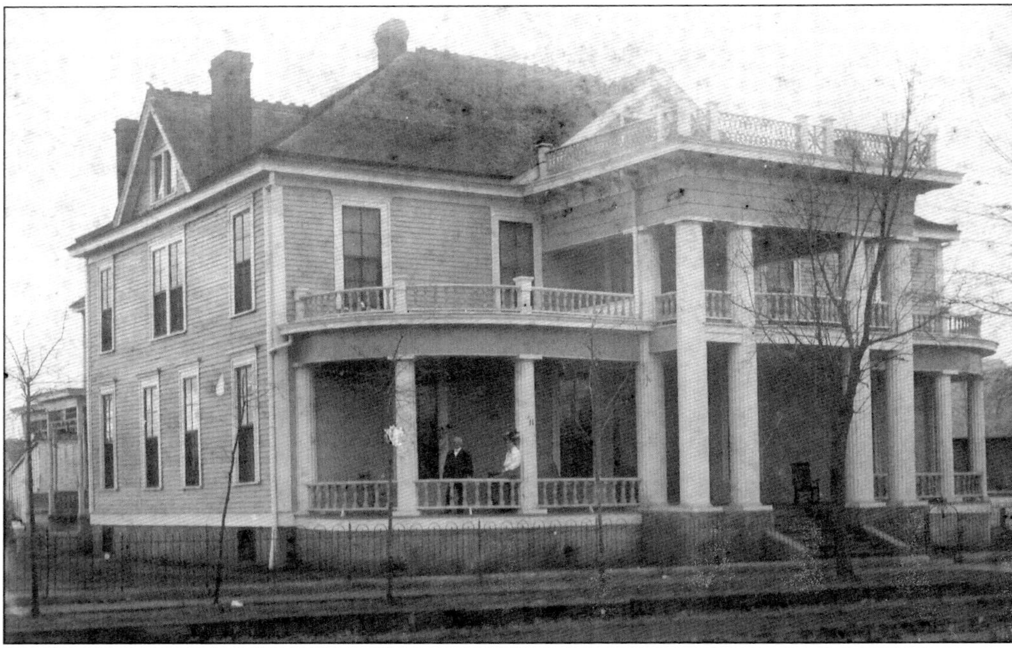

Hempstead County and the state of Arkansas came out of Reconstruction in 1874. Hope became a town that epitomized the New South philosophy with all the advancements of the modern age. With the railroad came families in search of new lives. The Barlow family established a hotel on Elm Street catering to railroad passengers. Around 1900, the family built the house shown above, which was moved in 1908 one block to 310 West Division Street because of the new Frisco and Louisiana and Arkansas rails. Below, at the R. M. Lagrone home on 300–312 South Pine Street, his wife, Marie, sits in the carriage while a servant tends the horse. (Courtesy of SARA.)

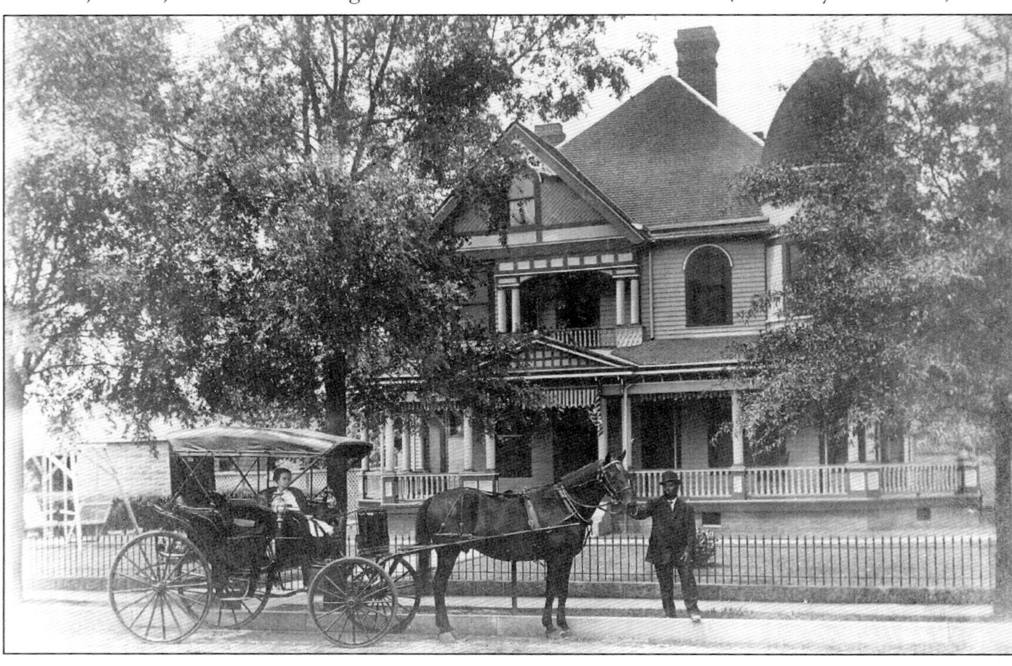

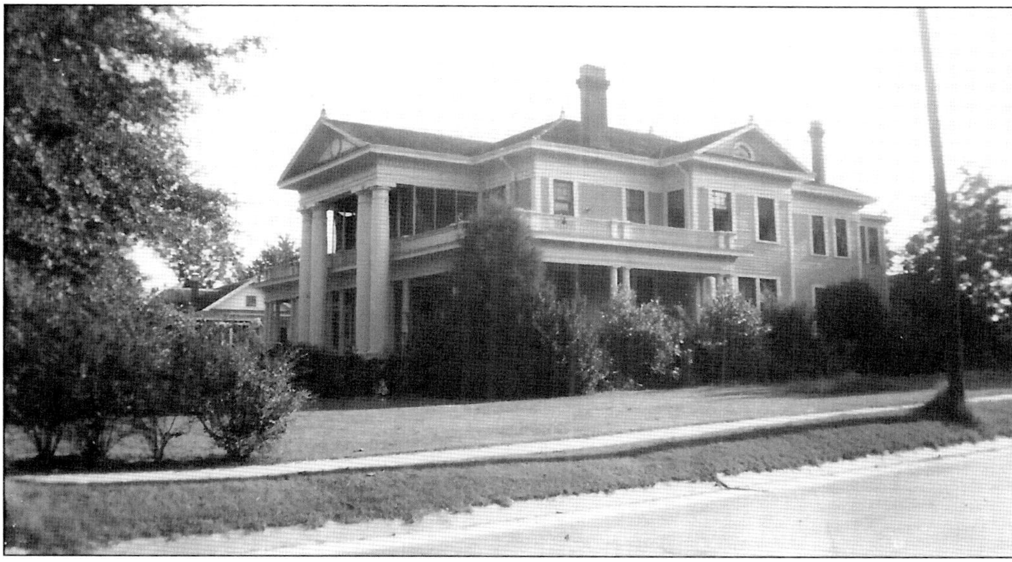

In 1909, K. G. McRae built this house at 304 South Edgewood Avenue. The home demonstrates the wealth located in the town of Hope during the first decades of the 20th century. (Courtesy of SARA.)

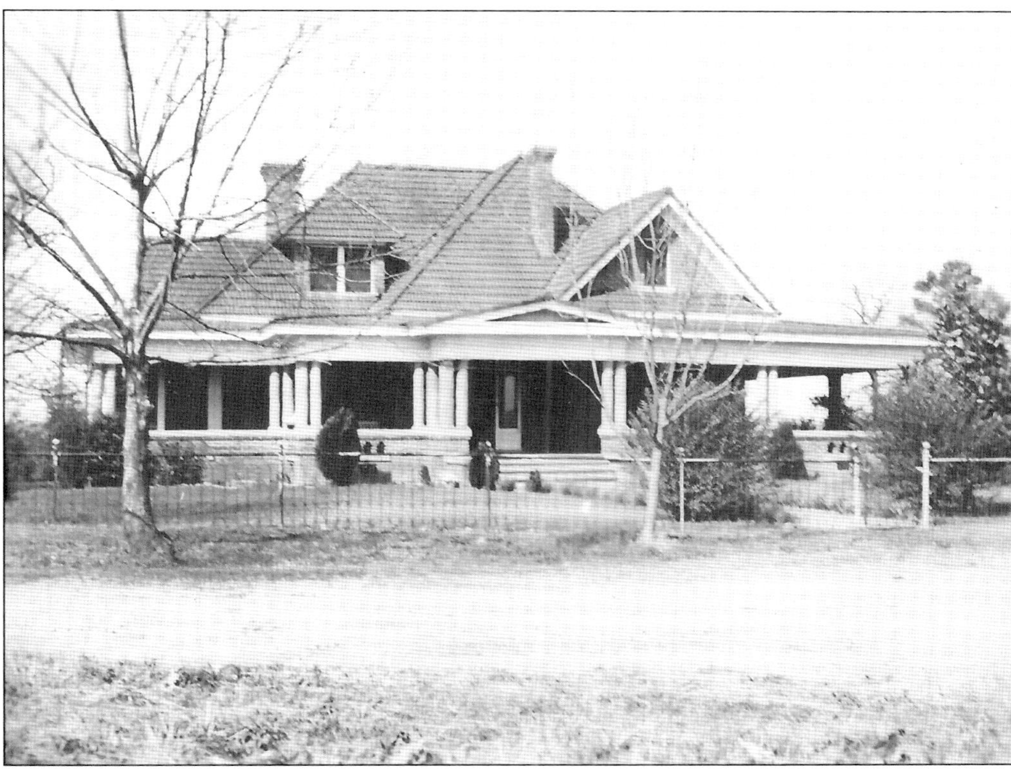

In 1913, N. P. O'Neal built a house out of the bricks from Hope Brick Works. In order to oversee the work being done at the factory, he built on-site at 1220 East G Street. In 1938, it remained a sturdy home. (Courtesy of Lloyd Paul Powell.)

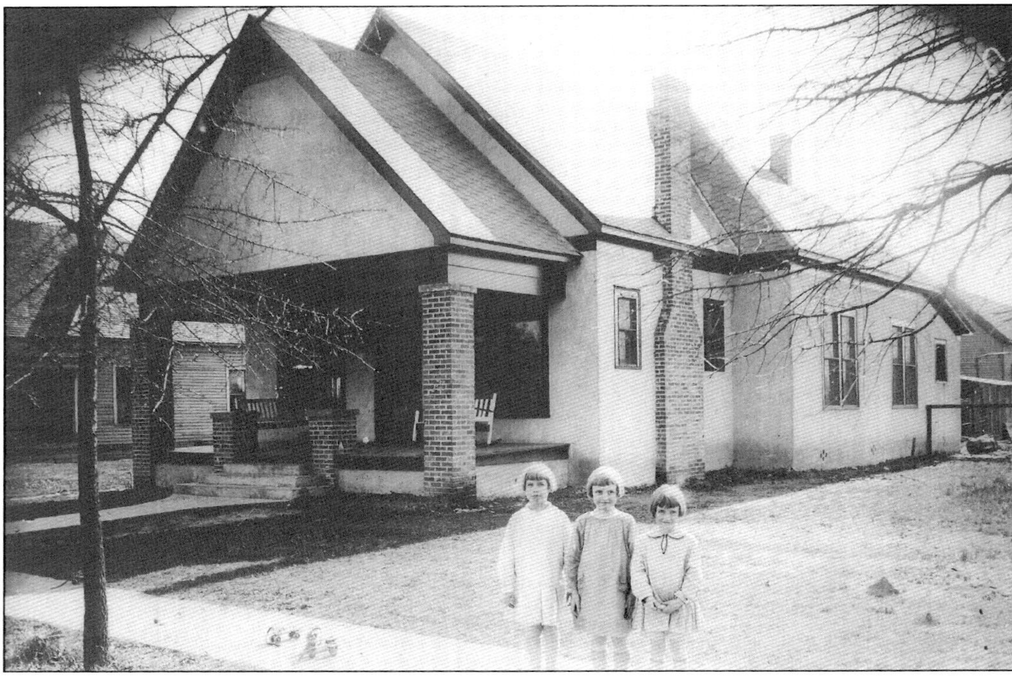

All the houses in town were not as grand as the Barlow or McRae residences, but they indicate a strong middle-class community. This home on 802 South Elm Street was remodeled in the 1920s and rented by the Carter family. The children are, from left to right, Evelyn Briant, Mary Nell Carter, and Jane Carter. (Courtesy of Mary Nell Turner.)

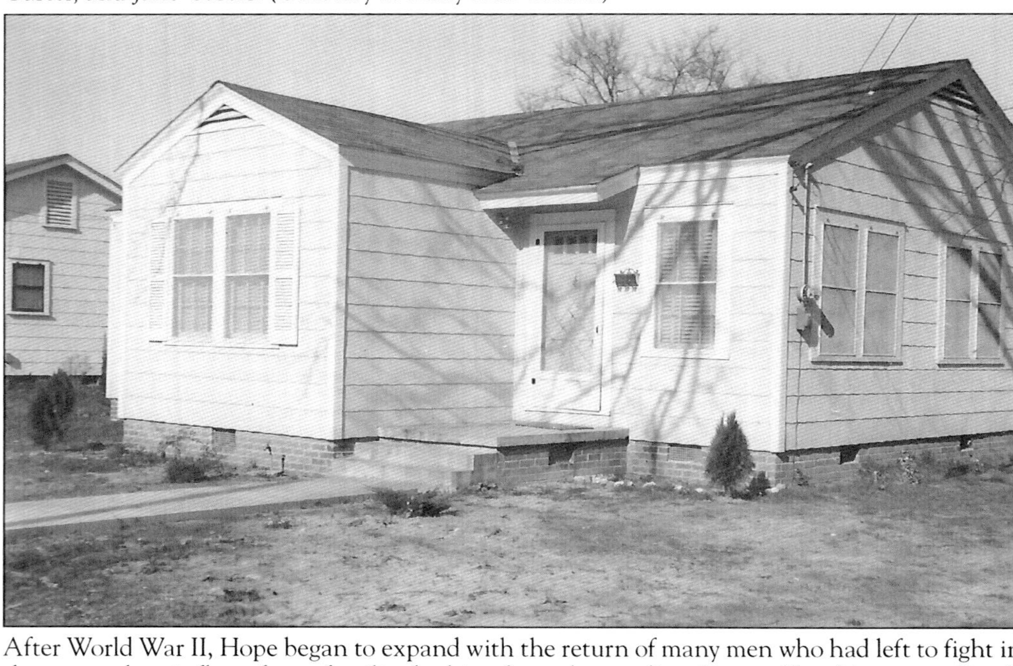

After World War II, Hope began to expand with the return of many men who had left to fight in the war and an influx of new families looking for a place to live. Homes like this one on South Grady Street were built in the new suburbs. (Courtesy of Lloyd Paul Powell.)

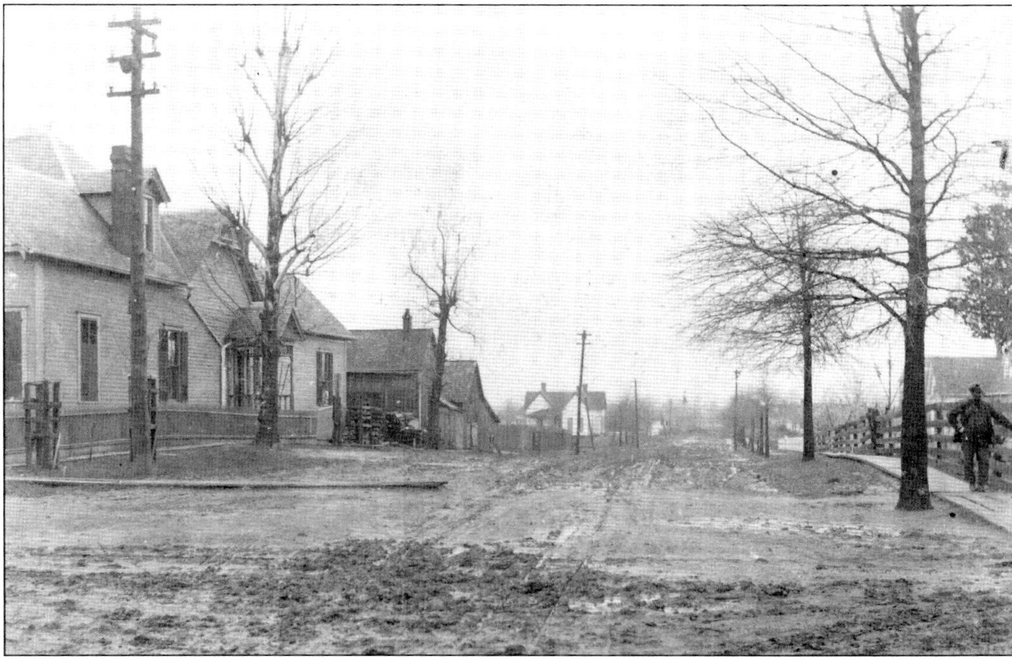

Hope's streets were originally dirt roads with plank sidewalks. New trees were planted with box frames built around them for protection. This scene was taken around 1905 looking west at the intersection of West Avenue B and Louisiana Street. The home of J. J. Ward at 122 North Louisiana is in the foreground on the left-hand side of the street. (Courtesy of SARA.)

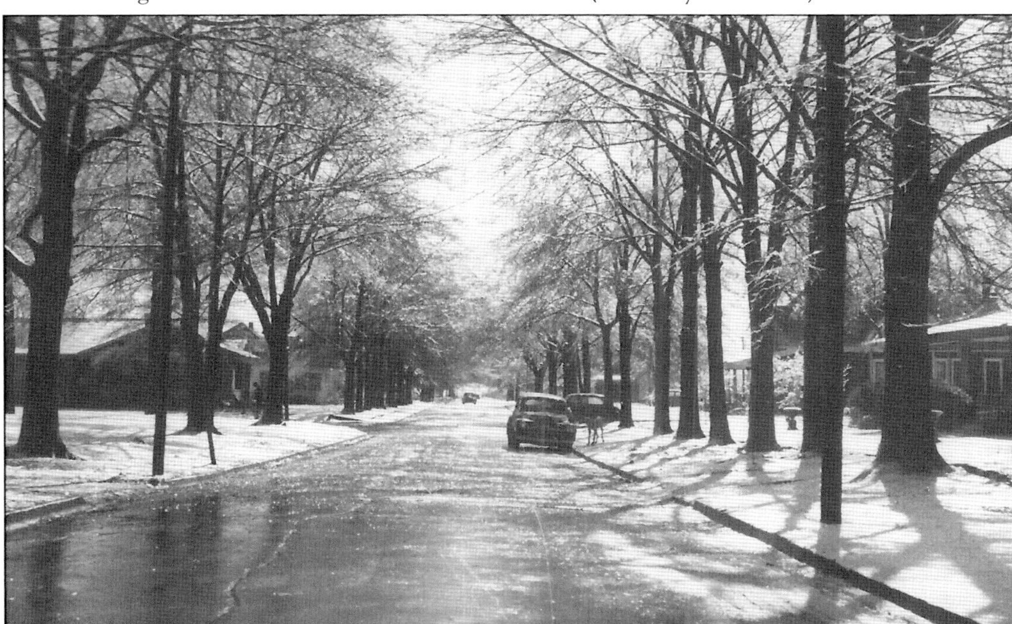

By 1950, small oak saplings that were planted had become towering trees that shaded many of the streets around Hope. Here is a stretch of South Hervey Street, from the intersection with Third Street, after a snowfall in 1949. (Courtesy of Lloyd Paul Powell.)

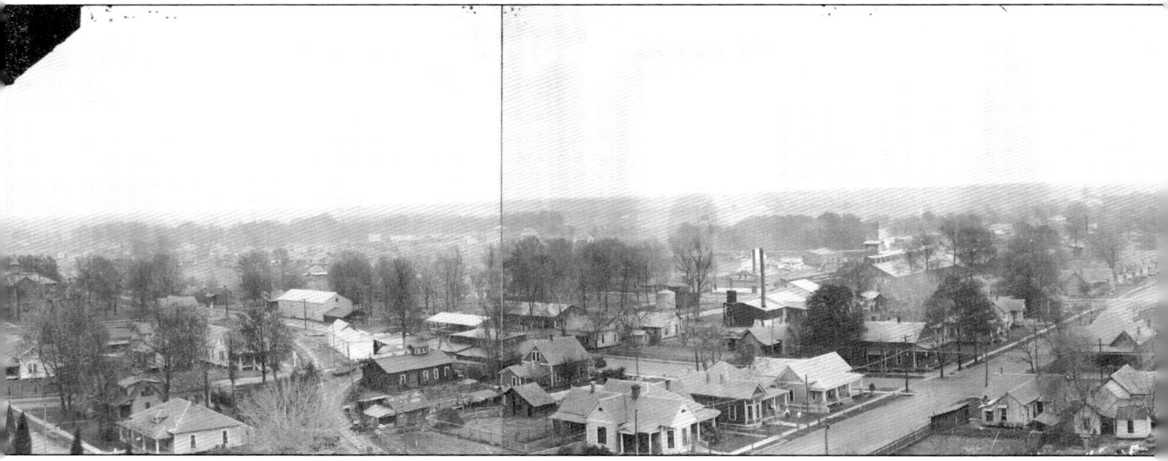

Around 1916, a photographer took this panoramic shot of downtown Hope from the water tower of the Hope Water and Light Company. Many of the town's major buildings can be seen. The new four-story National Building (below, left side of photograph), was completed in 1916 and housed Hope National Bank. At the time, it was the tallest building in Arkansas on an unpaved street.

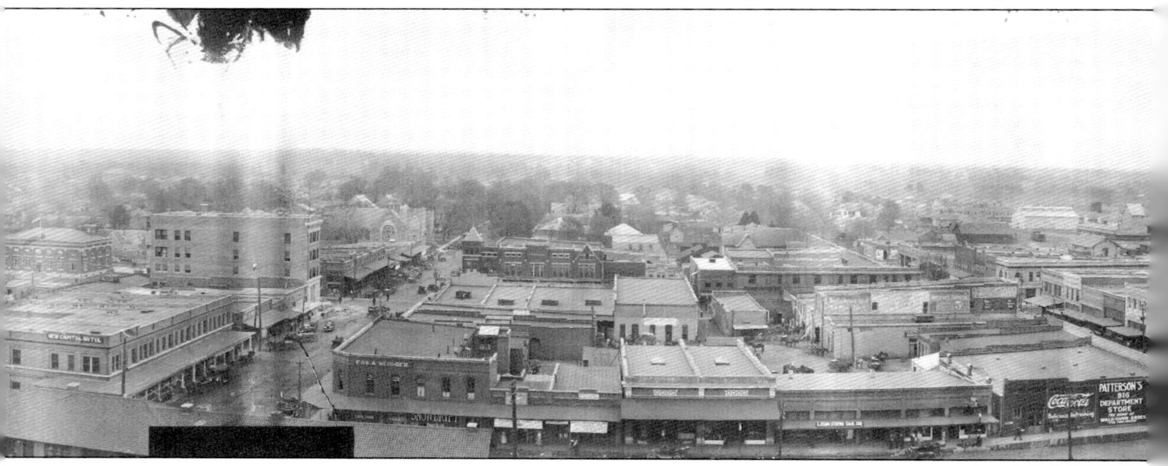

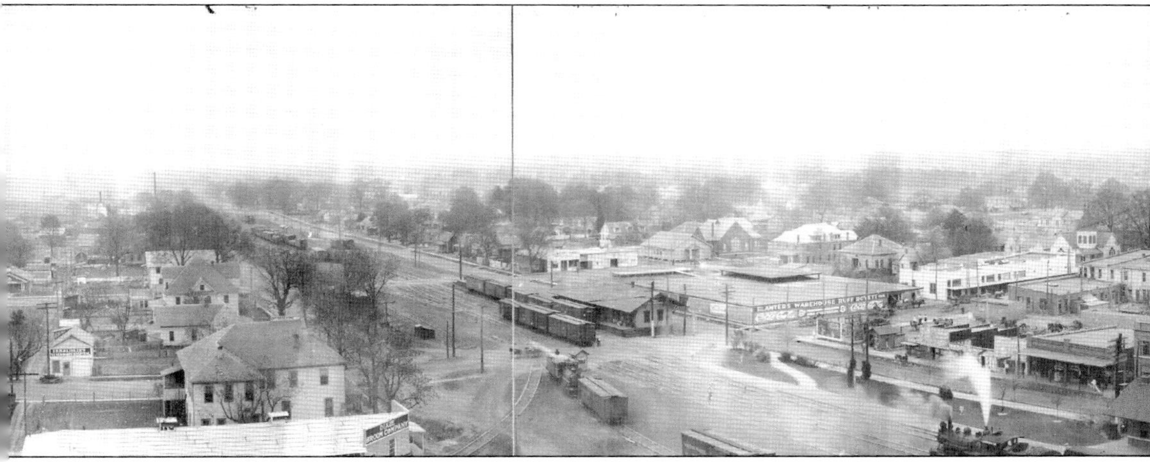

The depot was the center of this railroad town, which was divided north-south by the railway and east-west by Main Street. Church steeples rise across the community, and churches were located on the four corners downtown. Not shown in this photograph is the Christian church, located north of the depot, behind the photographer. (Courtesy of HVCM.)

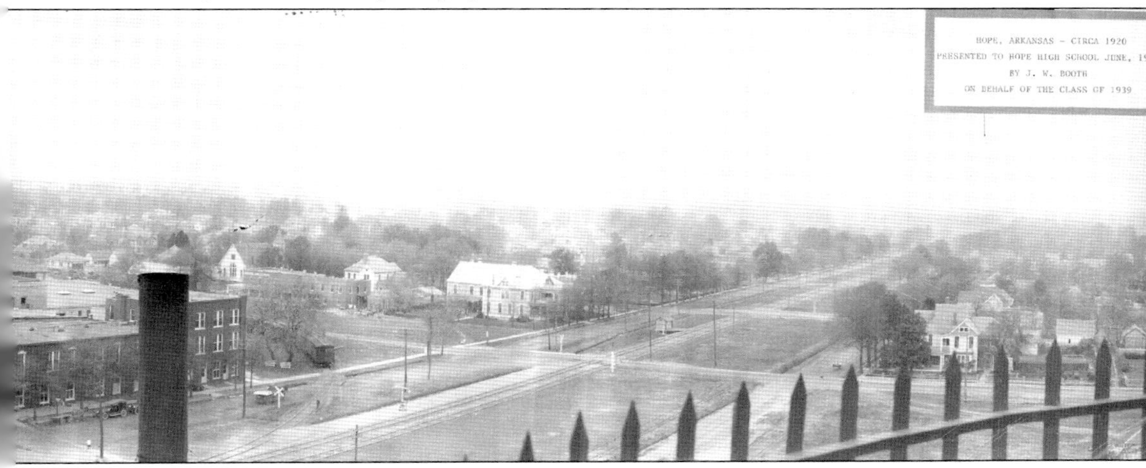

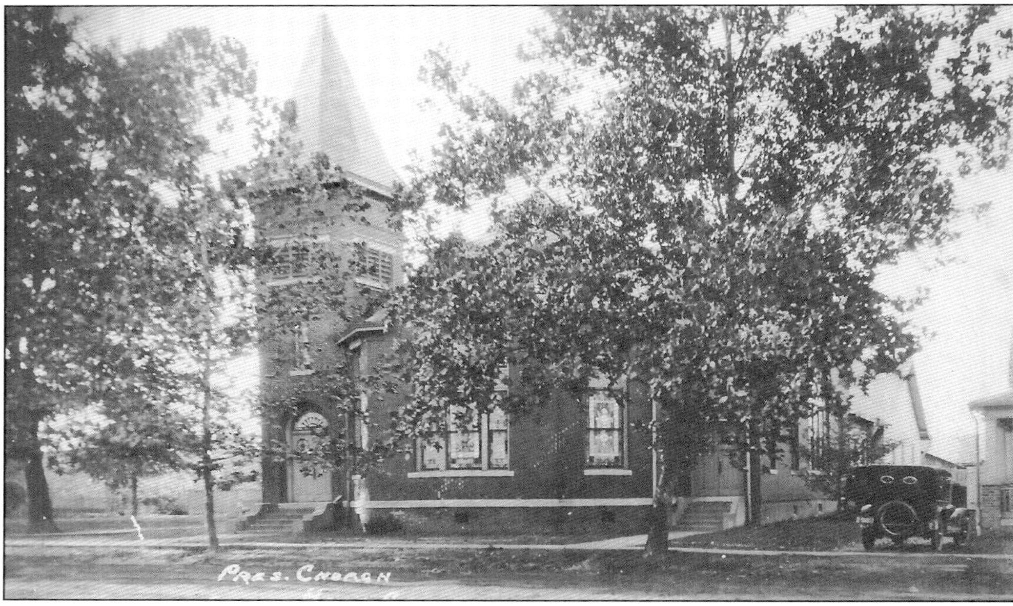

The First Presbyterian Church was located at the corner of South Hazel and East Second Streets. Its organization dates to June 8, 1861, when the church was located just north of Hope in a community named Greenwood. In April 1874, the congregation moved into the Hope city limits and, in 1883, decided to build a sanctuary at South Hazel and East Second. In 1897, this structure was destroyed by fire. By 1898, the church completed the building shown in the photograph above and held services in the sanctuary on January 2. The new Presbyterian church was based on the Akron plan (first used in 1872 at the First Methodist Episcopal Church in Akron, Ohio), which featured a sanctuary in the shape of a fan to optimize acoustics and seating, as seen in the curved pews in the photograph below. (Above, courtesy of SARA; below, courtesy of Earl Waggoner.)

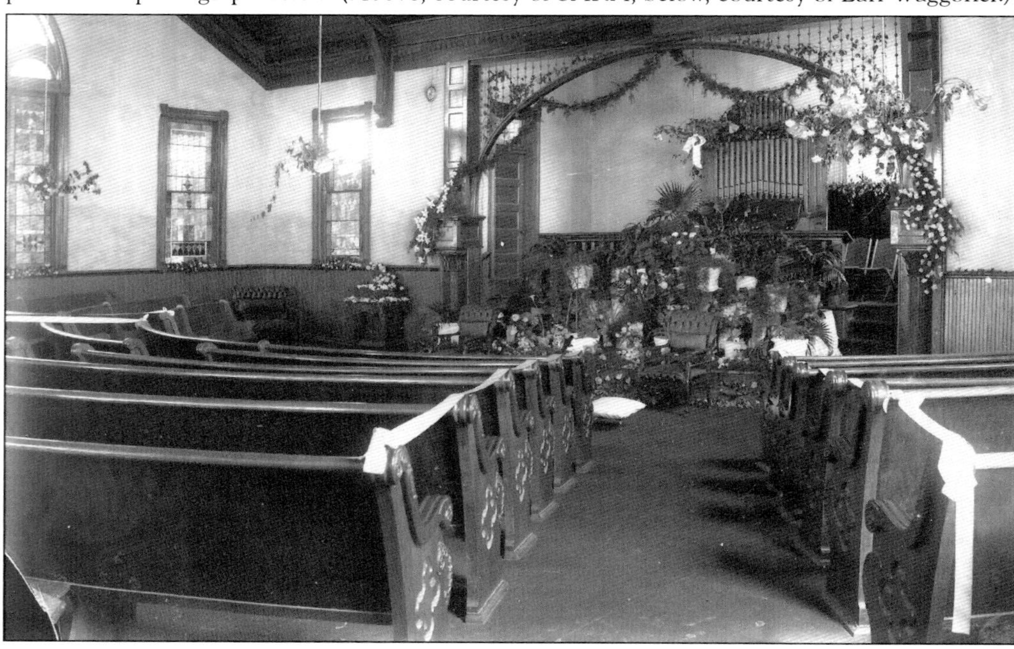

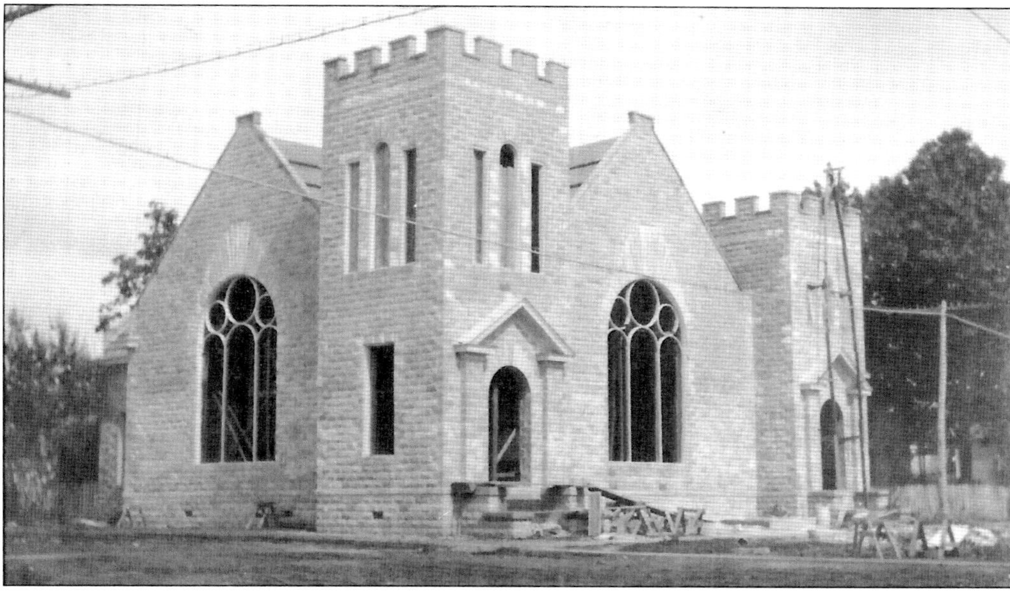

The First Baptist Church traces it founding back to 1868 at a location 3 miles south of Hope. Around 1876, the congregation moved to town and met in a one-room frame building at the corner of North Walnut Street and Avenue B. By 1884, First Baptist relocated to its present location at the corner of Third and Main Streets. In 1905, the church above was constructed of concrete blocks made locally by George Hinton at a factory he owned. On September 15, 1906, the first services were held inside the new sanctuary, shown in the photograph below. At the time, the auditorium was the largest in town and was used for various community functions. Like the First Presbyterian Church, the Baptist sanctuary was also based on the Akron plan. (Above, courtesy of AHC; below, courtesy of Mary Nell Turner.)

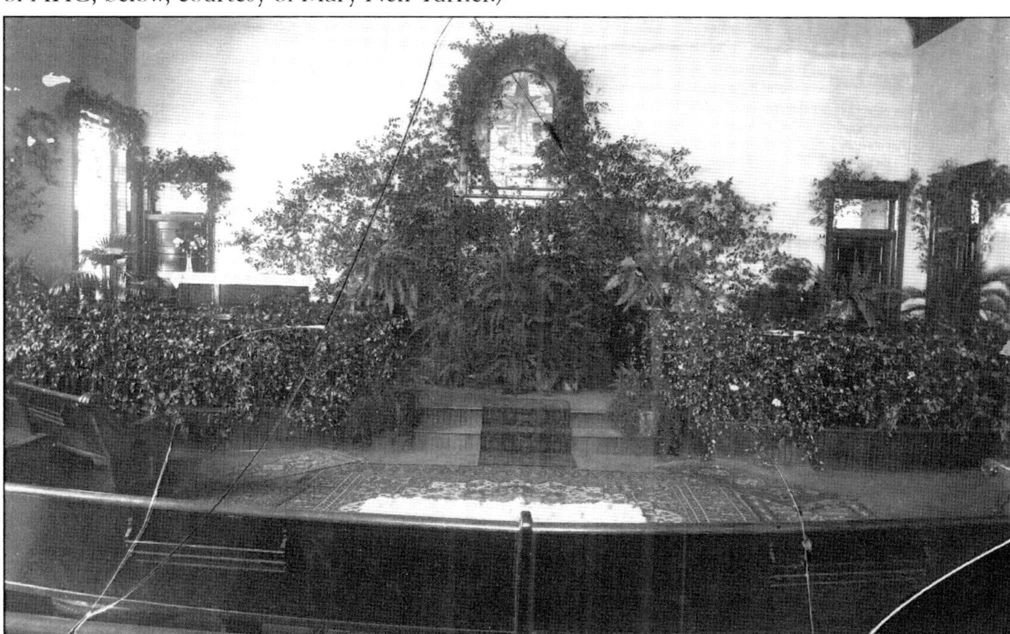

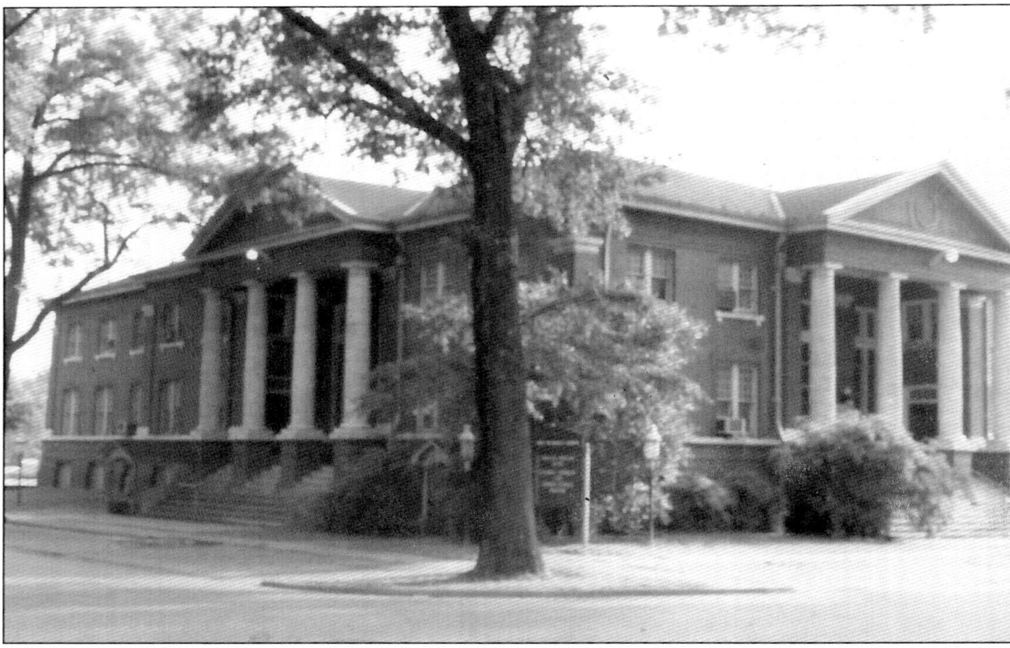

First United Methodist Church was organized in 1874 and built its first structure on a lot on the corner of North Pine Street and Avenue A donated to the congregation by the Cairo and Fulton Railroad. After a fire, the church moved to a location on Pine Street and built another wooden church. Due to growth, the congregation decided in 1916 to construct a larger building made of brick provided by N. P. O'Neal, owner of the Hope Brick Works. It was completed in 1918 at a cost of $50,000. Like many of the other churches in town, it was built on the Akron plan to provide an optimal amount of seating. In 1920, a plane crashed into the Pine Street steps just after the singing of the last hymn. No one was injured, but the congregation was greatly startled. (Both, courtesy of SARA.)

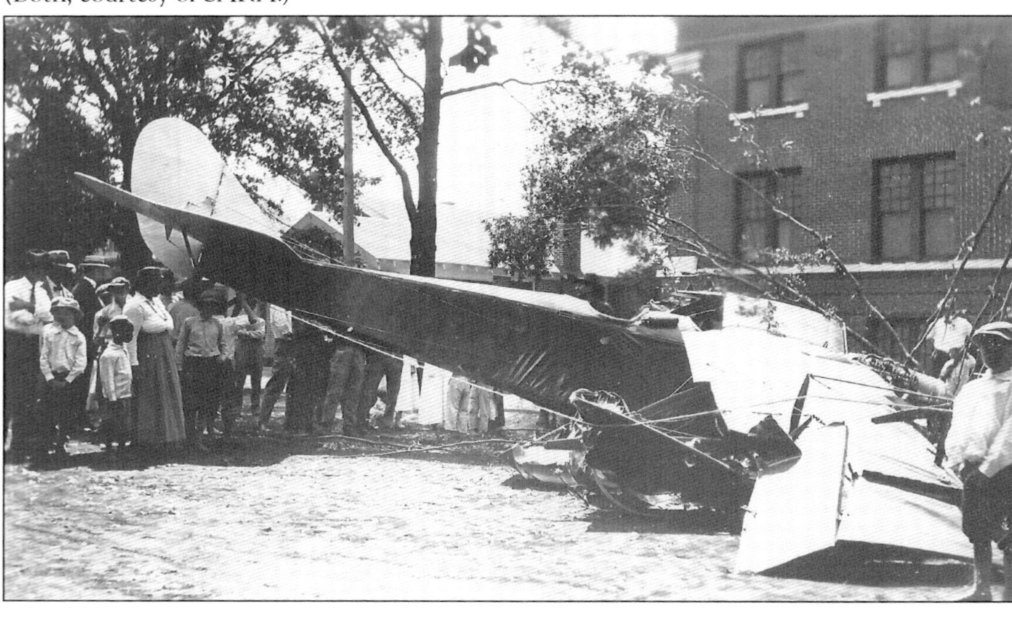

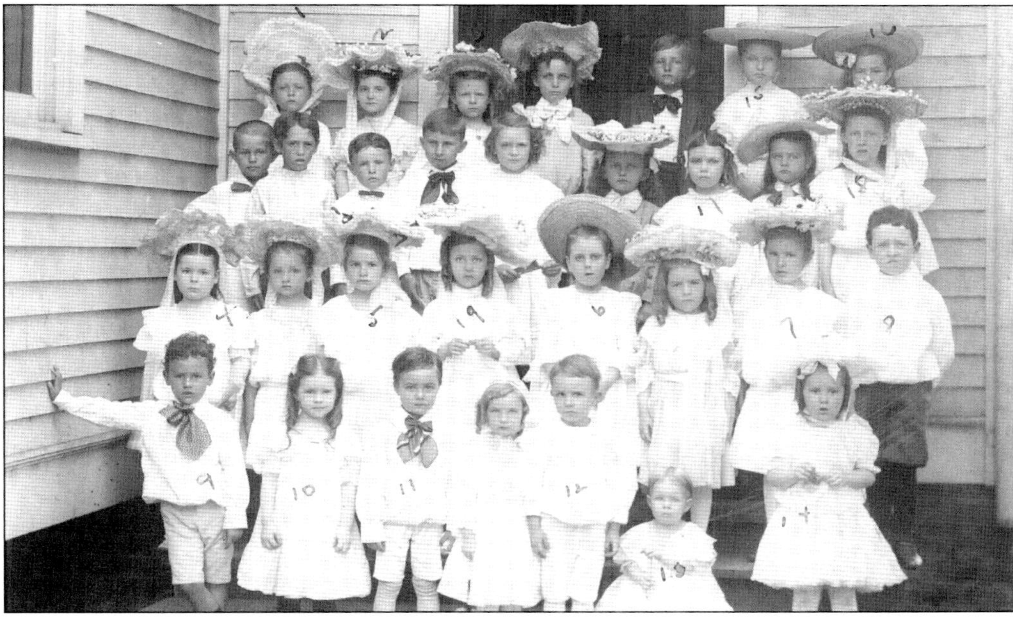

This photograph was taken of the children's Sunday school at First Methodist Church in 1906. From left to right are Irene Goodlett (1), Mary Kim Carrigan (2), Ethel Arnold (3), Ruth Weaver (4), Mildred Thompson (5), Willie Perkins (6), Dorothy Thompson (7), Tom Billingsley (8), Evan Jones (9), Margaret Arnold (10), Paul Lewis (11), Vaughan Thompson (12), Katherine Arnold (13), Marie LaGrone (14), Nell Lewis (15), Ollie Purdy (16), Marie Lewis (17), Annie Taylor (18), Thelma Carter (19). (Courtesy of First United Methodist Church of Hope.)

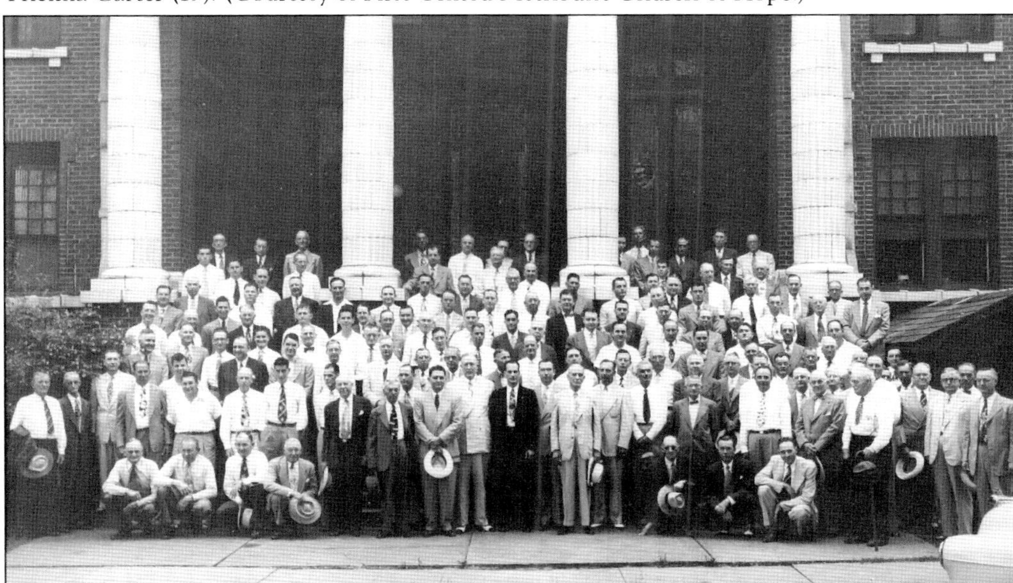

The Century Bible Class was a men's Sunday school class at First Methodist Church. Men from around the community and different Christian denominations attended the Sunday school class meetings. On June 10, 1951, the class had 200 men in attendance for the first time. (Courtesy of First United Methodist Church of Hope.)

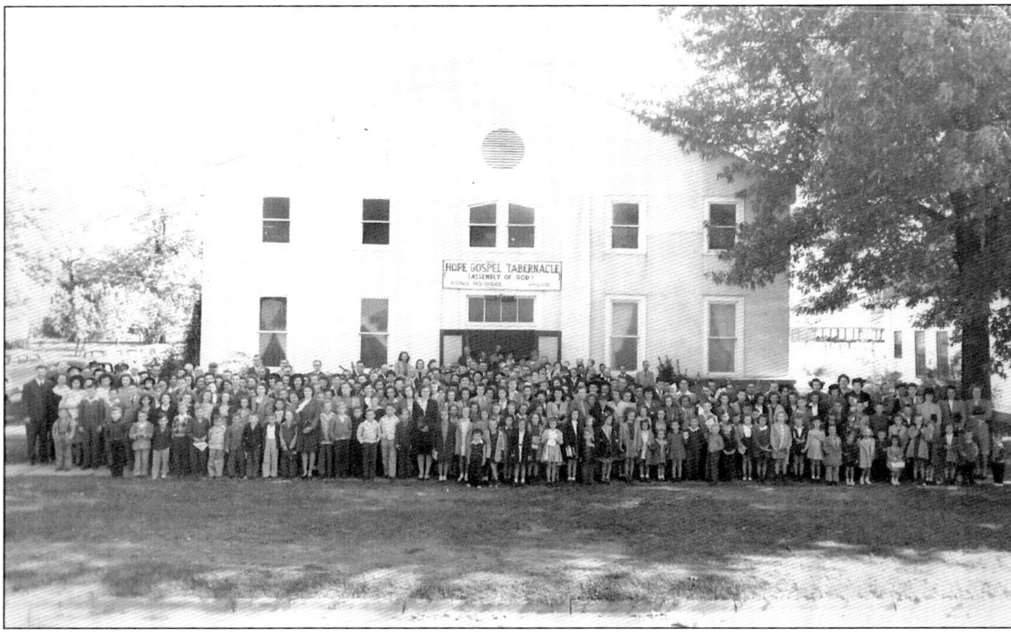

The Sunday school classes at Hope Gospel Tabernacle pose for this *c.* 1950 photograph, during the pastorate of H. Paul Holdridge (April 15, 1945–March 4, 1951). The church was founded in 1934, and Rev. Phinis Lewis was its first pastor. It later became the First Assembly of God of Hope. (Courtesy of First Assembly of God of Hope.)

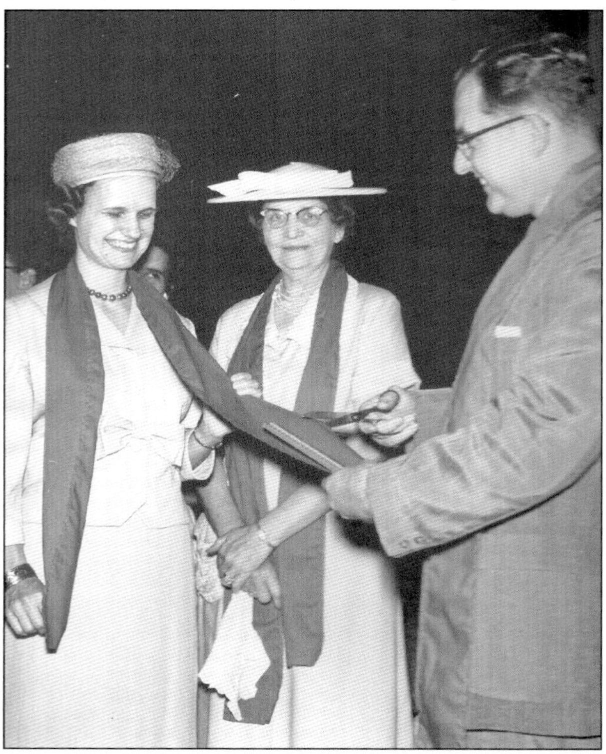

For seven Sundays in 1958, the Hope Gospel Tabernacle put on a loyalty campaign to raise attendance in Sunday school. Each teacher was given a 90-inch-by-6-inch bright red cloth strip to be worn around the neck. If attendance fell under the goal, a 10-inch piece was cut from the teacher's necktie. (Courtesy of First Assembly of God of Hope.)

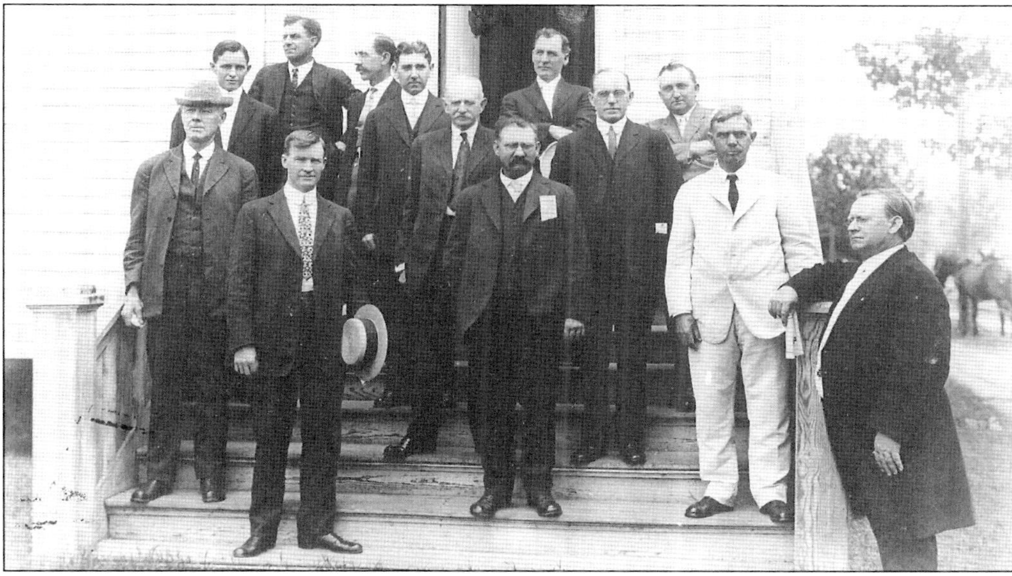

The First Christian Church was organized in 1882, and the congregation continues to meet in the same building at the corner of Avenue B and North Main Street. Shown here in this c. 1920 photograph are the elders and deacons, with the pastor, Rev. Basil E. Newton, standing to the far right. They are, from left to right, (first row) unidentified, Will Porterfield, ? Nelson, George B. Carter; (second row) Charles Neal, unidentified, Charles Richards, Rev. A. C. Tharpe, ? Brazell, Floyd Porterfield, W. W. Duckett, ? Coffee. (Courtesy of Mary Nell Turner.)

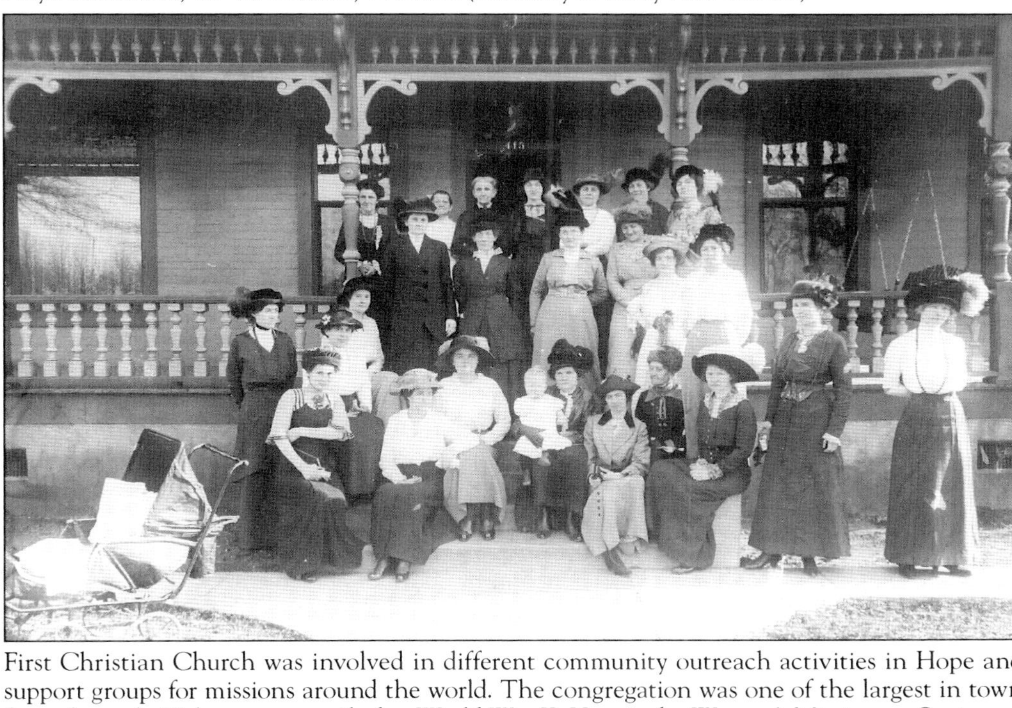

First Christian Church was involved in different community outreach activities in Hope and support groups for missions around the world. The congregation was one of the largest in town from the early 20th century until after World War II. Here is the Women's Missionary Society of the First Christian Church in 1913. (Courtesy of Mary Nell Turner.)

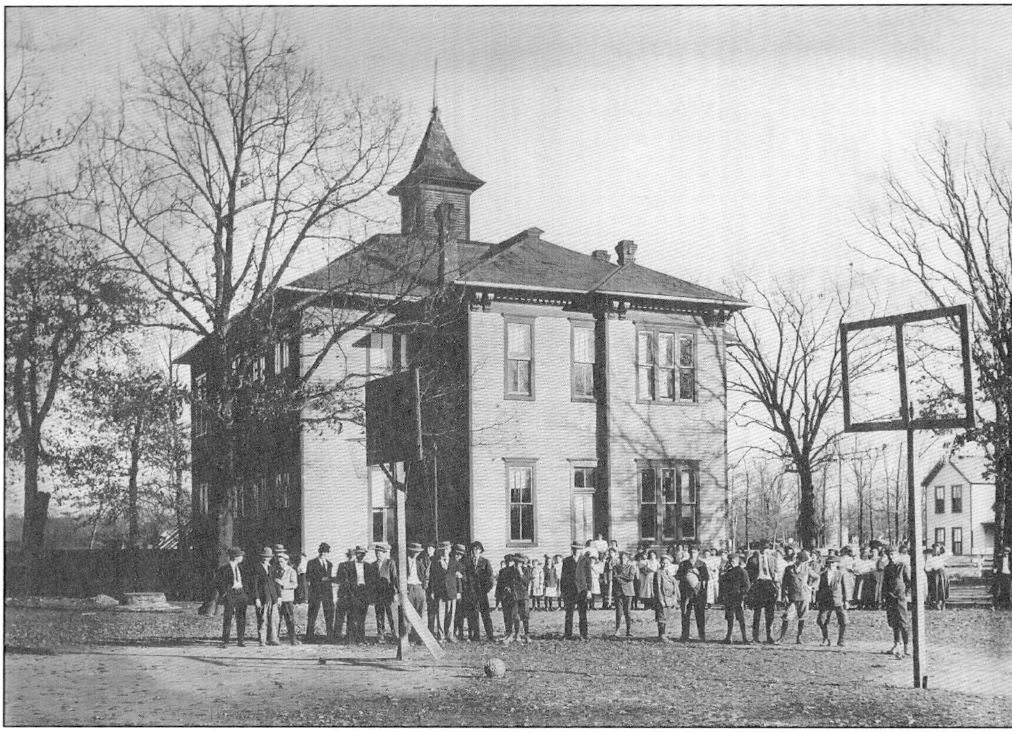

In 1888, the Hope school board constructed a red-frame, two-story building at the intersection of East Avenue D and North Main Street as a public school for the white population. From 1908 to 1922, it served as a high school. The photograph was taken in 1908. (Courtesy of SARA.)

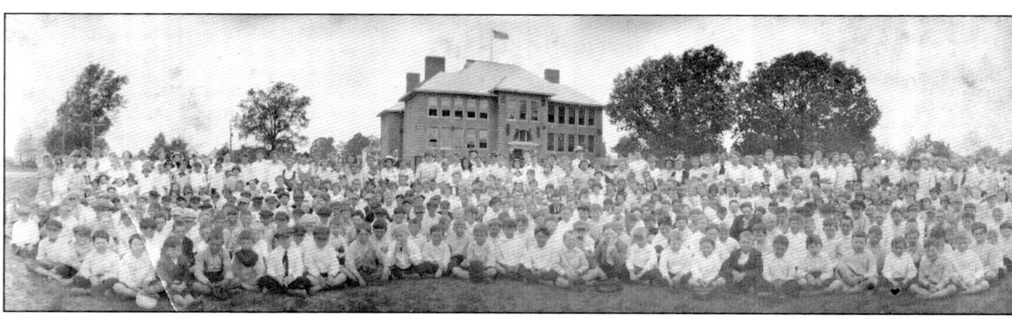

By 1905, due to increased enrollment, the school board purchased property in College Addition on the west side of Hope and, in 1908, built a new school for the elementary grades. The new building was the pride and joy of the citizens of Hope. On May 7, 1916, the student body of Garland School stands in front of the building for this group photograph. (Courtesy of SARA.)

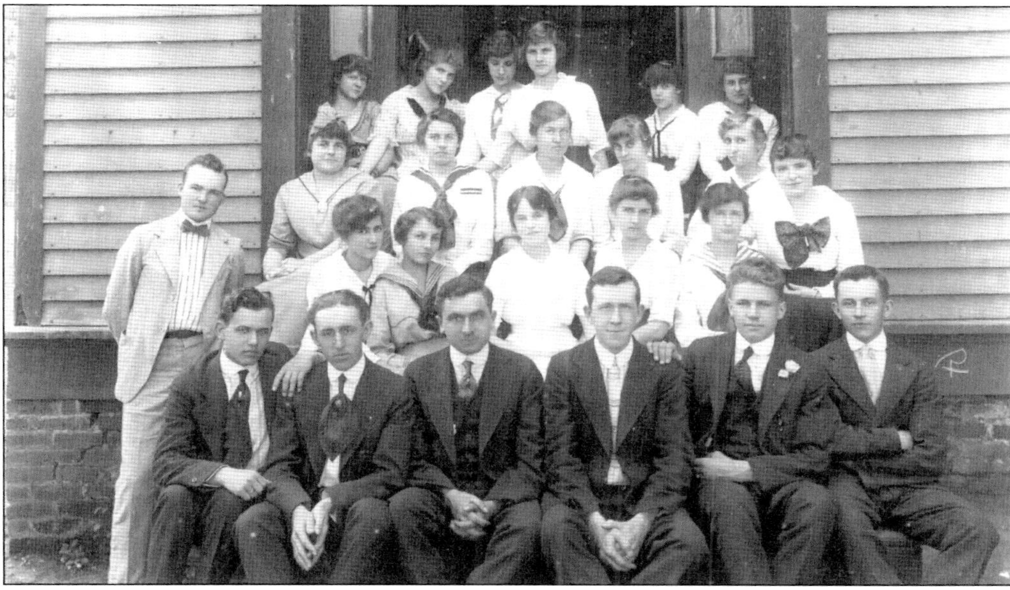

In the class at Hope High School in 1916 are, left to right, (first row) Robert Vasey, Arthur Thomas, Carter Haynes, Walker Newcomb, Curtis Cannon, and Charley ?; (second row) Sunney Teoche, Gillian Teoche, Julis Briggs, Genie Chamberlain, Kathleen Broach, Evrie Hart, and Van Golsten; (third row) Fay Crosnoe, Snow Sparks-Morron, Willie Perkins, Eunice Lipscomb, and Audie Moses; (fourth row) Ahel Arnold, Mae Briant, Dorothy Thompson, unidentified, Helen Williams, and Effie May Bridewell. (Courtesy of SARA.)

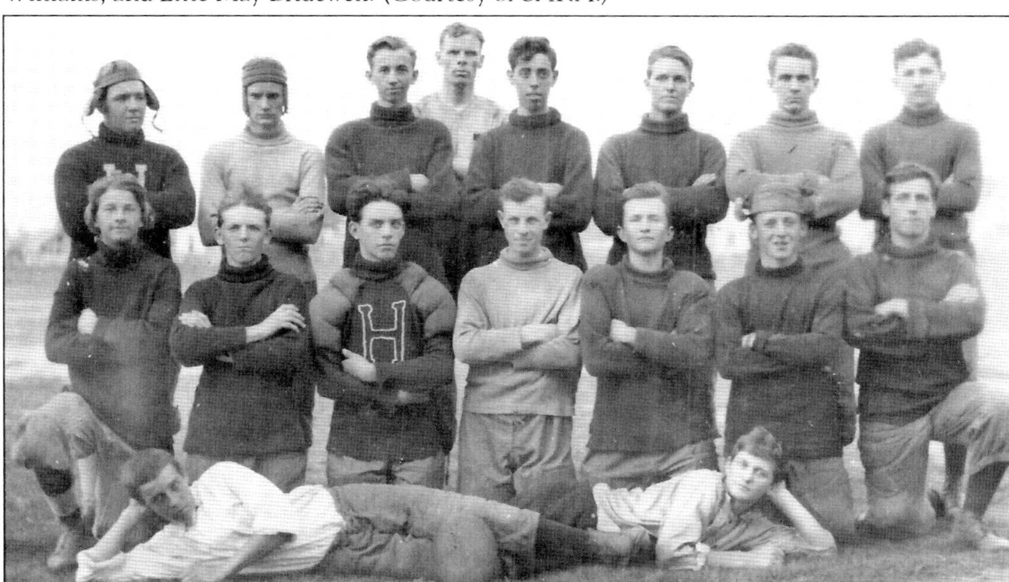

In 1914, football was becoming a popular sport at schools across America. The Hope High School Bobcats are, from left to right, (first row) T. P. Boyett and Raymond Robison; (second row) Alton Bowden, Jim Gentry, McRae Andrews, Roscoe Dyer, Homer Doup, Basil Newton, and Ruffin Boyett; (third row) Malcolm Porterfield, Otha Sullivan, Hale Robison, Ike Wiesiger, Ernest O'Neal, Paul Cornelius, Charles Walker, and coach W. E. Rodgers. (Courtesy of SARA.)

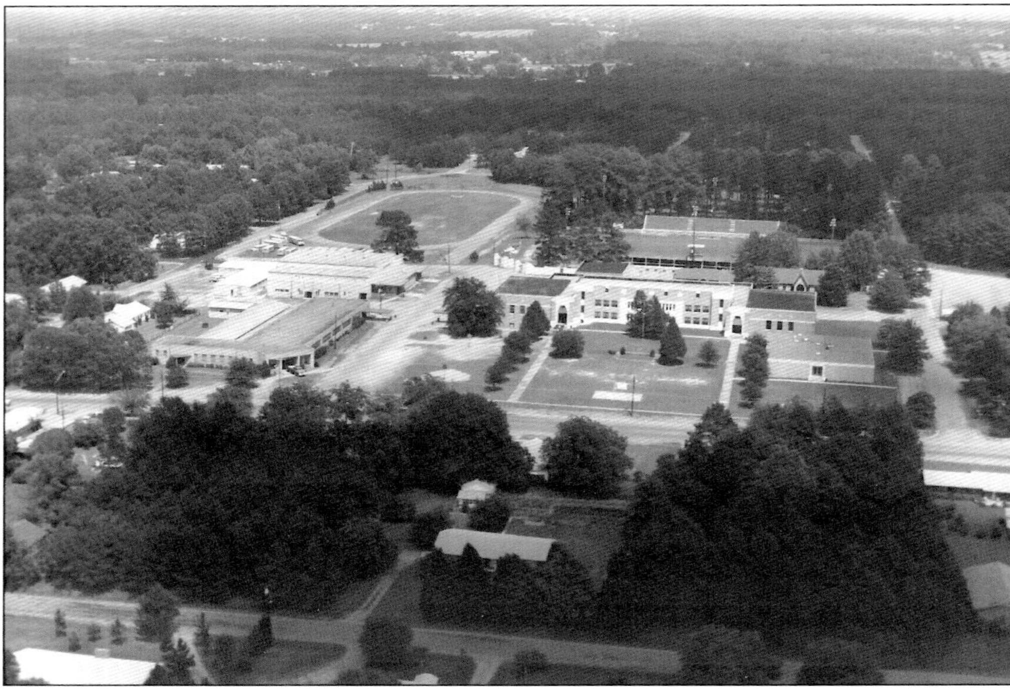

After 1922, Hope High School was moved from a wooden structure on the north end of town to Garland School, where it stayed until the building was condemned in 1930. In 1931, a new high school was constructed south of town on Main Street at a cost of $150,000. It included an intercom system that was the first of its kind in Arkansas. (Courtesy of SARA.)

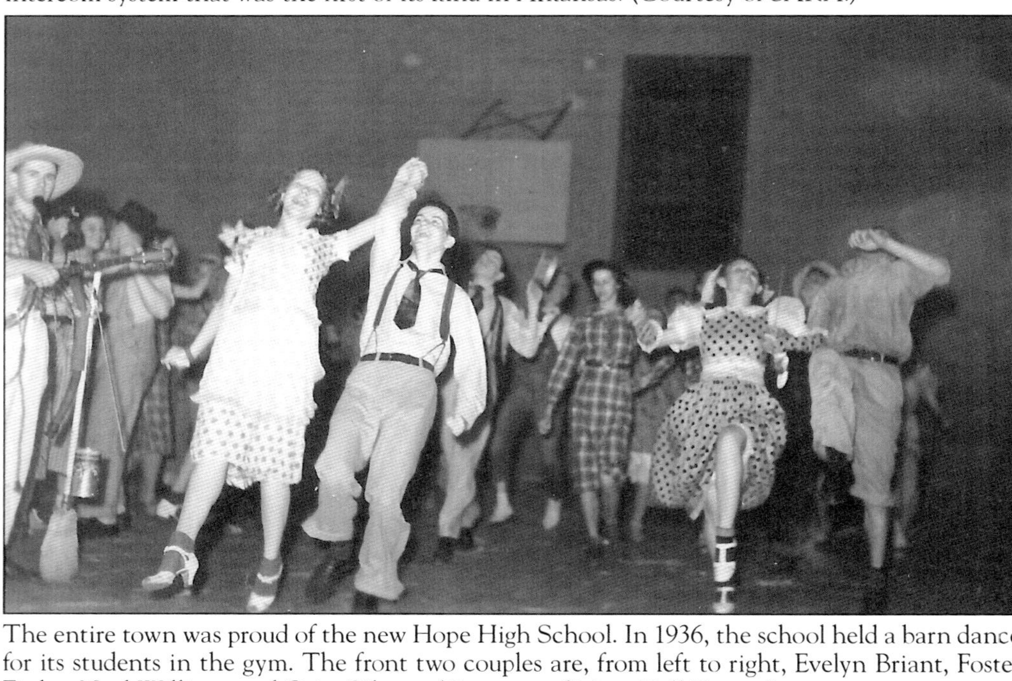

The entire town was proud of the new Hope High School. In 1936, the school held a barn dance for its students in the gym. The front two couples are, from left to right, Evelyn Briant, Foster Finley, Neel William, and Orin Gibson. (Courtesy of Mary Nell Turner.)

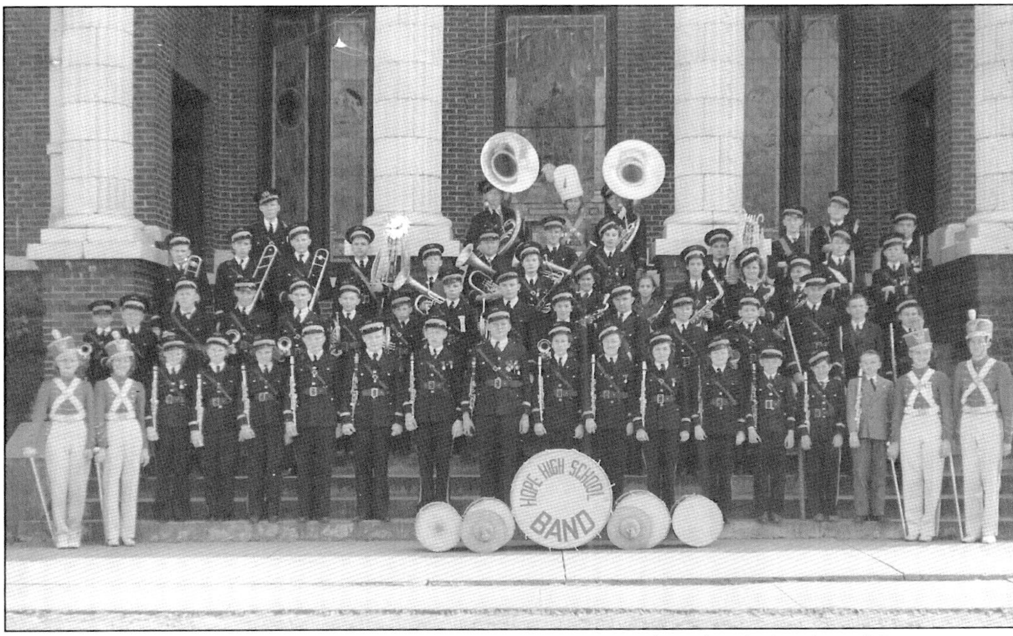

Music was an important part of the curriculum at Hope High School. As the athletic program increased, so did the need for a band. The 1955 band poses on the front steps of First Methodist Church. Members are wearing military-style uniforms that were popular during that era. (Courtesy of HVMC.)

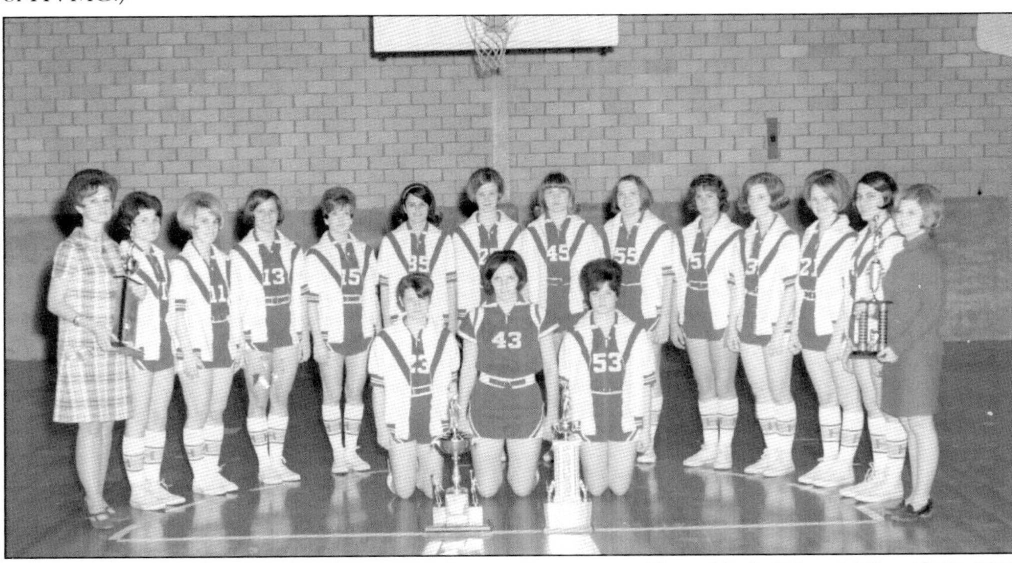

Athletics for both boys and girls increased over the years at Hope High School. The 1967–1968 Ladycats were the Class A state runners-up in basketball. From left to right are (first row) Sandra May, Sharon East Rowe, and Jo McKamie Ross; (second row) Charlotte Gibson Britton (coach), Jenny Callicott Hampton, Vicki Reeves McClelland, Carol Anthony Robinson, Gail Hartsfield McGill, Donna Byers Carozza, Mary Beth Millican Moore, Kay Coleman Caldwell, Kathryn Coleman Dickinson, Retha Adams Powell, Nellie Churchwell Hopkins, Debbie Powell Putman, Junanne Reynolds Brown, and Sue Russell Gilbert. (Courtesy of Kathryn Dickinson)

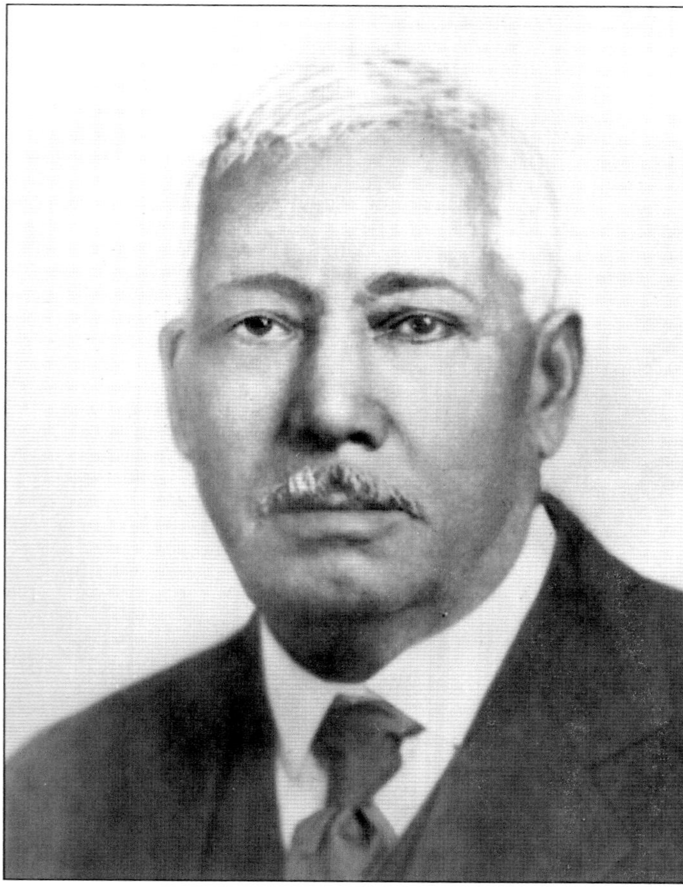

Before 1969, education in Hope was segregated. In keeping with the vision of Booker T. Washington of educating the African American community, Henry Clay Yerger (above) moved to Hope in 1886 and took charge of the school for the African American community. He was born December 4, 1860, near Spring Hill, Arkansas, just south of Hope, and died in 1935 at age 75. Through Yerger's guidance, the facility grew to include a high school and, in 1895, a training school for African American teachers. It moved from its original location on South Hazel Street to Shover Street around 1896 and became known as Shover Street School. In 1915, a second story was added to the building (below) to meet a need for classroom space. (Left, courtesy of SARA; below, courtesy of Hazel Simpson.)

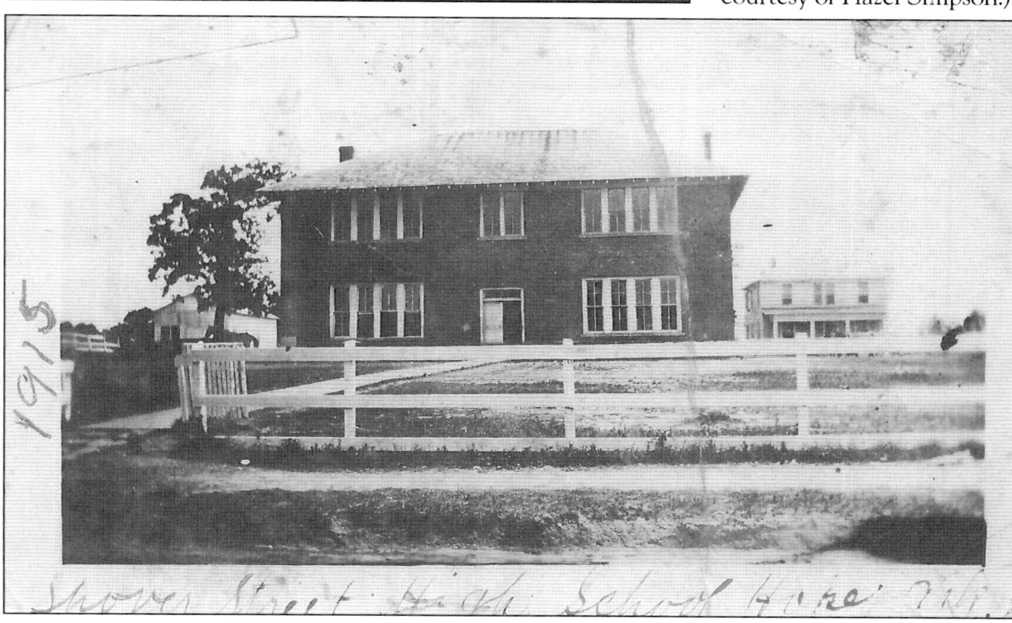

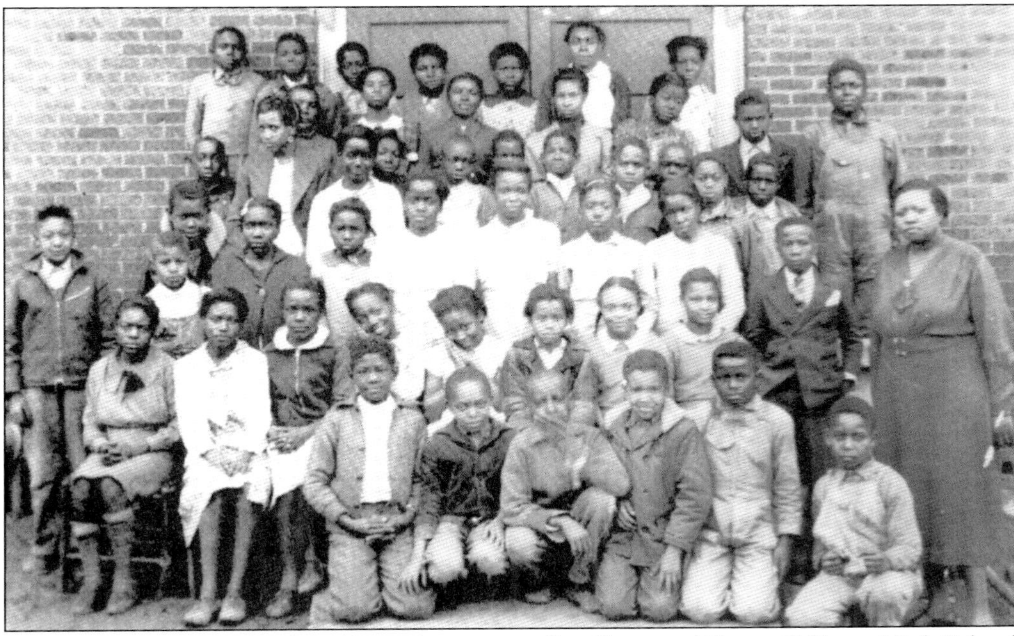

In October 1931, the school on Shover Street was officially named Henry C. Yerger High School. Other buildings were added to accommodate students attending not only from Hope but from other parts of the state of Arkansas. Shown here is the fifth-grade class taught by Emma Cooper (standing far right) in the mid-1930s. In 1935, the school included 900 students and 17 teachers. (Courtesy of Hazel Simpson.)

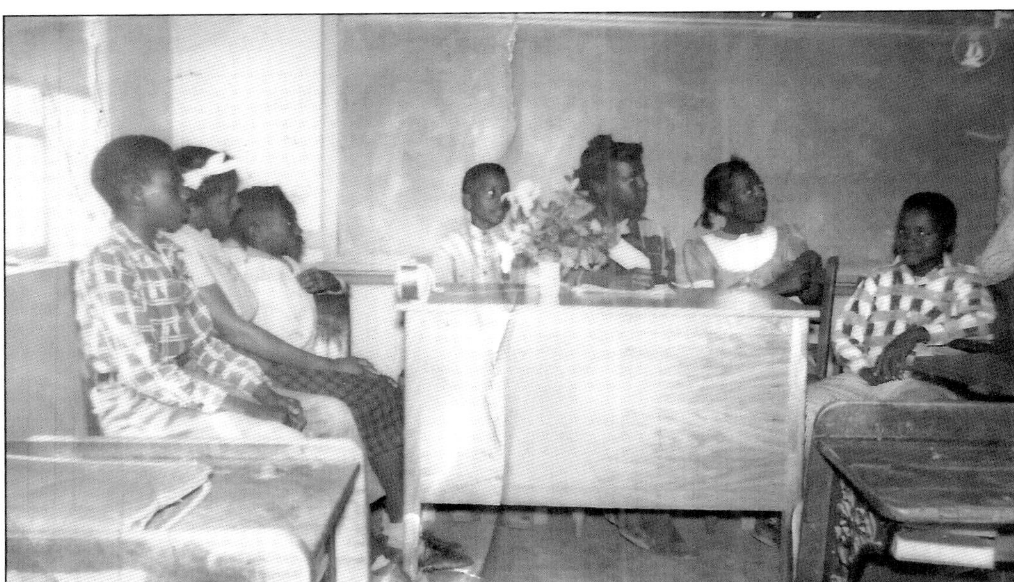

After World War II, a high school annex, new elementary buildings, and an adult education program, which included a program for World War II veterans, were added to the school. Shown in the photograph are some of the sixth-grade students in 1953. Hazel Simpson is second from the right. (Courtesy of Hazel Simpson.)

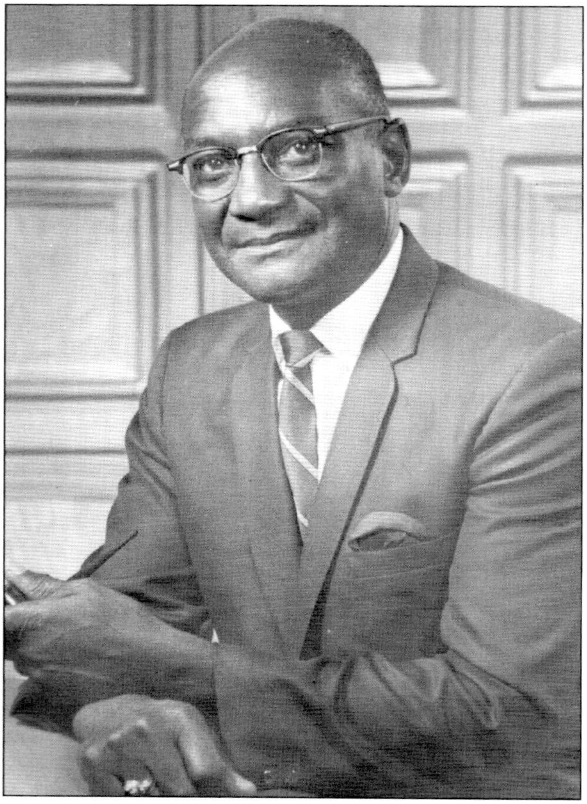

William V. Rutherford was principal of H. C. Yerger School from 1949 to 1969. During his time as principal, the school reached full accreditation standards and became a member of the North Central Association of High School and Colleges on March 28, 1958. After integration, Rutherford continued to work in the Hope public school system until he retired in 1972. (Courtesy of Hazel Simpson.)

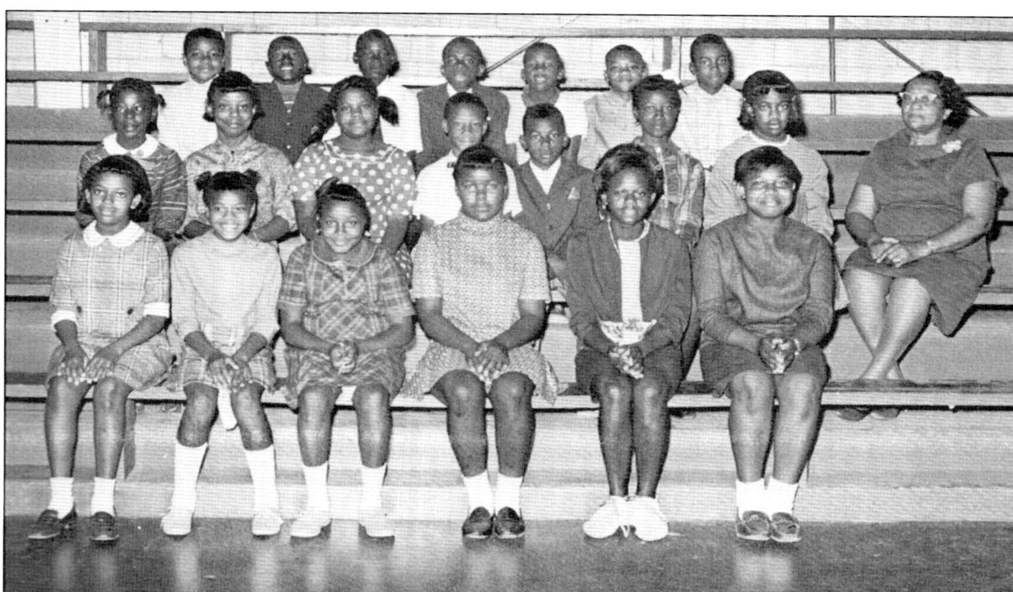

This photograph of E. Bizzell and her fifth-grade class was taken for the 1968–1969 school year at H. C. Yerger School on Shover Street. This was the last class before integration. (Courtesy of Hazel Simpson.)

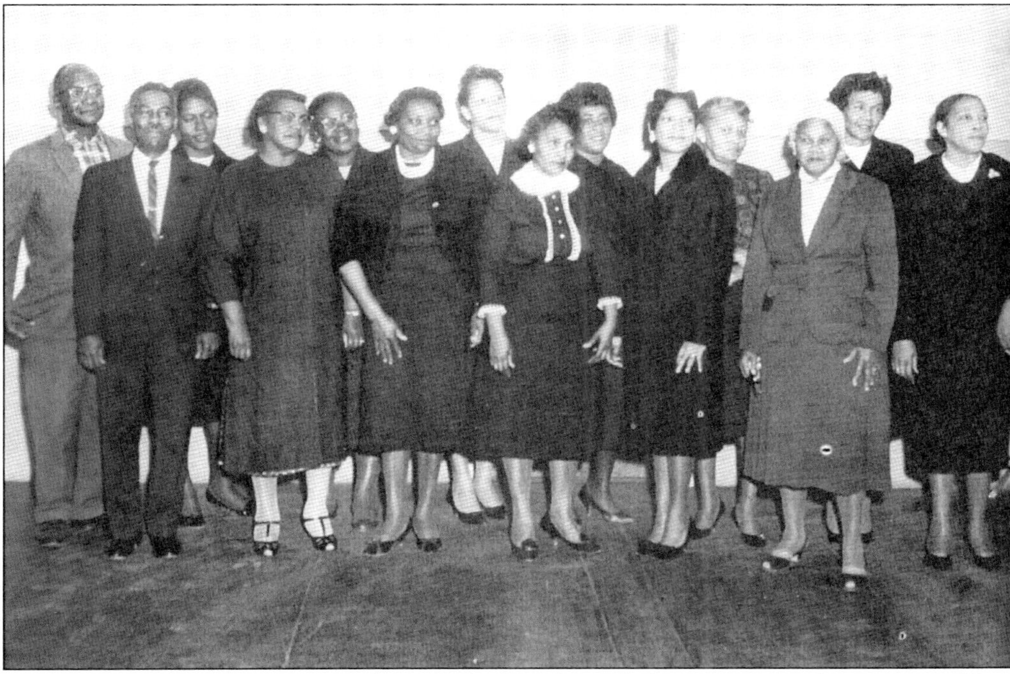

Equipment for school events, such as football and band, does not come free. Pictured here is the Band Parents Club from 1961 that raised money to secure uniforms, instruments, and transportation for the H. C. Yerger High School band. Rose Wilson was president of the club. (Courtesy of Hazel Simpson.)

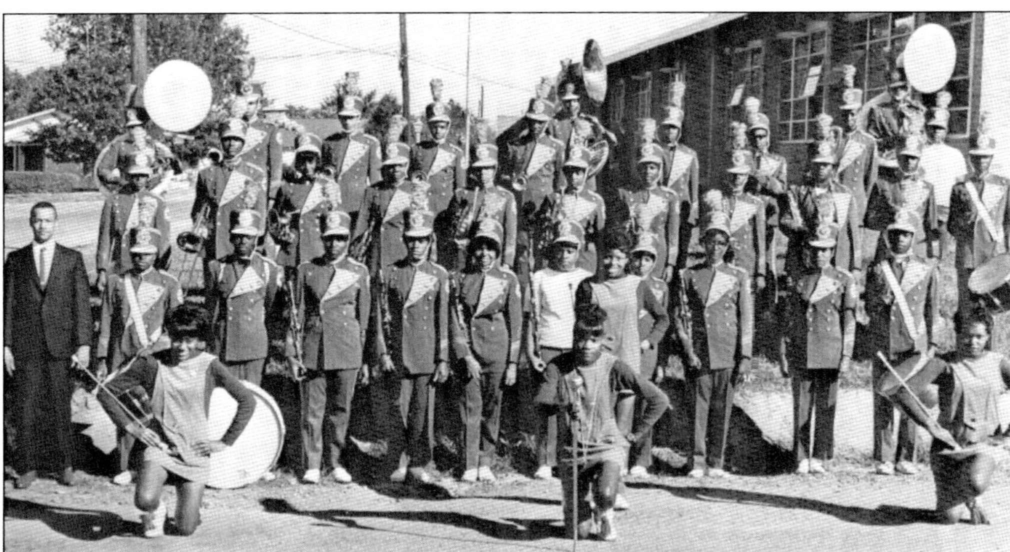

The H. C. Yerger High School band performed for the last time during the 1968–1969 school year. The colors of their uniforms were blue and gold. Afterwards, all interested musicians would be in one band at Hope High School. (Courtesy of Hazel Simpson.)

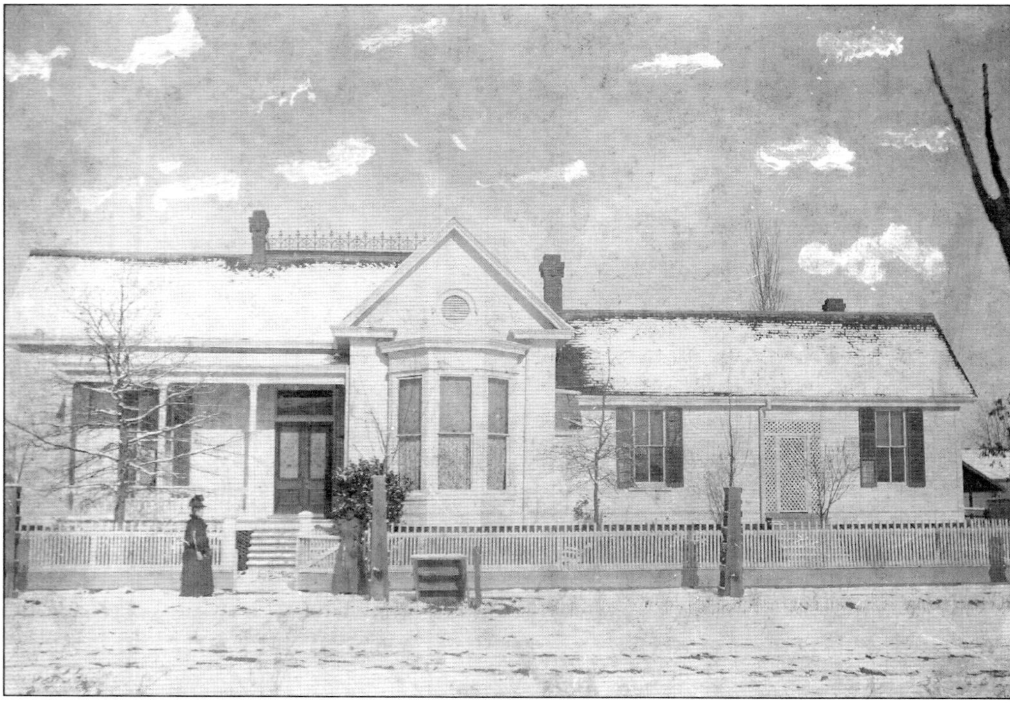

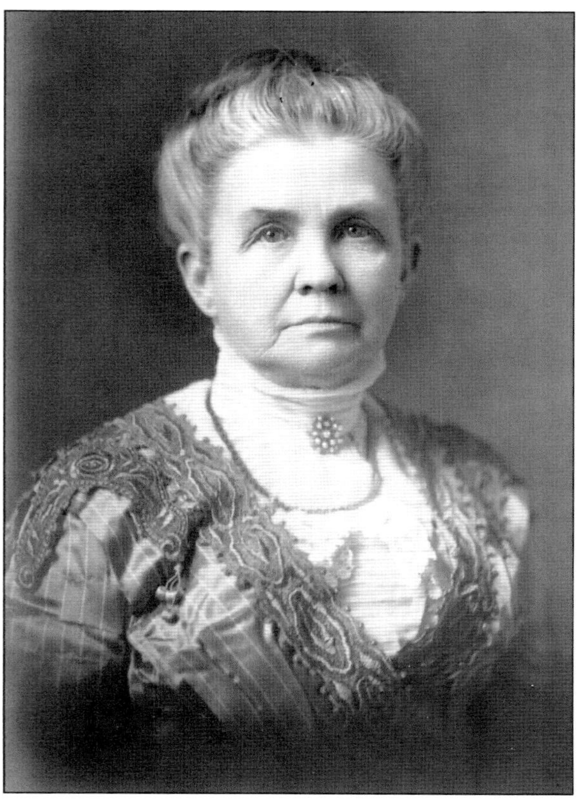

After the Civil War, veterans and ladies in the South formed different societies to help remember the men and women who lost their lives and fought for the Southern cause. On October 14, 1896, at the home of Mrs. Catherine A. Forney, the Arkansas state division of the United Daughters of the Confederacy (UDC) was organized. The house (above) was located on the corner of Elm Street and West Avenue B. Mrs. Catherine A. Forney (left) is called the Mother of the UDC in Arkansas. As part of this organization, she also founded the Pat Cleburne Chapter of the UDC earlier that year, on March 7, at Hope. This was the first UDC chapter in Arkansas and second west of the Mississippi River. (Both, courtesy of Historic Washington State Park.)

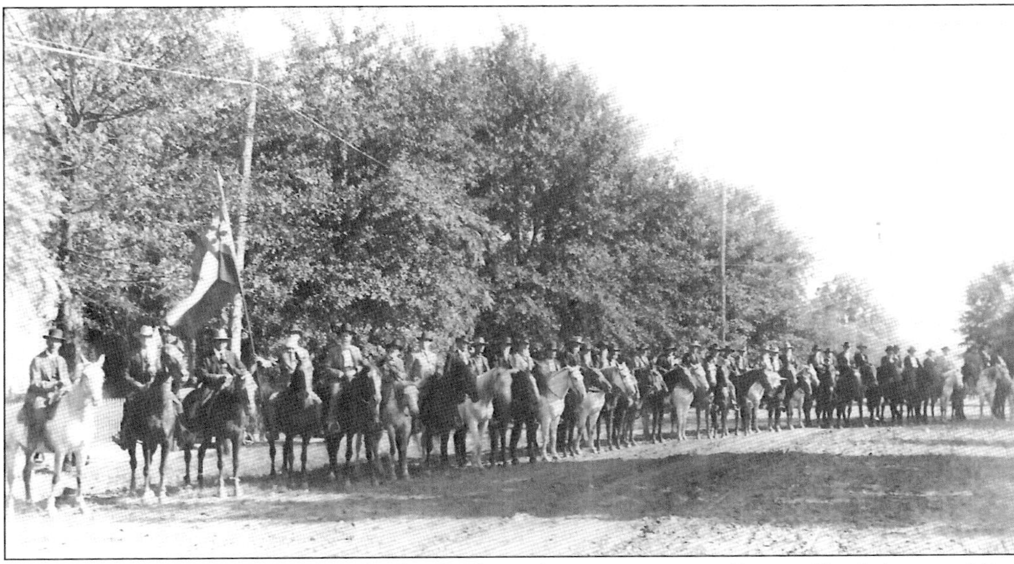

After the Civil War, veterans from both sides formed veteran societies. Former Confederate soldiers called their organization the United Confederate Veterans (UCV). Every year in Hope, on the opening day of the local fair, veterans would be honored. Around 1900, surviving members of the first unit to leave Hempstead County pose on horseback along South Main Street. (Courtesy of AHC.)

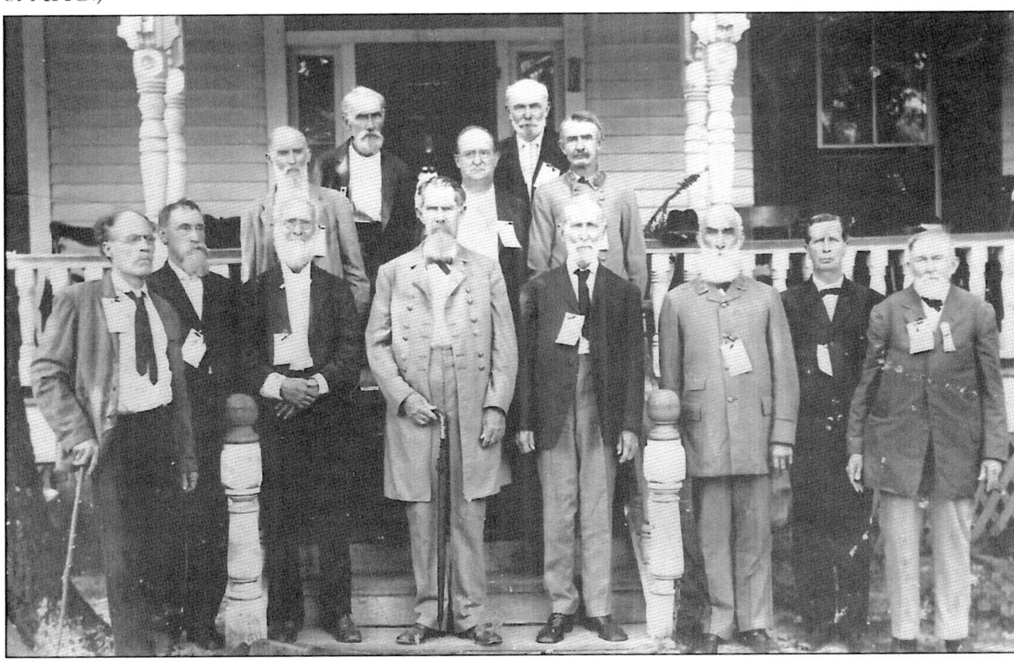

Around 1915, some of the few surviving Confederate veterans in Hope stand in front of Capt. W. B. Folsom's house at 408 East Second Street. From left to right are (first row) W. H. "Bill" Lewis, Jim Kidd, Rev. Horace Jewell, Col. W. W. Folsom, Judge A. H. Carrigan, Major Green, F. T. Wright, and "Squire" W. C. Wallace; (second row) Capt. C. A. Bridewell, B. P. Haynes, and Capt. Henry Black; (third row) Henry Robinson and Judge J. M. Hanegan. (Courtesy of SARA.)

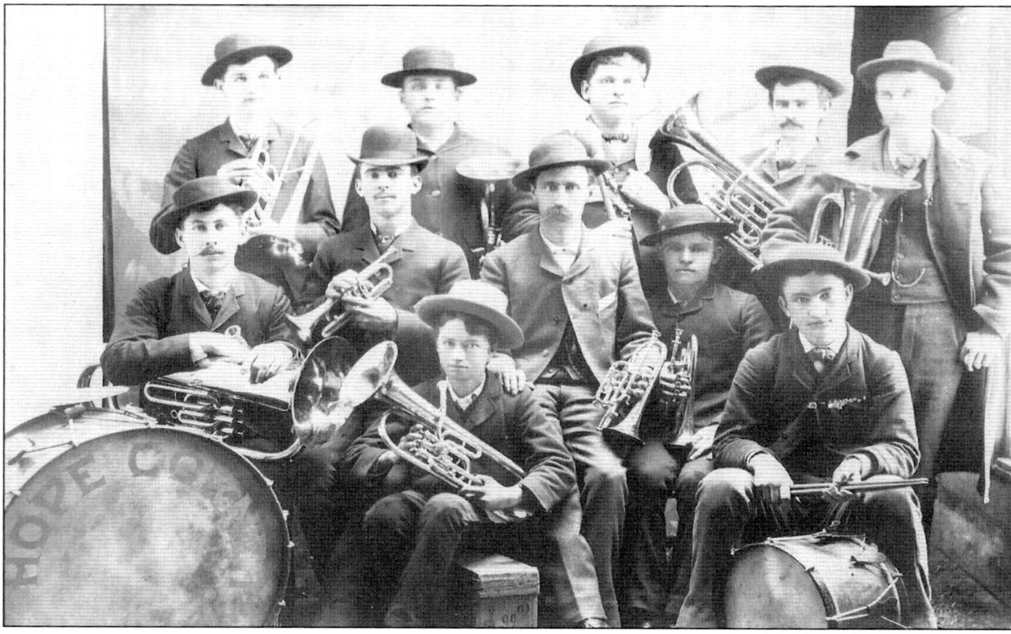

A brass band was a popular activity in many local towns across the country. In 1885, Hope had its own Cornet Band. Some men identified are, from left to right, (second row) Sam Knighton, S. H. Briant, and Ed McCorkle Sr.; (third row) Capt. Ruff Boyett, second from left. (Courtesy of SARA.)

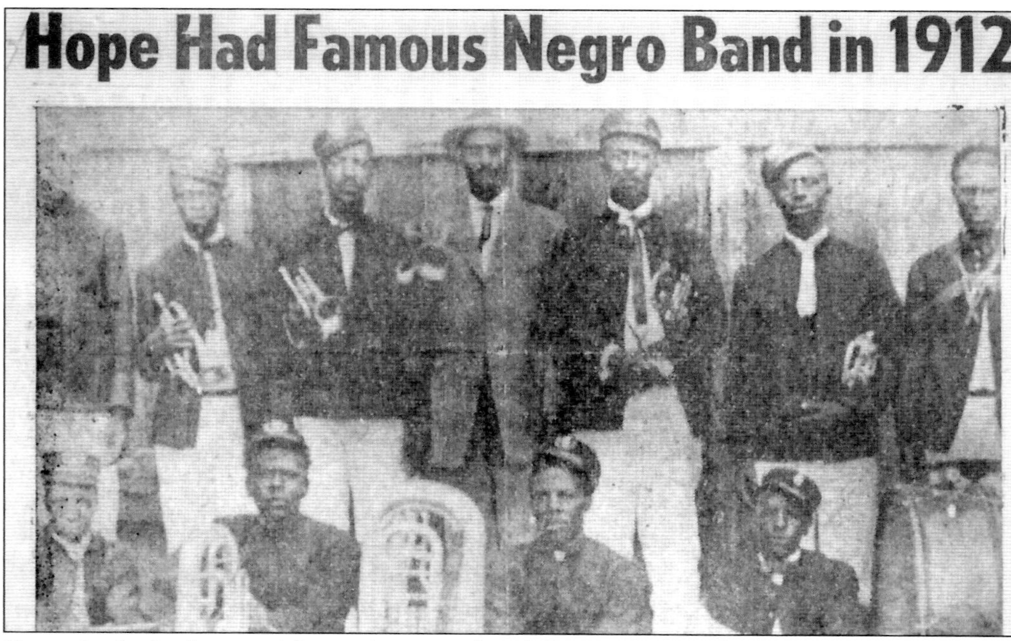

Hope Had Famous Negro Band in 1912

Hope also had a famous African American band that was reported in the newspapers in 1912. The Black Giants, from left to right, are (first row) Red Dees, Joe Jackson, Ernest Smith, and Bis Royal; (second row) John [W]ard, Arthur Steel, Alex Gibson, Joe Button, Arthur Levins, and Elliot Curry. (Courtesy of AHC.)

Scouting has been a popular community organization within the town of Hope for both boys and girls. After World War II, local Boy Scout troops sponsored an annual spring kite-flying contest that would take place north of downtown at the airport near the Cotton Compress. Shown here is Jerry O'Neal of Troop 62 with his 14-foot-tall kite. (Courtesy of Don and Mary Parker.)

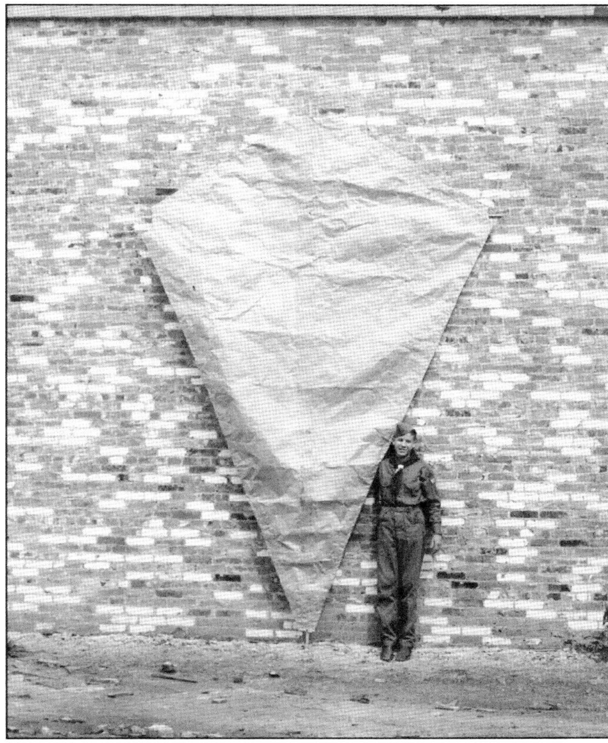

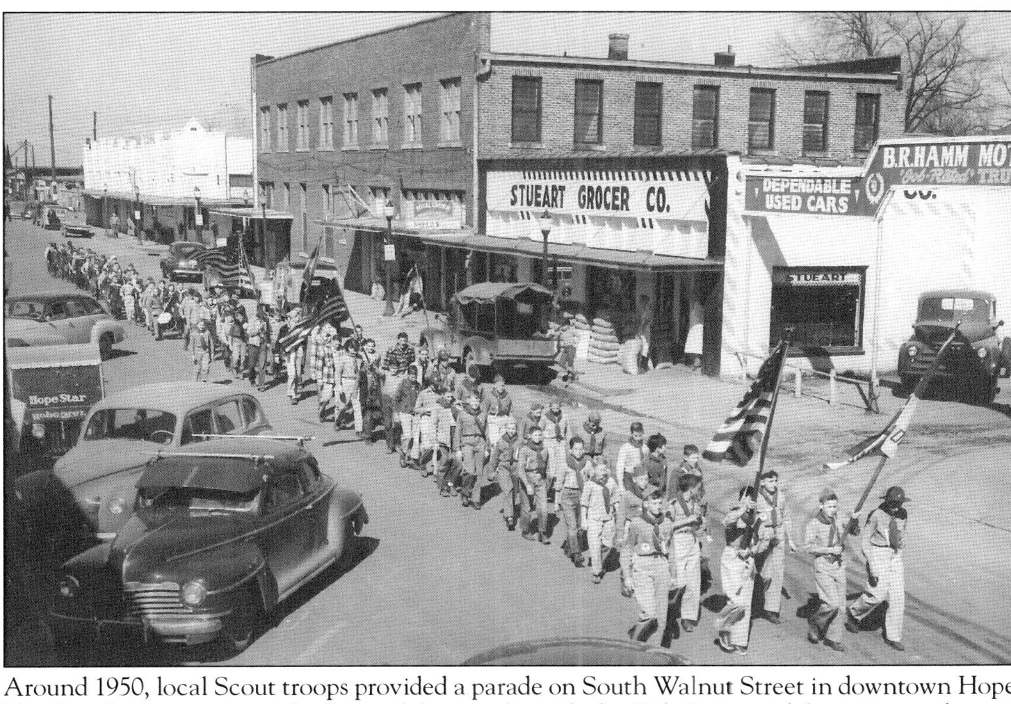

Around 1950, local Scout troops provided a parade on South Walnut Street in downtown Hope. The Boy Scout troop is in the front of the parade, with the Cub Scout pack bringing up the rear. (Courtesy of HVCM.)

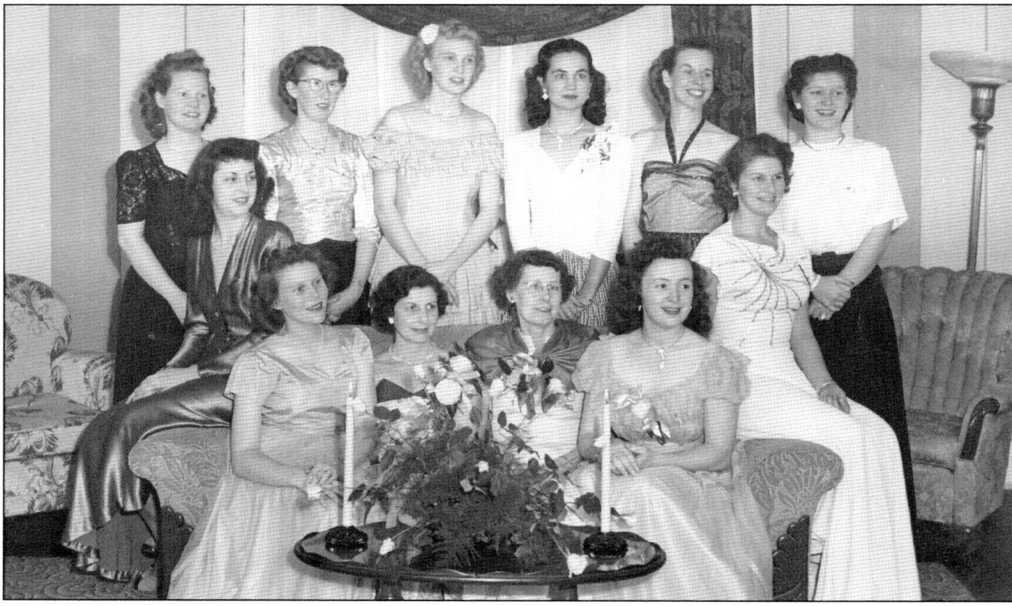

After World War II, civic clubs and organizations continued to be popular throughout Hope. In this photograph is an unidentified ladies group posing for a photograph. From left to right are (first row) unidentified, Nell Branch, ? Formby, unidentified; (second row) unidentified and Bonnie Anthony; (third row) Mary Ethel Perkins, two unidentified, Lucille Ruggles, Inez Compton, and unidentified. (Courtesy of Don and Mary Parker.)

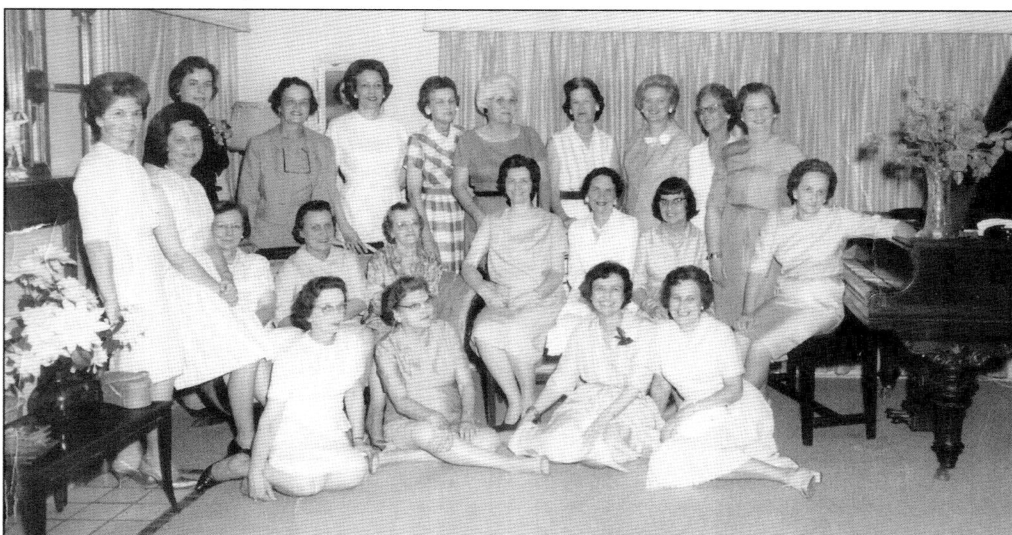

The Cosmopolitan Club was formed in Hope as a ladies group to discuss different pieces of literature. From left to right are (first row) Lilian Stewart, Mamie Jackson, Mary Nell Turner, Elizabeth Routon Arnett; (second row) Marilyn Robison, Marjorie Smith, Edith Haynes, Vivian Brown, Phoebe Perkins, Mary Ann Herndon, Ruth Hanegan, Ruth Jones, Marietta Moses; (third row) Sue Balentine, Cornelia Broach, Princess Wyatt, Laneil Lawrence, Lessie Whitman, Virginia Jones, Elizabeth Bryant, Mary Wood McKenzie, and Mary Virginia Horton. (Courtesy of Mary Nell Turner.)

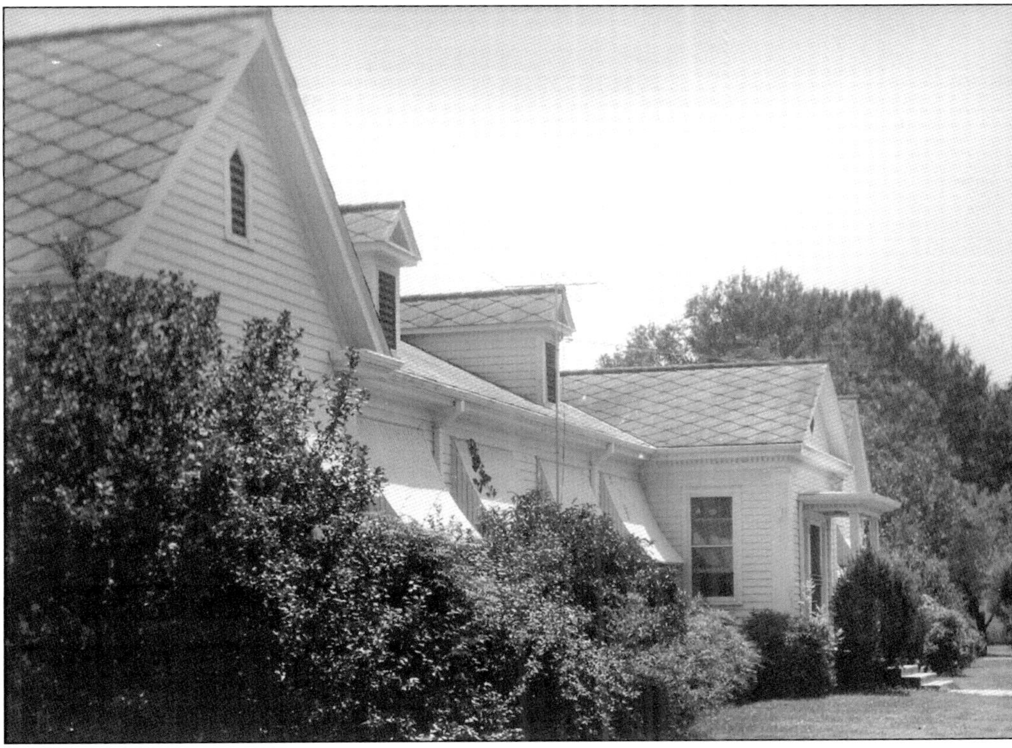

The first documented hospital in Hope was started in 1925 on the second floor of a building at the corner of Second and Walnut Streets. In 1927, through the efforts of Dr. W. R. Anderson, pastor of the First Presbyterian Church, a hospital association was formed. In 1929, it bought property on South Main and South Walnut Streets and built the Julia Chester Hospital shown here. (Courtesy of Lloyd Paul Powell.)

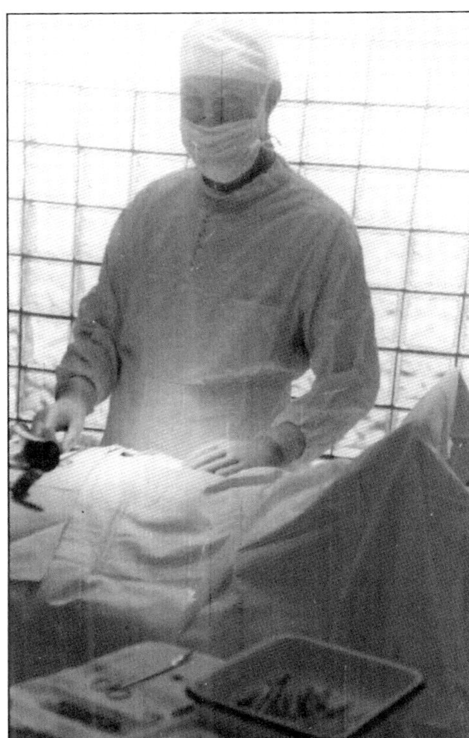

After World War II, one of Hope's favorite doctors was Jim Martindale. The scene for the *c.* 1950 photograph has been staged before he is about to perform surgery at Julia Chester Hospital. Many Hope Baby Boomers were born at this hospital, including Pres. Bill Clinton. (Courtesy of Nancy Finley.)

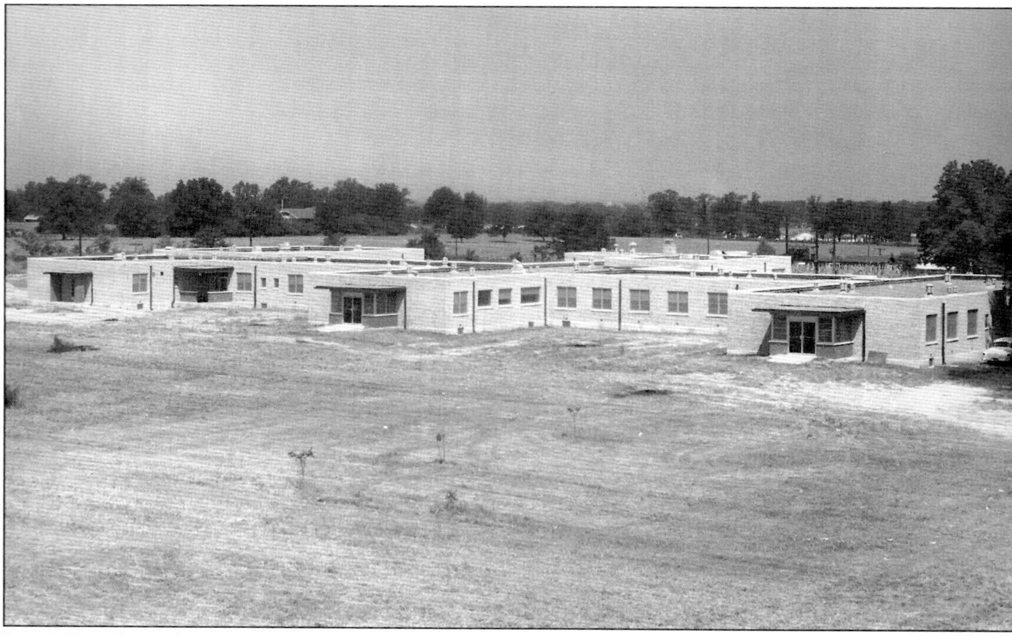

In 1955, Julia Chester Hospital was closed and converted into a nursing home. The Hope and Hempstead County Hospital Association decided it was time for a new building to meet the needs of the community and constructed a new hospital south of town on Main Street. (Courtesy of Don and Mary Parker.)

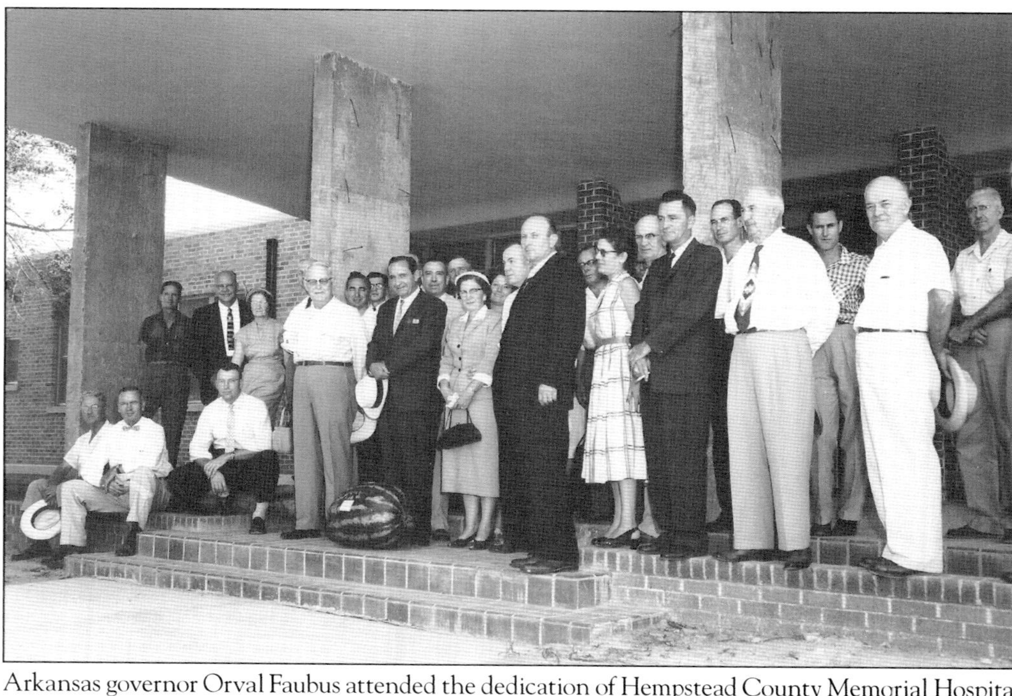

Arkansas governor Orval Faubus attended the dedication of Hempstead County Memorial Hospital in September 1955. He is seen in this photograph standing behind a Hope watermelon with town residents and members of the hospital association around him. (Courtesy of SARA.)

Three

Commerce

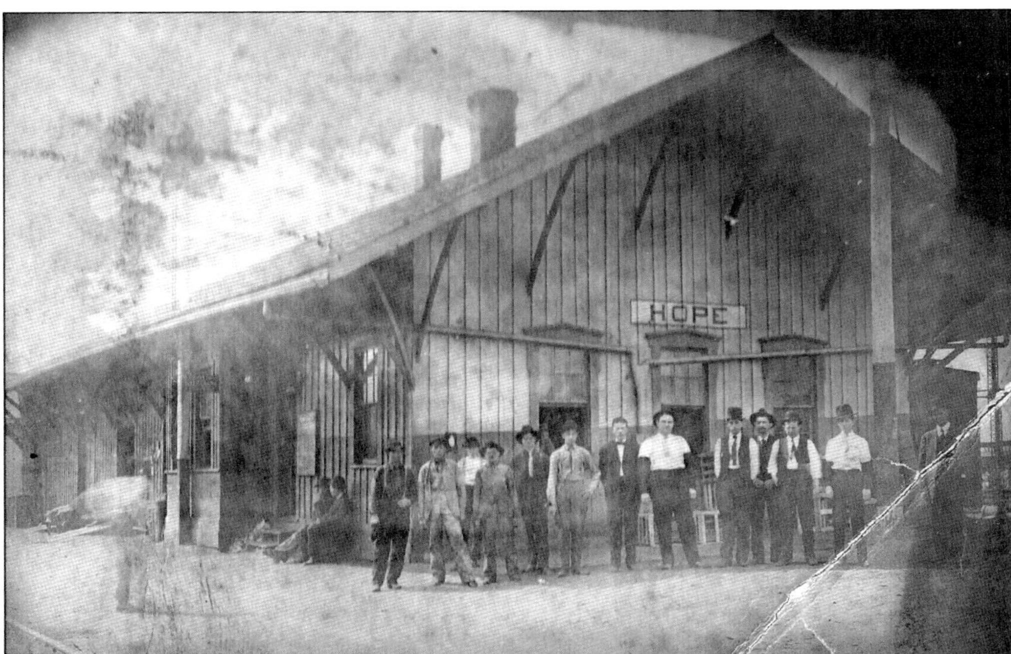

This depot was one of the first buildings constructed by the St. Louis, Iron Mountain, and Southern Railroad in 1874. Originally located on the north side of the track, the depot moved in 1912 to the south side, at the corner of East Division and South Walnut Streets. In this 1912 photograph, three men identified are John Churchman (fourth from left), Charles Shiver (sixth from left), and Walter Wright (eighth from left). (Courtesy of SARA.)

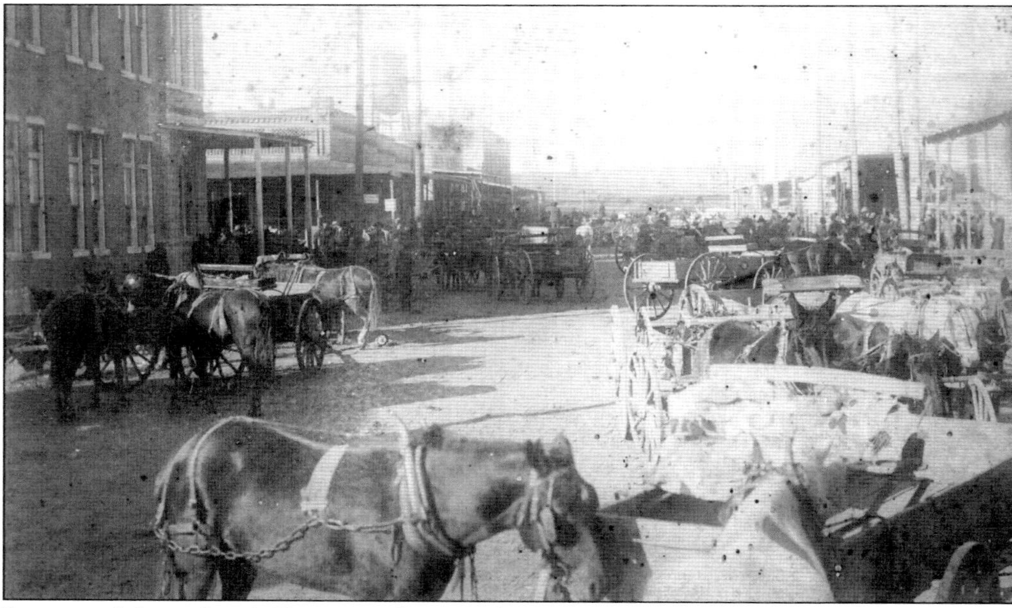

Because of the railroad, Hope was the main business location in Hempstead County. Goods could easily be brought in and shipped out through Hope to the entire country. The railroad line connected directly to St. Louis, Missouri. In 1912, the Missouri Pacific Railroad built a new brick depot on Main Street to benefit three nearby hotels, the Barlow, the Snyker, and the Capitol. The photograph above shows the new brick depot in the distance on Main Street. In the photograph below, the busy nature of Hope can be seen on Second Street, crowded with people and wagons. (Both courtesy of SARA.)

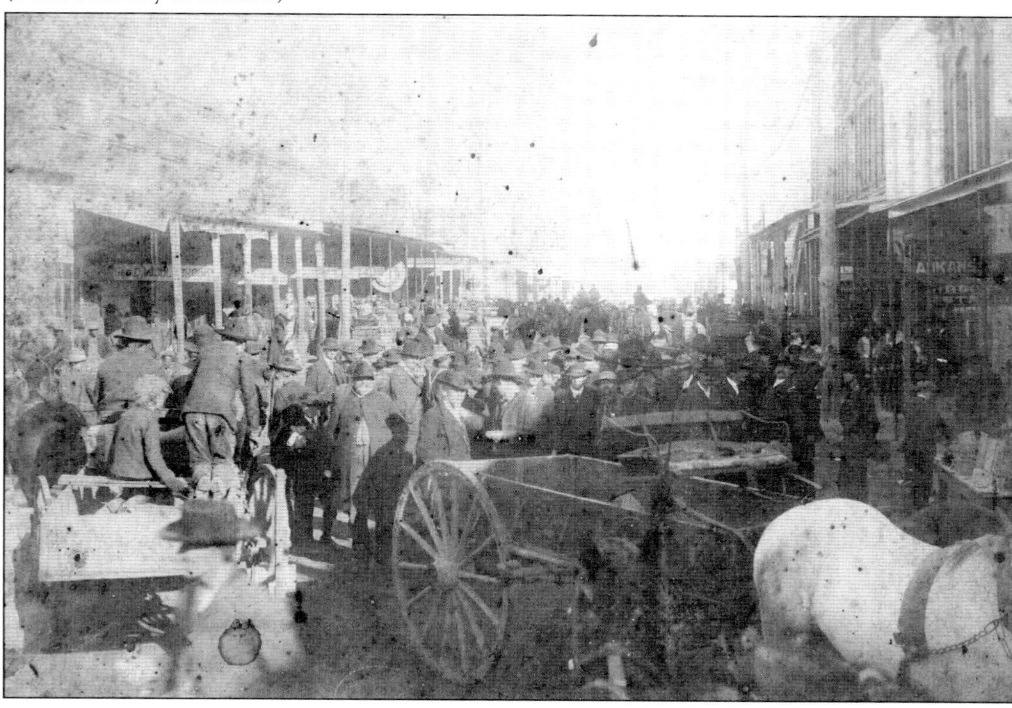

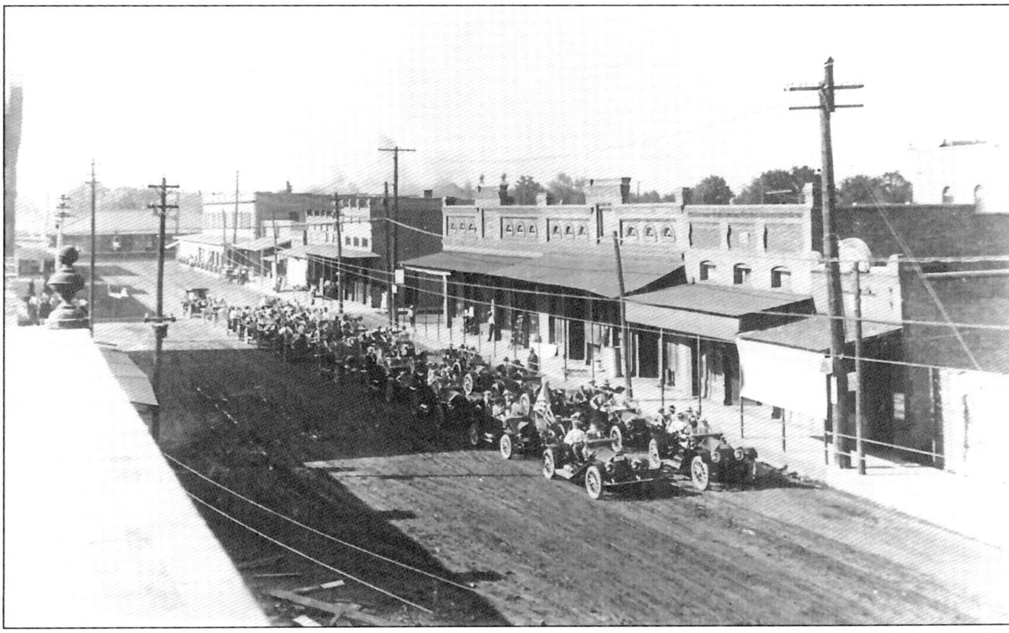

By 1910, a sewer system and natural gas lines were installed in the principal areas of Hope. New factories, like Hope Heading Factory, United Cotton Seed Oil Mills, and Hope Basket Factory, were also beginning. Around this time, cars parade along South Main Street downtown. (Courtesy of SARA.)

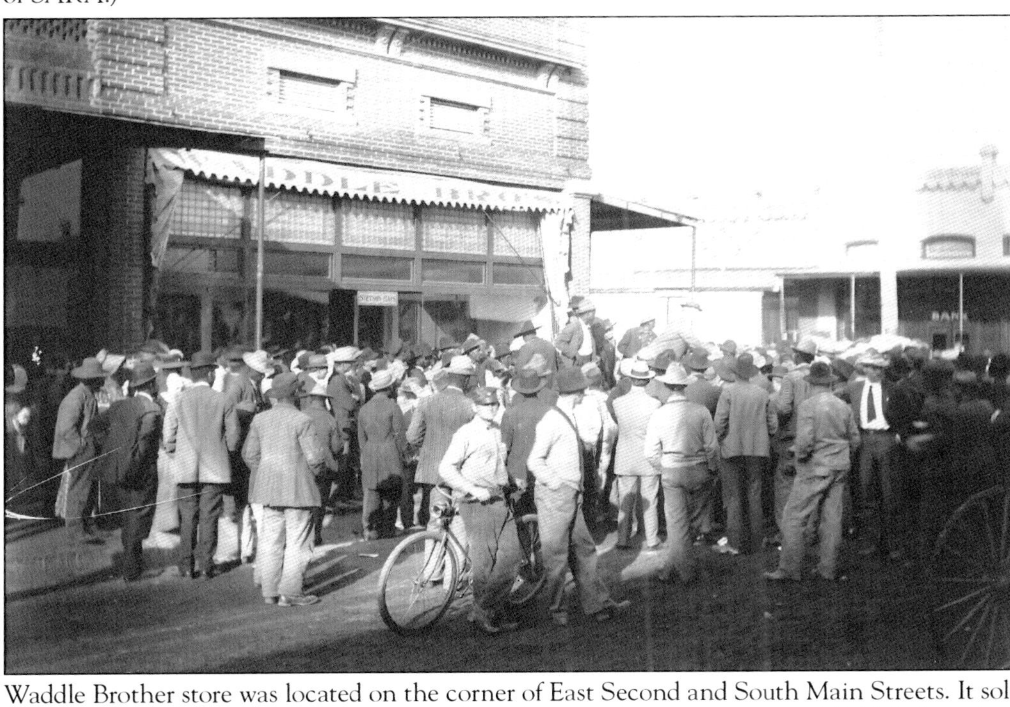

Waddle Brother store was located on the corner of East Second and South Main Streets. It sold a variety of goods, including Stetson hats. This photograph was taken around 1915, before Hope National Bank (seen across the street) built a new four-story building. (Courtesy of HVCM.)

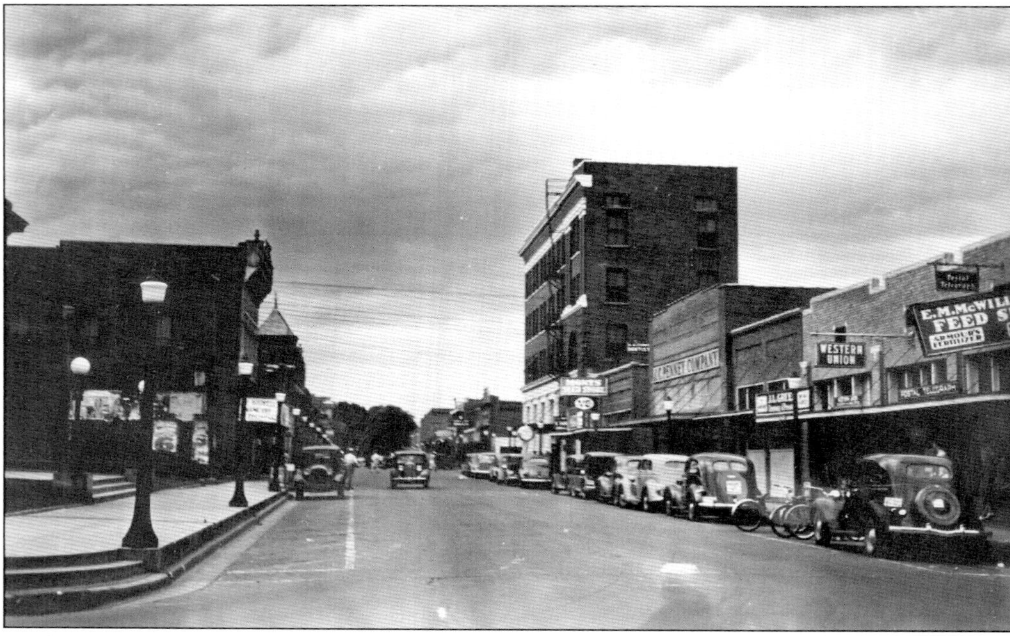

By the 1920s, all downtown and principal residential streets had been paved. Hope continued to develop during World War II and the decades following the 1940s. The above photograph was taken around 1945 looking west up Second Street at the intersection with Walnut Street. Stores such as Western Union and Ernest M. McWilliams's food and feed store can be seen. The photograph below shows businesses one block down Second Street looking west from the intersection with Main Street. Businesses such as Scott's and Owen's department stores are on the left-hand side of the street; at the end is the Saenger Theatre, which featured the latest movies from Hollywood. (Above, courtesy of Don and Mary Parker; below, courtesy of HVCM.)

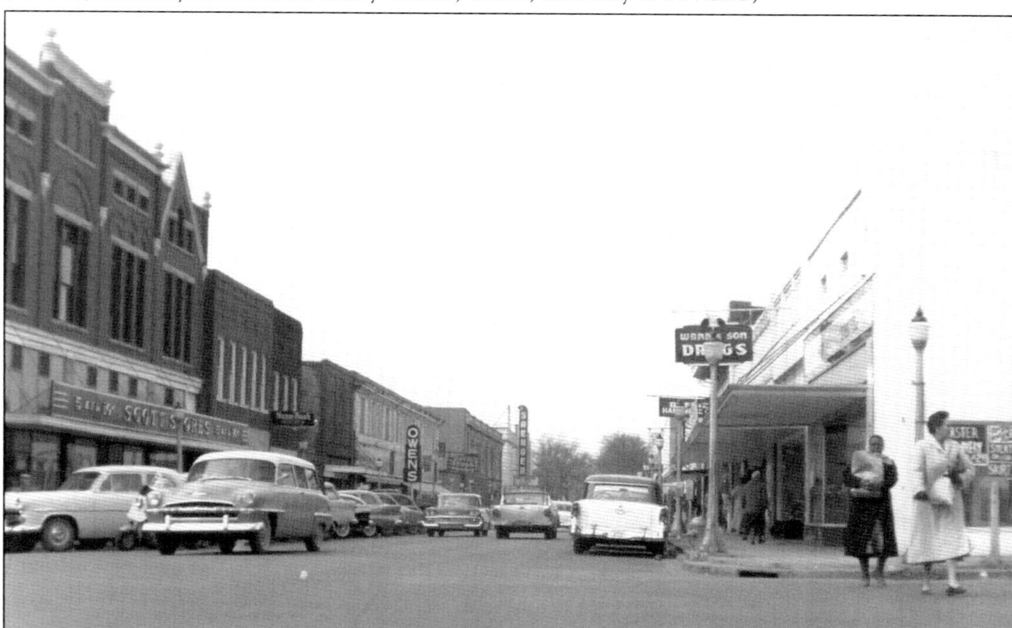

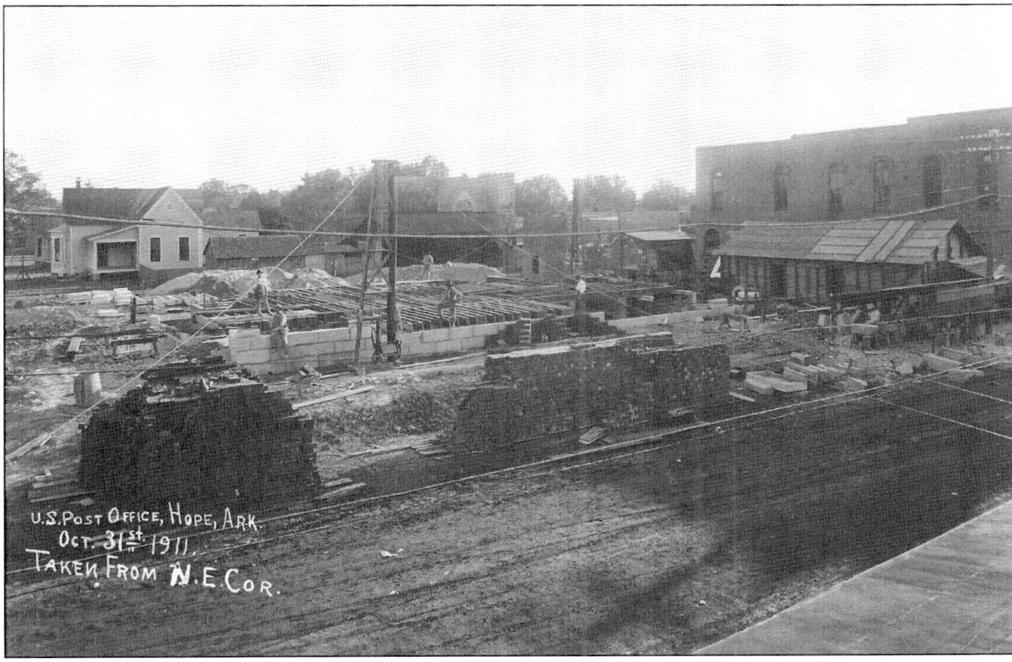

On October 31, 1911, a foundation was put in place for a new U.S. Post Office in downtown Hope. It was located on the corner of Walnut and Second Streets. In the background is the concrete-block First Baptist Church. (Courtesy of HVCM.)

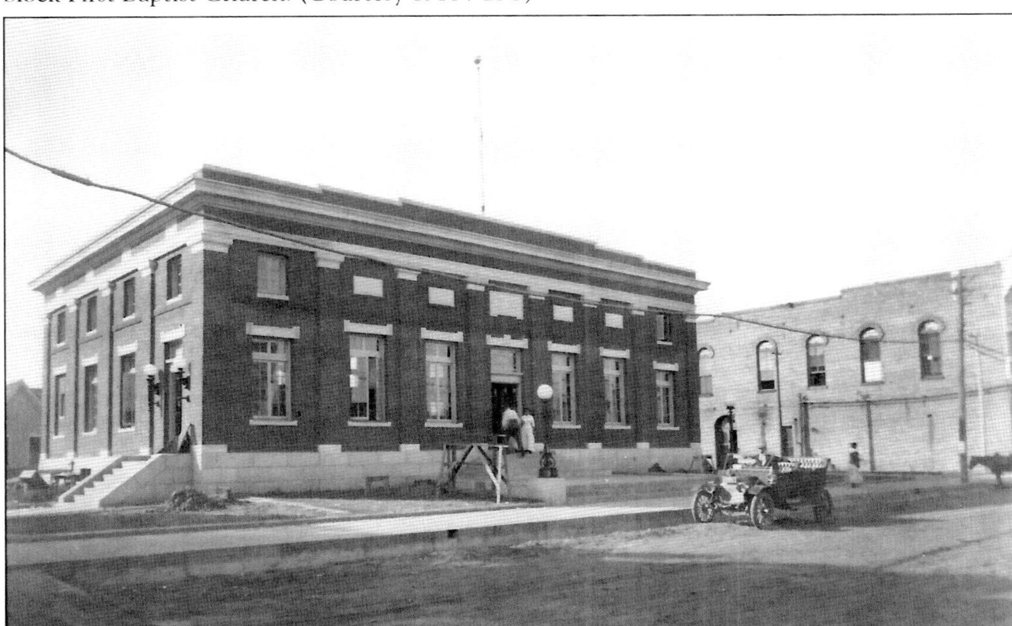

By 1912, the post office was open for business. Built at a cost of $50,000, it was a handsome structure in the Colonial Revival style. When a new post office opened in 1965, this building was sold to the Hope public school district to serve as administrative offices. (Courtesy of Mary Nell Turner.)

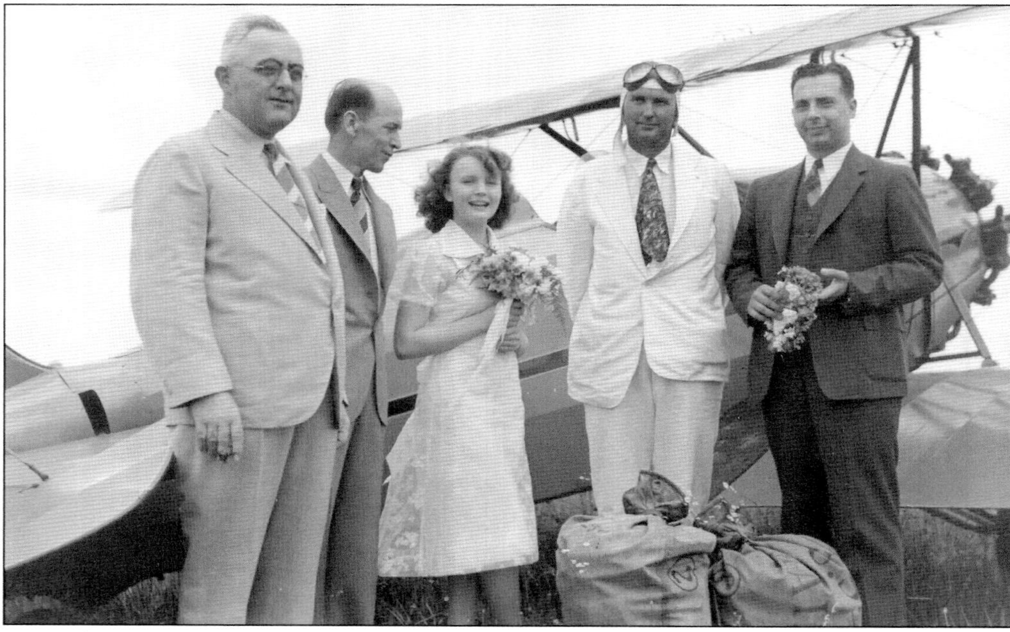

Around 1935, Hope received its first airmail service. The plane landed at the local Hope airport, a large open field just north of town near modern-day Compress Street. In the photograph, from left to right, are unidentified, Robert Wilson (postmaster), Mary Wilson, unidentified, and Mayor Albert Graves. (Courtesy of HVCM.)

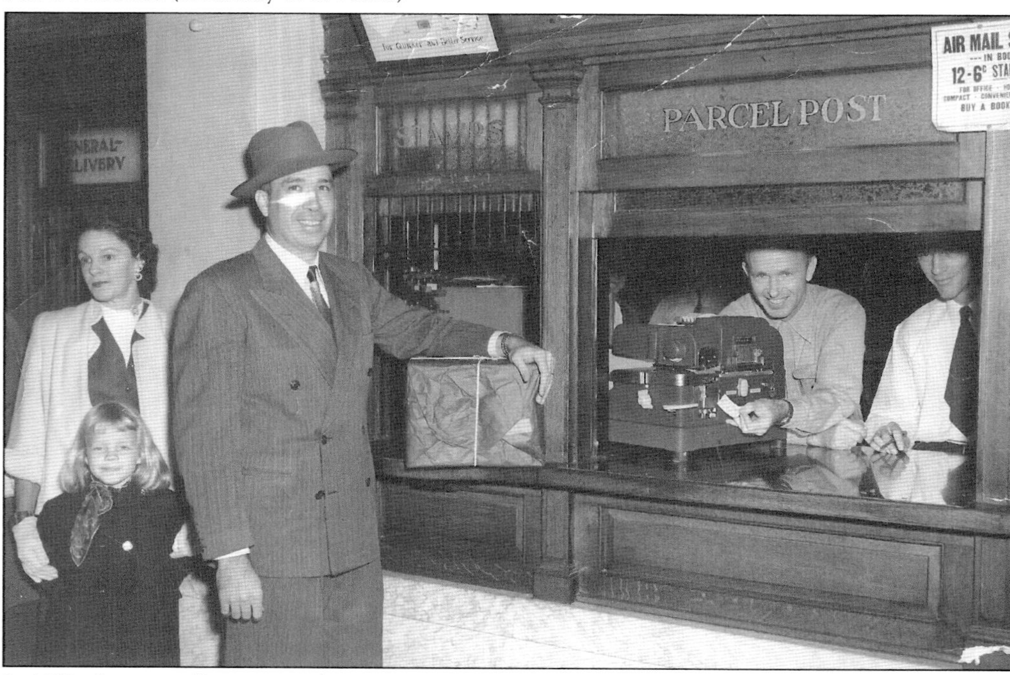

In 1952, the post office acquired a new postage meter for large packages. Seen here in the photograph are, from left to right, Margaerite Forster, Susan Forster, Mayor John L. Wilson, Clyde Browning, and McDowell Turner. (Courtesy of Mary Nell Turner.)

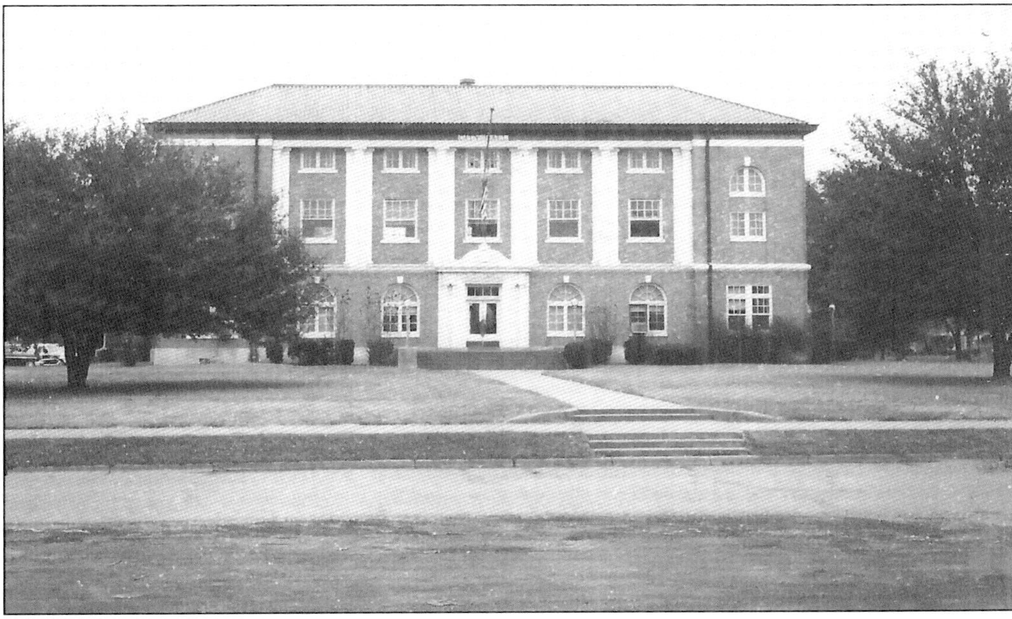

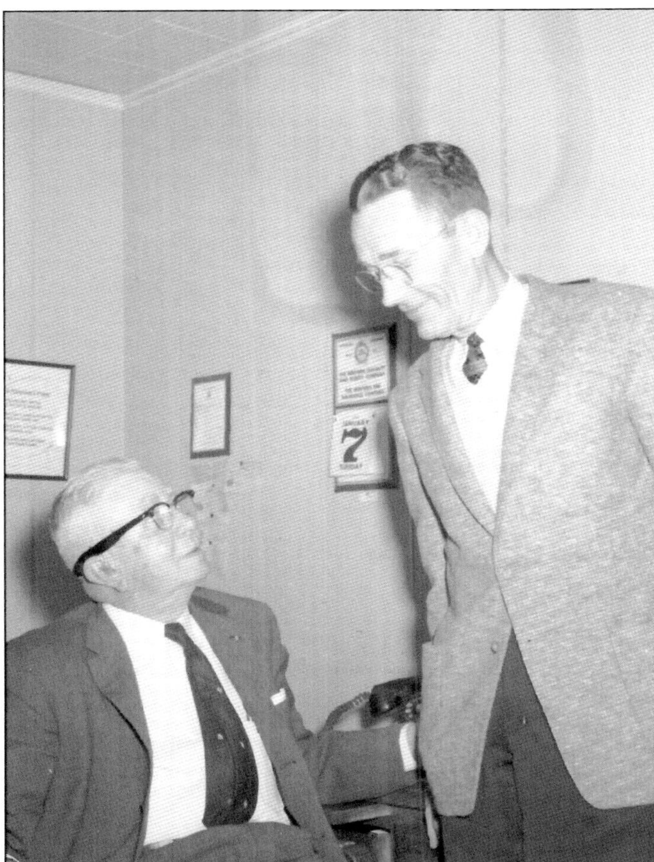

In 1926, a grand city hall (above) for Hope was completed without a bond issue. The first floor consisted of offices, and the upstairs held a large auditorium for various civic and community functions. The "Broadway of America" highway, earlier known as the Bankhead highway, passed directly in front of the building on Avenue A. For many years, Hope was run by a strong mayoral system, with the mayor coordinating all city functions. In 1957, the town voted to change to a city manager administration, and Hope became the first municipality in Arkansas with that type of government. Hope's first city manager was Garland Medders. In the photograph to the right, Medders is seen with local civic leader and long-time resident Roy Anderson. Medders was originally from Texas, where he served as city manager for several towns. (Above, courtesy of SARA; right, courtesy of AHC.)

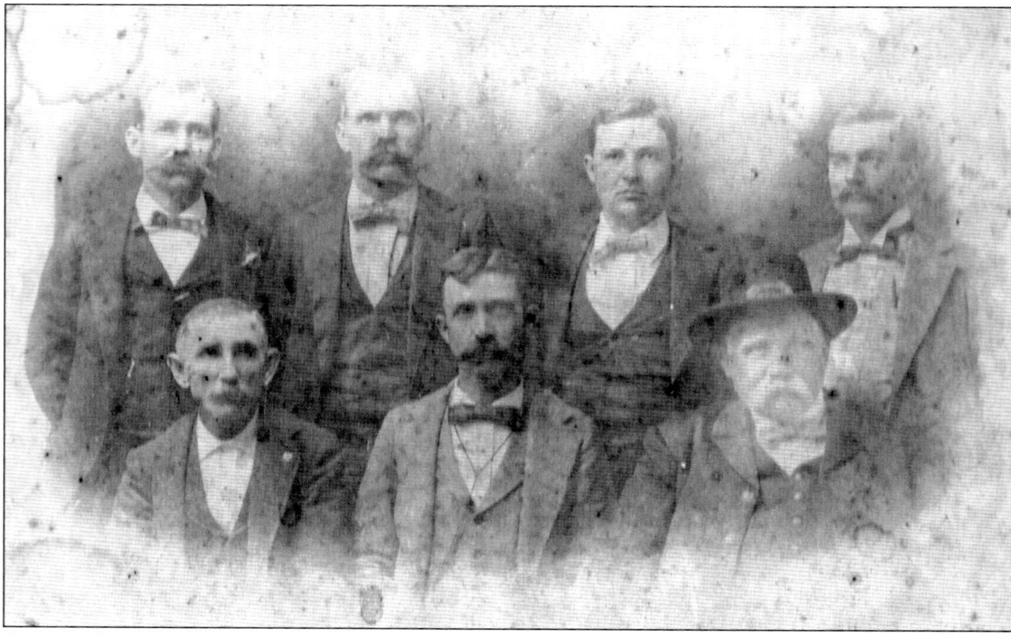

On April 19, 1898, city officials pose for a photograph after being sworn in. They are, from left to right, (first row) J. T. Barr (alderman), John Spragins (mayor), and "Pappy" Kyle (city marshal); (second row) T. R. Billingsley (city recorder), W. W. Duckett (alderman), S. V. Bracy (alderman), and J. B. Stone (alderman). (Courtesy of SARA.)

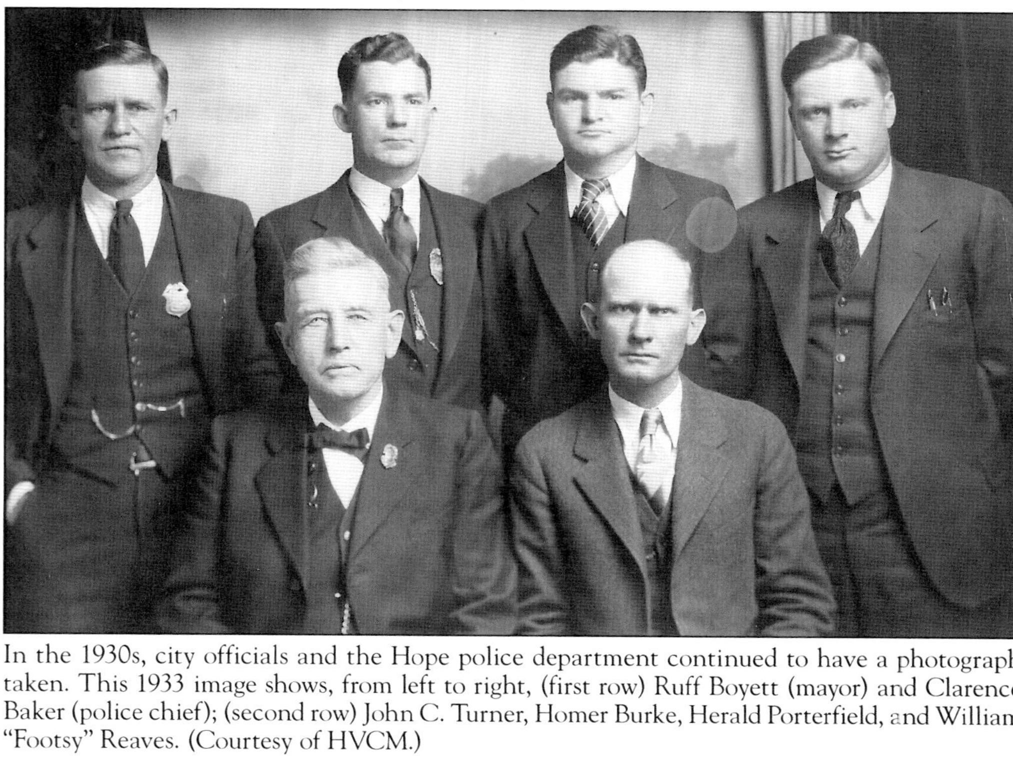

In the 1930s, city officials and the Hope police department continued to have a photograph taken. This 1933 image shows, from left to right, (first row) Ruff Boyett (mayor) and Clarence Baker (police chief); (second row) John C. Turner, Homer Burke, Herald Porterfield, and William "Footsy" Reaves. (Courtesy of HVCM.)

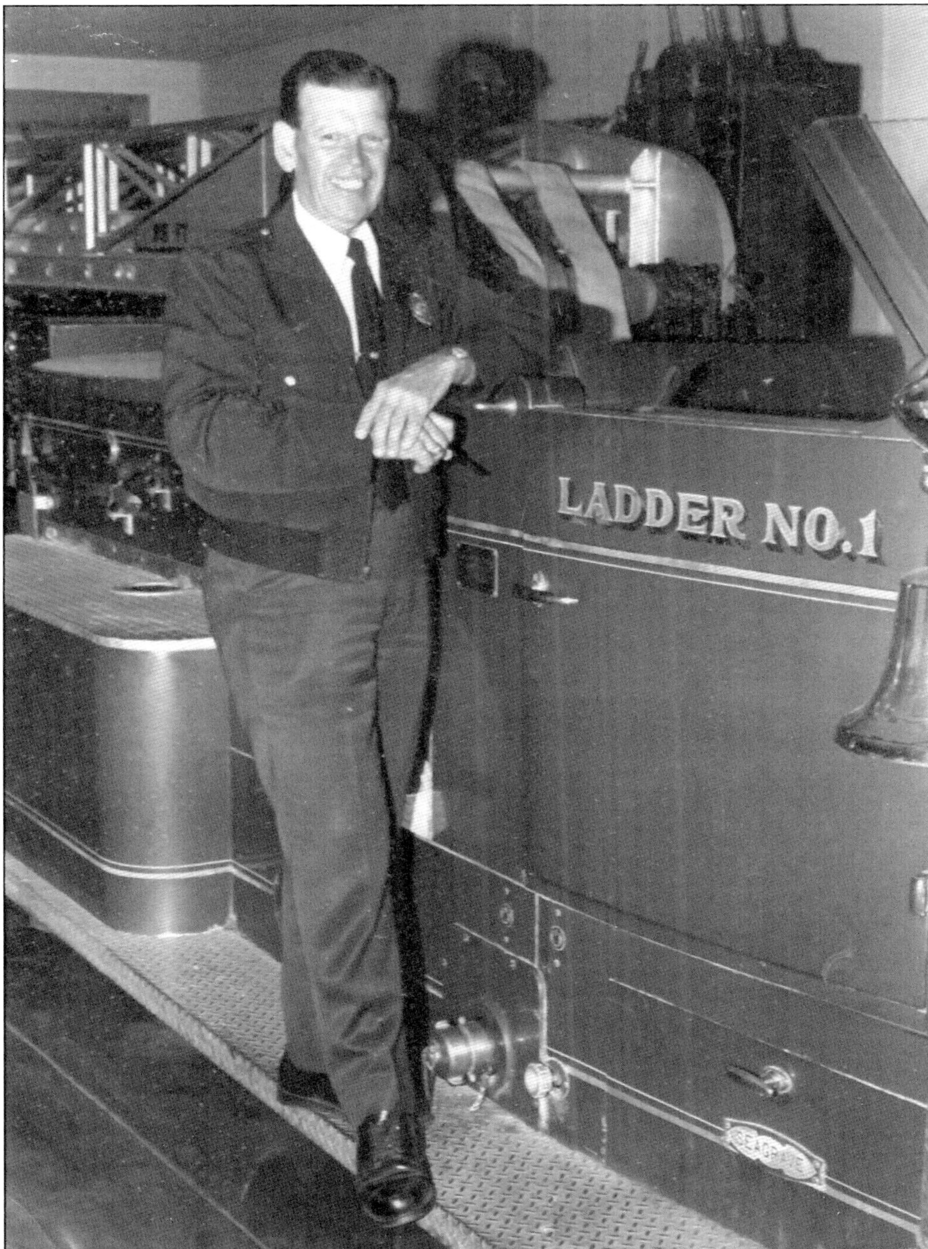

In 1939, the Hope Fire Department received a new building funded by the Public Works Administration. It was built on the northwest corner of Second and Laurel Streets. One of the longest-serving fire chiefs was Jim Cobb, pictured here around 1960 next to ladder truck No. 1. Except for four years on a tour of duty with the military police, Cobb worked in the fire department for 35 years from May 1941. He began his fire department service fighting a blaze at the Bruner Ivory Handle Company that burned two-thirds of the building. On his last day as a fireman in May 1976, he responded to one last call, at the Arkansas Machine Specialty Shop located on the north side of town. (Courtesy of Linda Lee.)

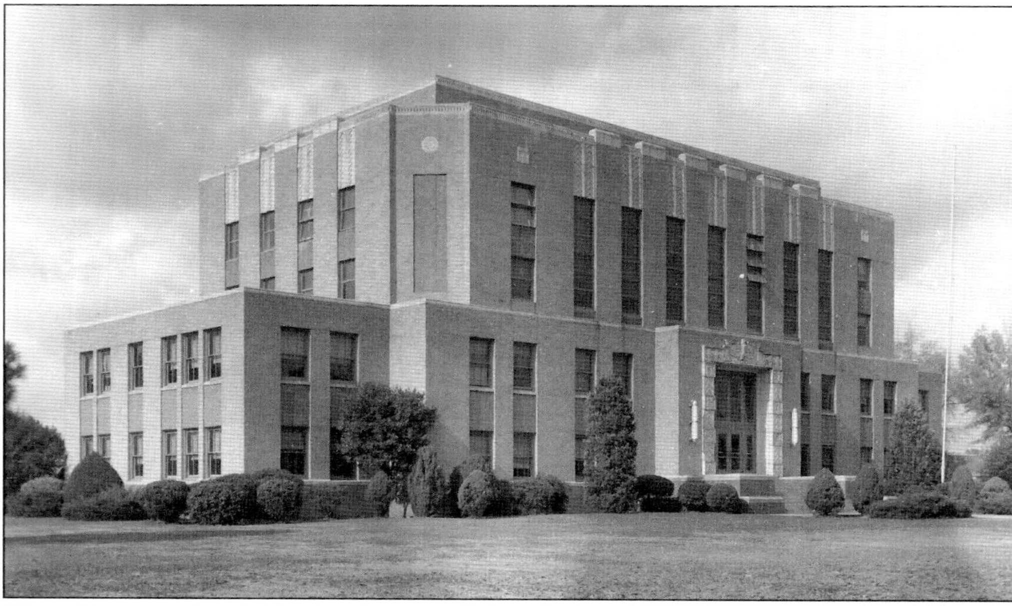

When Hope was founded by the Cairo and Fulton Railroad in 1873, Washington was the county seat. Located 10 miles north of Hope, it had been the seat of Hempstead County since 1824. As Hope grew over the years, Washington declined in both population and size. Four different times—in 1878, 1882, 1910, and 1914—the county put forward a vote to approve moving the seat of government. Finally, in 1939, a new courthouse was built in Hope on the original site of Garland School under the direction of local general contractor B. W. Edwards. Members of the local Freemasons, Whitefield Lodge No. 239, dedicate the cornerstone to the building. (Above, courtesy of Don and Mary Parker; below, courtesy of Mary Nell Turner.)

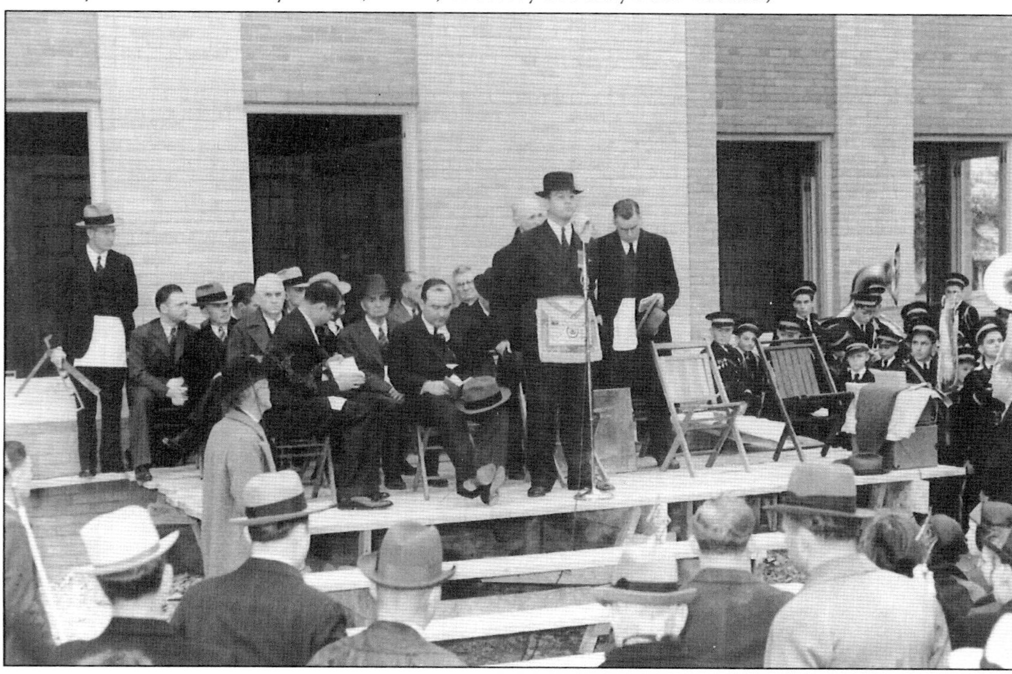

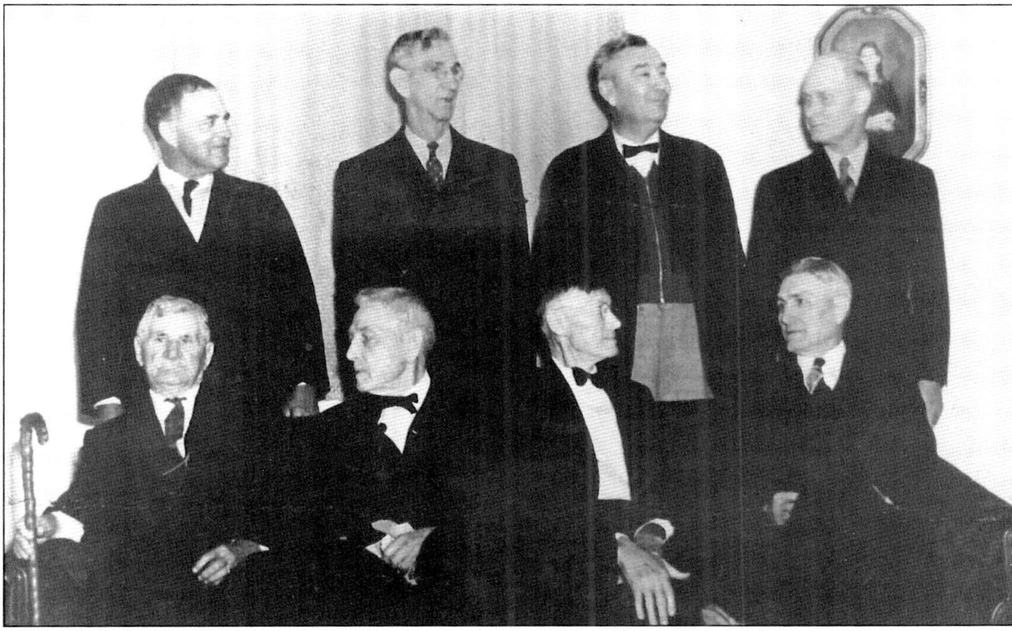

Eight former sheriffs of Hempstead County gathered around 1938 to remember their service to the county. They are, from left to right, (first row) Ed Velvin (1909–1912), Ruff Boyett (1913–1916), Bob Keel (1917–1920), and Jim Dodson (1921–1924); (second row) Jim Bearden (1925–1926, 1936–1942), Dorsey McRae (1927–1930), John L. Wilson (1931–1934), and Clarence Baker (1935–1938). (Courtesy of SARA.)

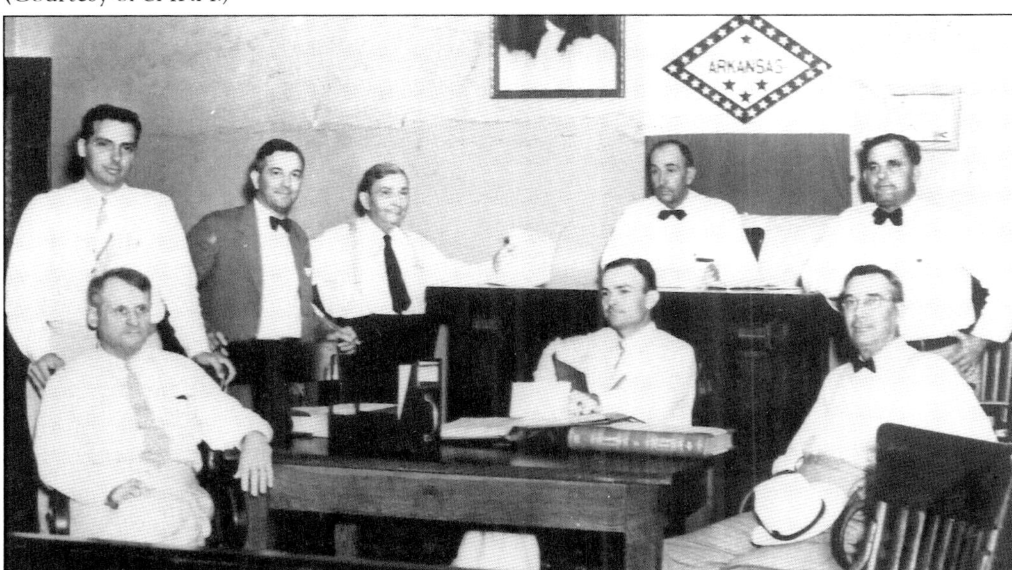

Hempstead County officials, along with others, had a photograph taken in 1938, their last year at the courthouse in Washington. Sitting, from left to right, are Steve Carrigan Jr. (attorney), Ray McDowell (county clerk), and John L. Wilson (judge). Standing behind, from left to right, are Albert Graves Jr. (attorney), Ed McFaddin, (later associate justice of the Arkansas Supreme Court), John P. Gibson, Frank Rider (county judge), and Jim Bearden (sheriff). (Courtesy of SARA.)

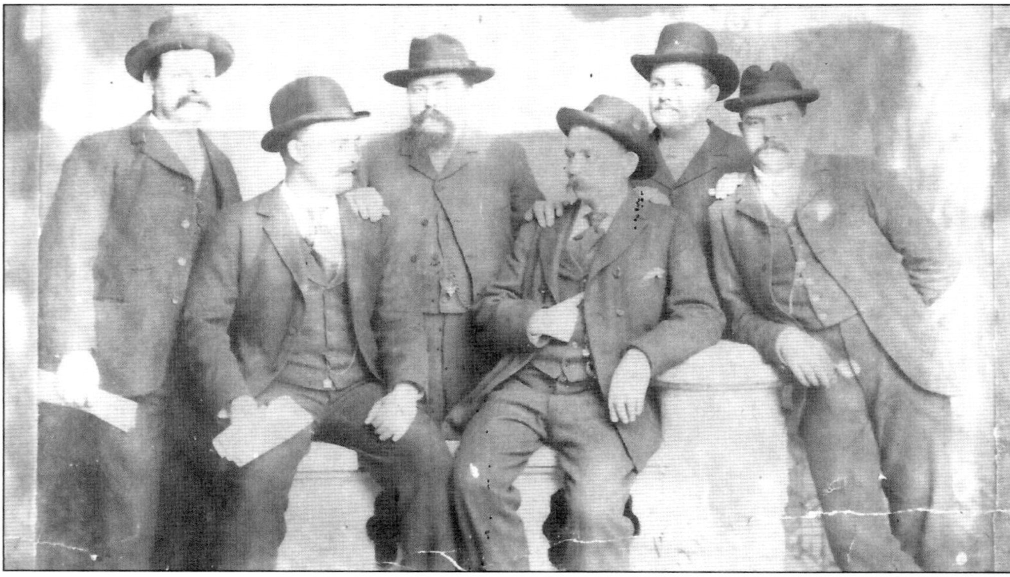

When Hope was founded, alcohol was readily available in the area. Around 1890, a photograph advertising J. W. McCullouch and the Green River and Mountain Dew Distillery circulated, with two of the representatives being from Hope. The men are identified, from left to right, as William Josey (Hope, Arkansas), Jim Facuette (Little Rock, Arkansas), Uncle Sam Wilson (Hope, Arkansas), Drummer (Kentucky), Parson Harris (Dardanelle, Arkansas), and Obe Thompson (Fulton, Arkansas). (Courtesy of AHC.)

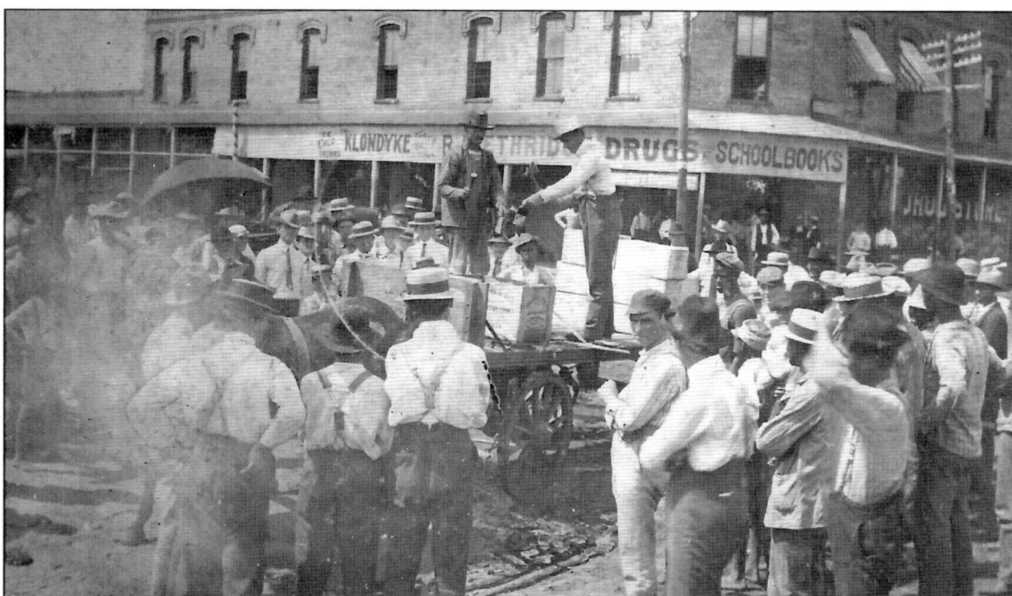

Hope had temperance societies that pushed for the abolition of alcohol in the county. Around 1915, the Hempstead County sheriff is seen in this photograph with a wagon containing confiscated liquor. He is smashing the cartons with a hatchet in front of the general public to ensure it was destroyed. They are in front of the Missouri Pacific passenger depot at the intersection of Front and South Main Streets. (Courtesy of SARA.)

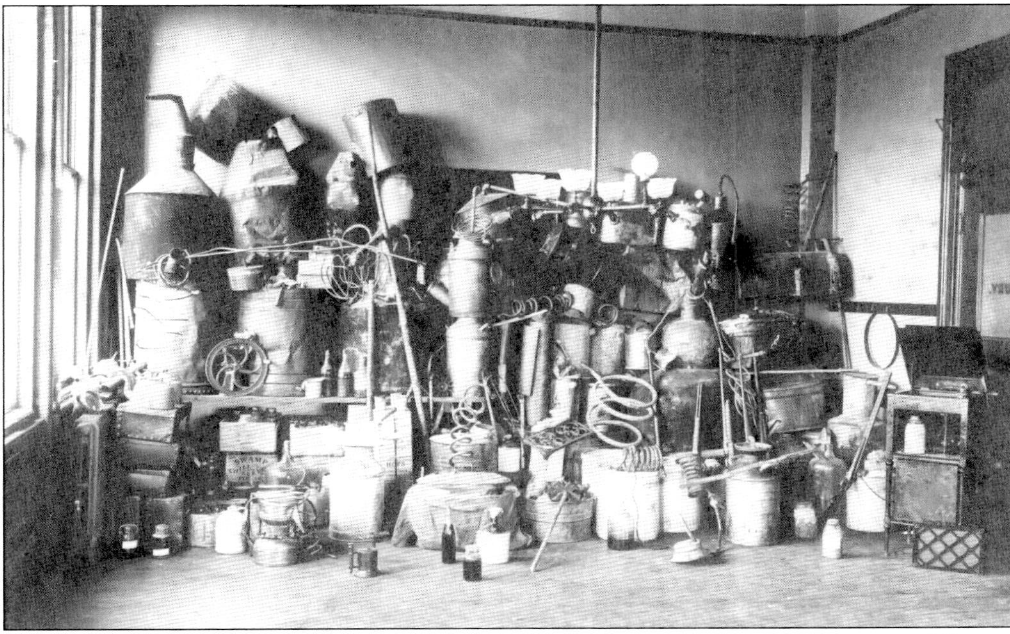

In 1920, Prohibition became law nationwide. During the 1920s and until 1933, Hempstead County officials, with the help of city officials in Hope, confiscated various whiskey stills. These stills are located in the grand jury room in the courthouse at Washington, Arkansas, around 1930. A whiskey jug sits in the phonograph on the far right. (Courtesy of SARA.)

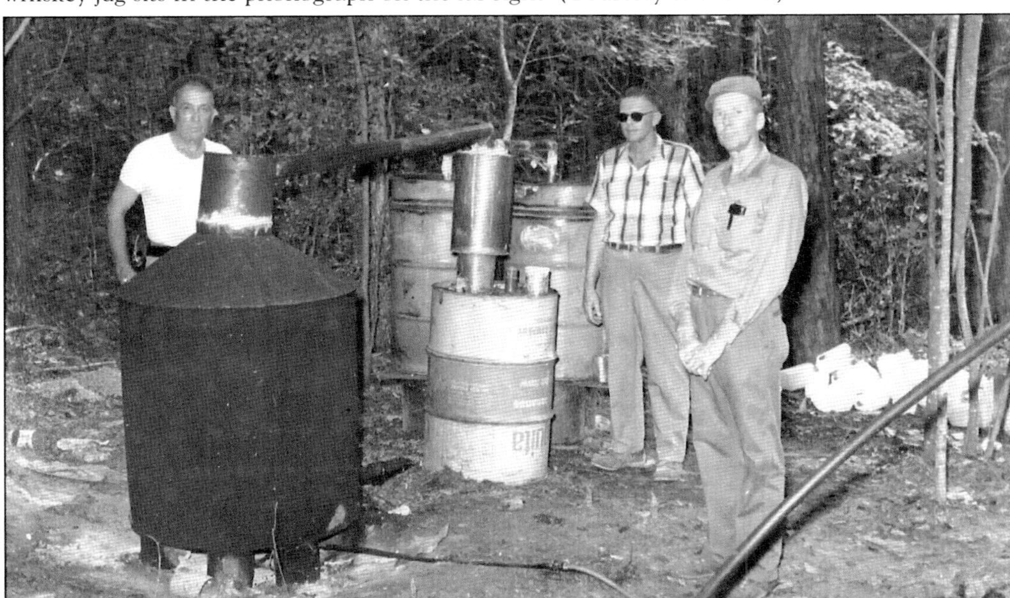

After World War II, the citizens of Hempstead County voted to become a dry county, where the sale of all alcoholic beverages is prohibited. To this day, alcohol cannot be sold publicly in Hope or Hempstead County. In this photograph from the late 1960s, Hempstead County sheriff Jimmy Griffin (wearing sunglasses) and Dep. Herbert Griffin (on far right) confiscate a whiskey still, while ? Bickerstaff (far left) looks on. (Courtesy of Hazel Jordan.)

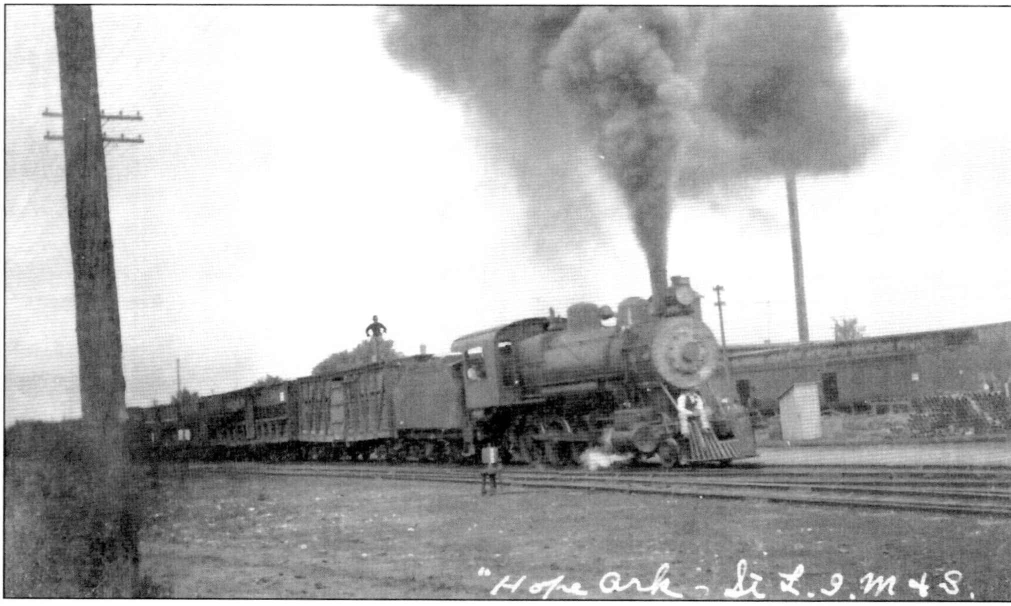

The railroad was a major industry that brought a variety of commerce to Hope. When Hope was originally laid out, the main rail line running northeast to southwest across the state of Arkansas was owned by the Cairo and Fulton Railroad. In 1874, it was renamed the St. Louis, Iron Mountain, and Southern Railroad. Trains from across the country would come through Hope carrying freight and passengers. Above is a train on the Iron Mountain line coming into Hope around 1910. This railway connected major cities like St. Louis, Missouri, and Dallas, Texas. Below are employees of the train line inside the depot in 1908. By 1917, the company was reorganized and became the Missouri Pacific Railroad Company. (Above, courtesy of AHC; below, courtesy SARA.)

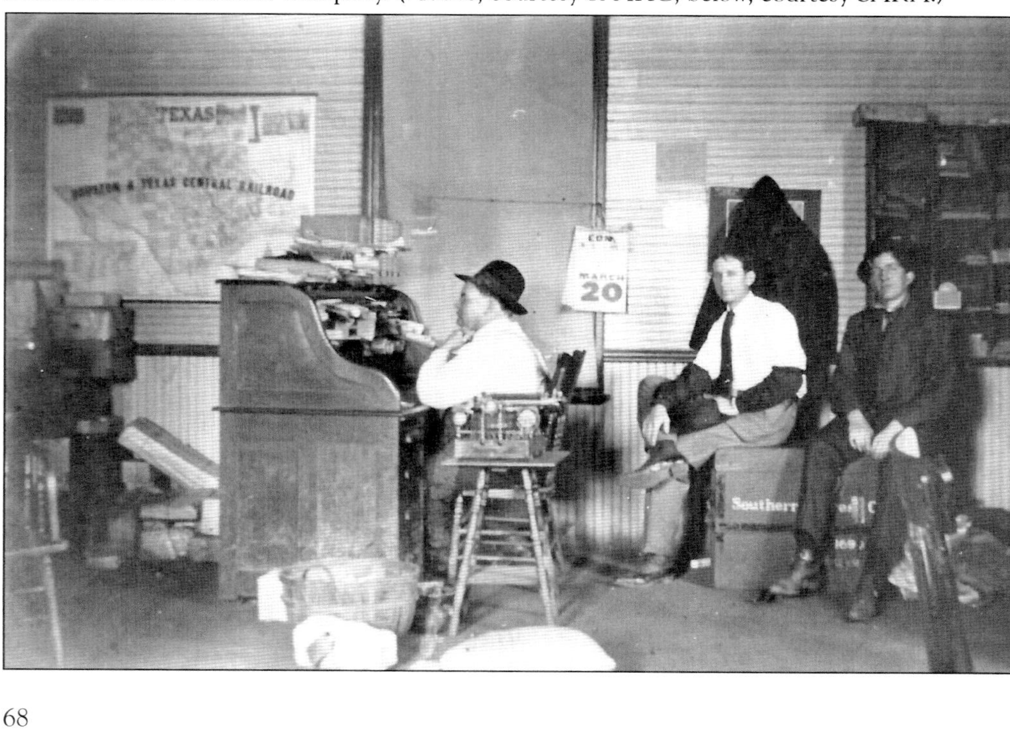

Townspeople around Hope enjoyed the busy nature of the trains and railroad yards. The railroad was seen as progress, and the places one could go seemed endless. In this c. 1915 photograph, three young men pose on top of a caboose on the St. Louis and San Francisco Line that connected Hope to Oklahoma and Shreveport, Louisiana. Downtown Hope can be seen in the background. (Courtesy of Lloyd Paul Powell.)

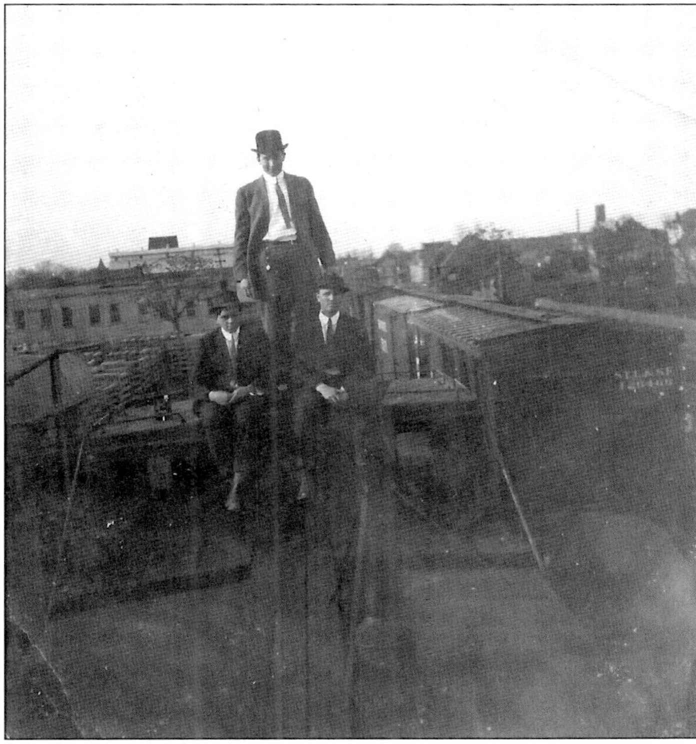

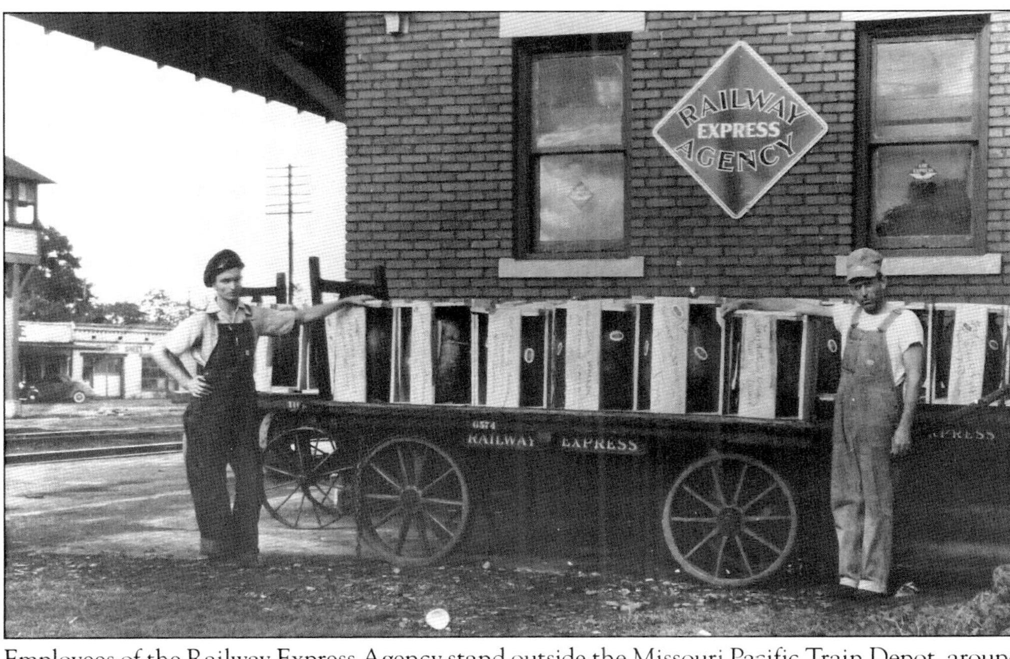

Employees of the Railway Express Agency stand outside the Missouri Pacific Train Depot, around 1945. They are waiting to ship out watermelons grown in Hempstead County to the rest of the country. Arthur Whitehurst is standing on the left. The gentleman on the right is unidentified. (Courtesy of HVCM.)

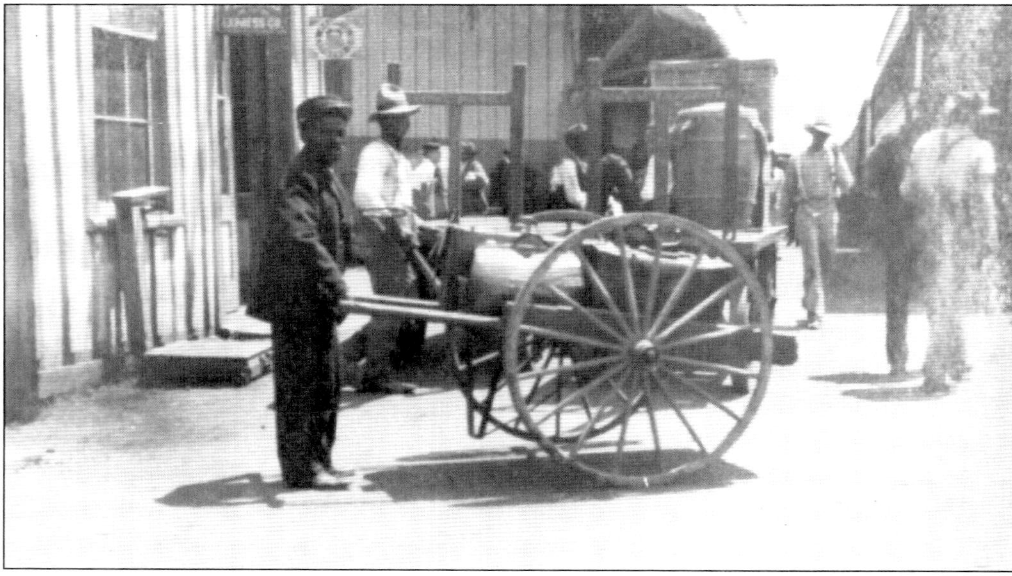

"Uncle Jim" handled baggage for passengers of the St. Louis, Iron Mountain, and Southern Railroad around 1910. He is shown here pushing a cart with several bags ready to be loaded on the next train leaving Hope. The depot is in the background. (Courtesy of AHC.)

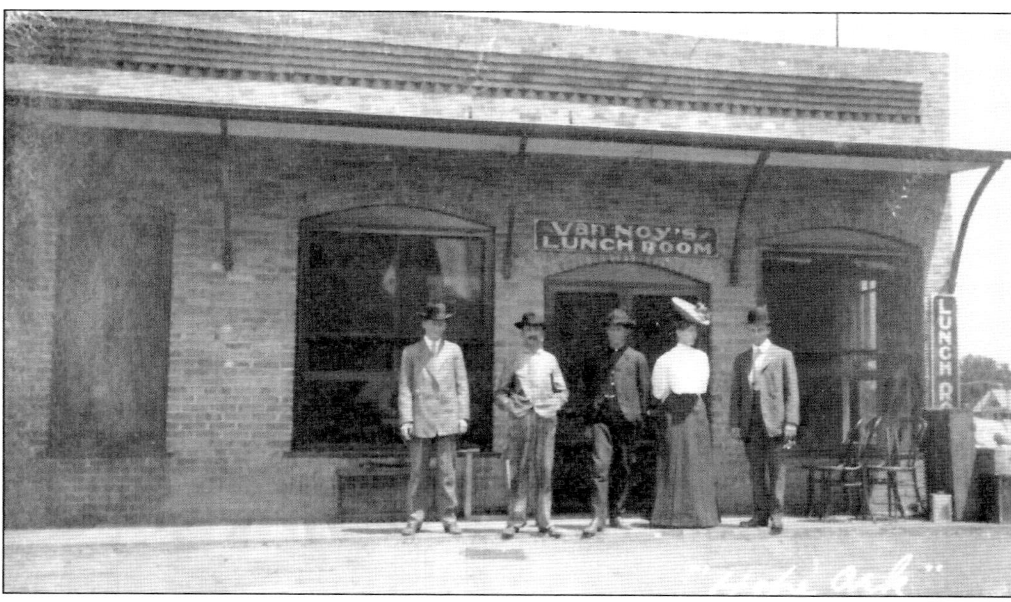

Passengers waiting for their next train would sometimes have to stay awhile in Hope, thus creating a need for service businesses. Van Noy's Lunch Room was one such spot. This photograph was taken around 1910. (Courtesy of AHC.)

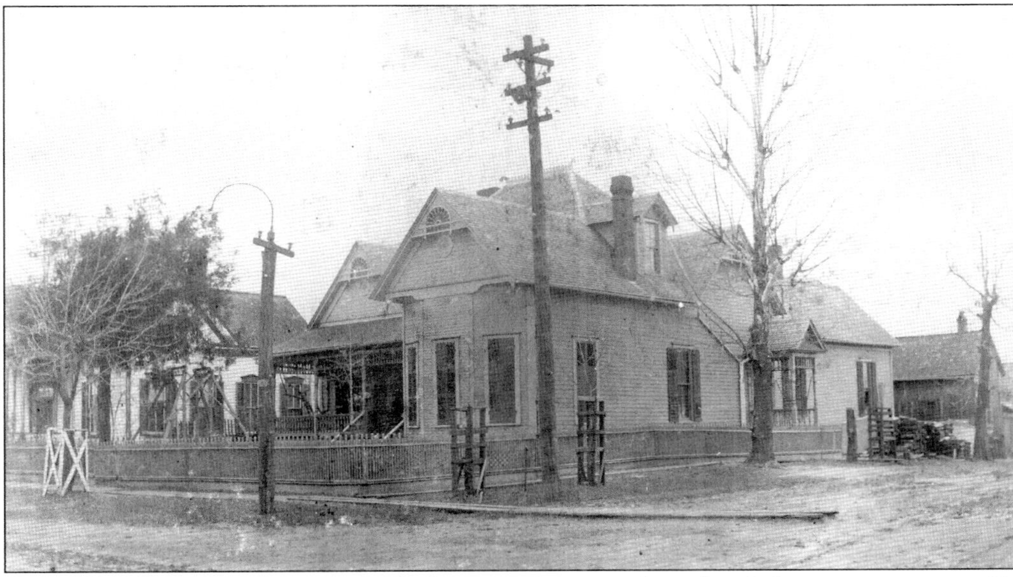

The original town plat for Hope was laid out in relation to the railroad. Streets running parallel to the main line were numbered consecutively on the south side and arranged alphabetically on the north side. Streets running perpendicular to the track were named after trees. Above is the J. J. Ward home on 122 North Vine Street next to West Avenue B, around 1902. About this time, the St. Louis and San Francisco (Frisco) and Louisiana and Arkansas railroads decided to run lines through Hope, and Vine Street became Louisiana Street, with a railroad going down its center. Below is the same J. J. Ward residence after the rails were put in. Steep embankments were cut for the railway. (Both, courtesy of SARA.)

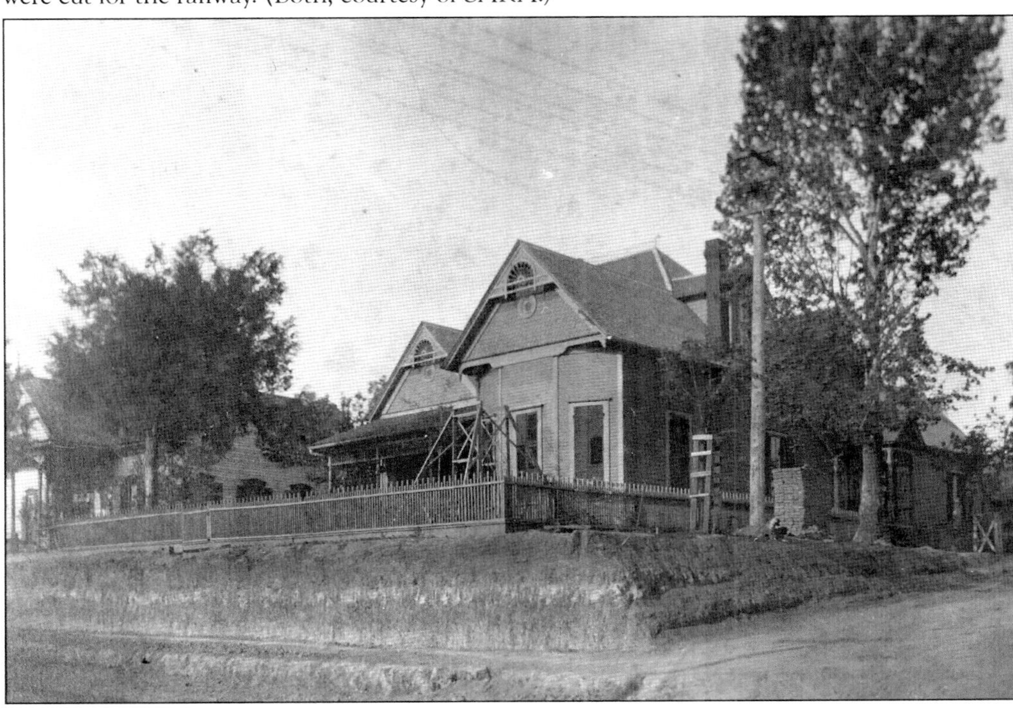

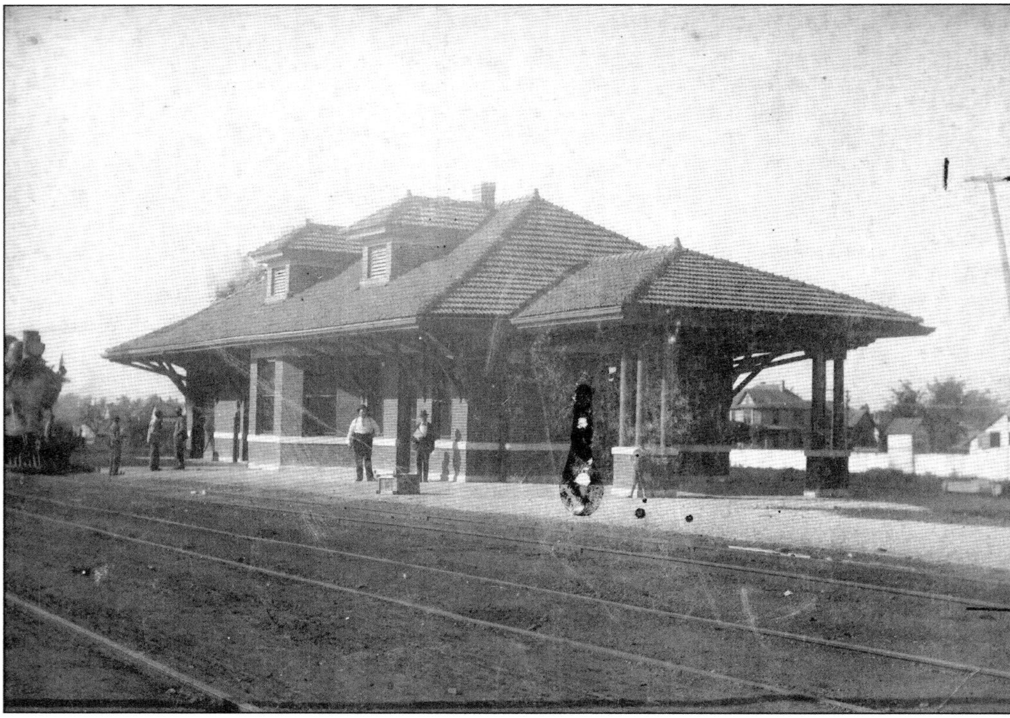

With a new railroad running through Hope, a new depot was needed for passengers traveling on that line. Around 1902, the St. Louis and San Francisco (Frisco) Railroad built a brick depot. The design was similar to one later built on the main line off Main Street. The photograph was taken around 1910. (Courtesy of SARA.)

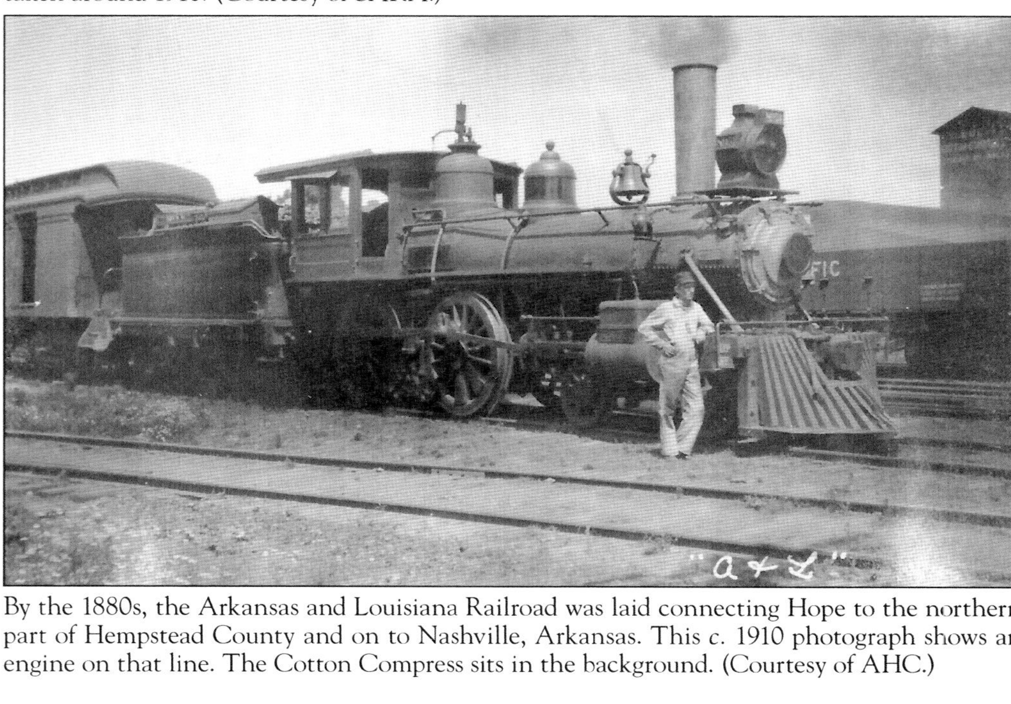

By the 1880s, the Arkansas and Louisiana Railroad was laid connecting Hope to the northern part of Hempstead County and on to Nashville, Arkansas. This c. 1910 photograph shows an engine on that line. The Cotton Compress sits in the background. (Courtesy of AHC.)

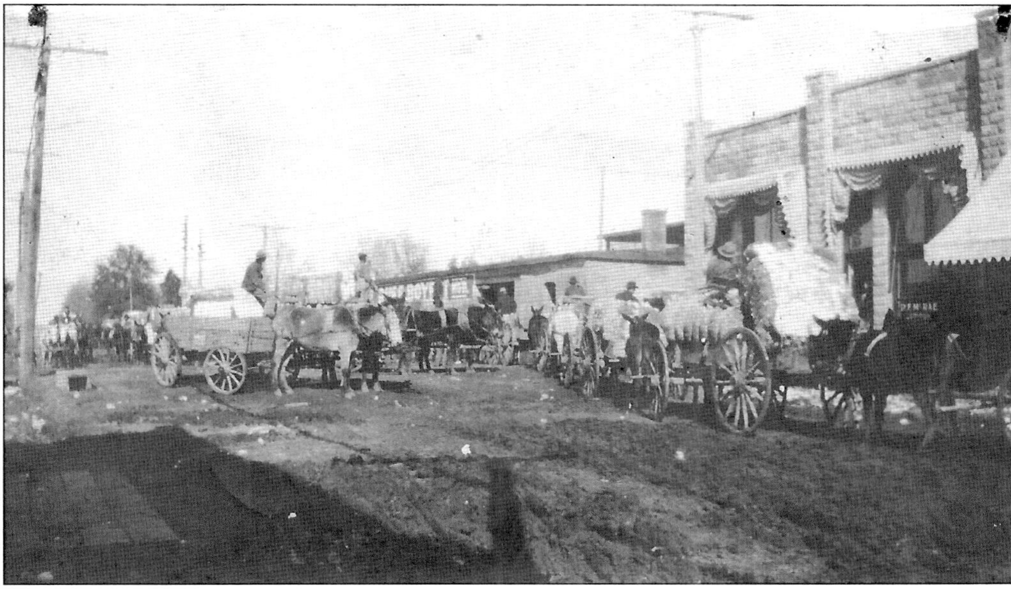

Cotton was still king in the South even after the Civil War, and Hope and Hempstead County were known for quality long staple cotton. By 1914, cotton was selling for 7¢ a pound. Farmers and merchants would bring bales to Hope to be bought and placed on trains for shipping. Above are wagons filled with cotton bales along South Walnut Street near the intersection with Second Street around 1915. South Walnut was known as "Cotton Row" because of the different cotton buyer offices located there. As seen in the photograph below, the line of cotton bales would sometimes stretch past the southwestern boundary of the city limits. (Above, courtesy of SARA; below, courtesy of Keenan and Peggy Williams.)

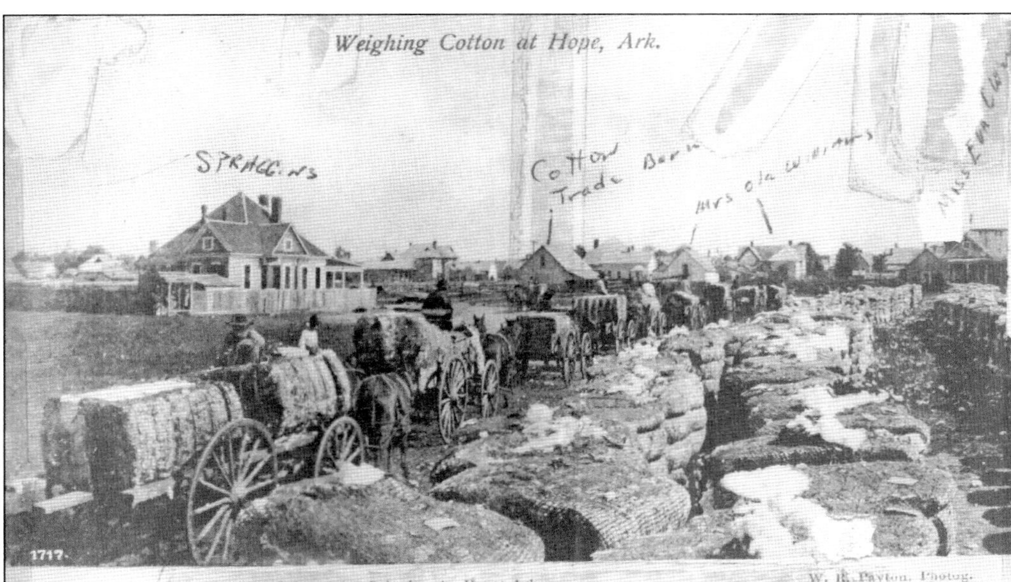

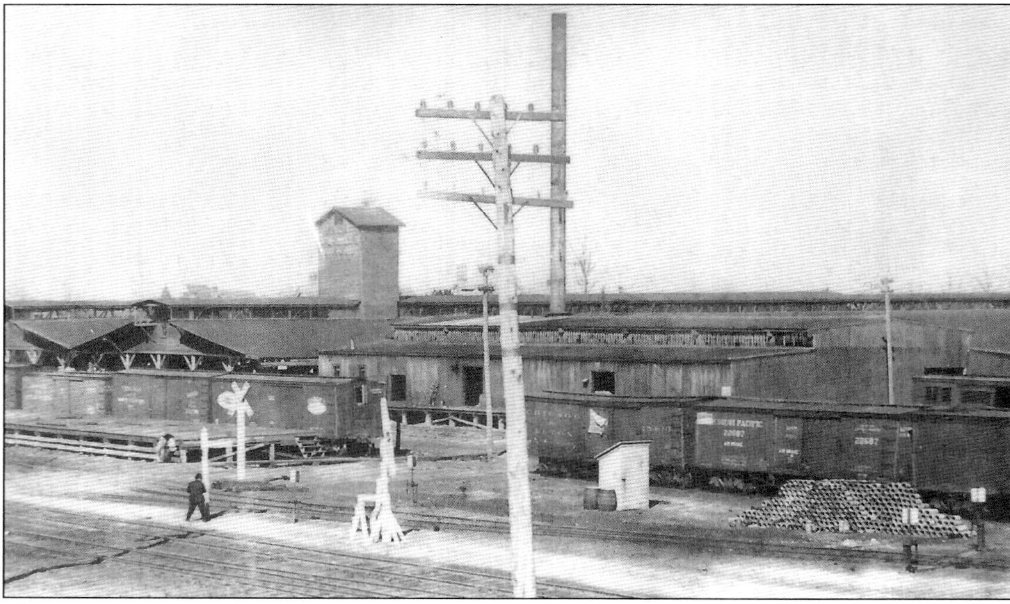

The first cotton compress in Hope covered an entire city block and began in the 1890s. The compress housed the different bales of cotton that would come into the town to be shipped. In 1888, an advertisement for Hope declared that over 10,000 bales of cotton had been shipped during the 1887–1888 season. Above is the view of the Cotton Compress for the main railroad line coming into Hope around 1905. A 1911 view (below) of the Cotton Compress is from Louisiana Street, where bale upon bale of cotton can be seen, with the steeple of the First Christian Church on Avenue B in the background. The Hope City Hall was later built on the site after the compress was moved north to a point accessible to the Frisco and Nashville branch railroads. (Both, courtesy of SARA.)

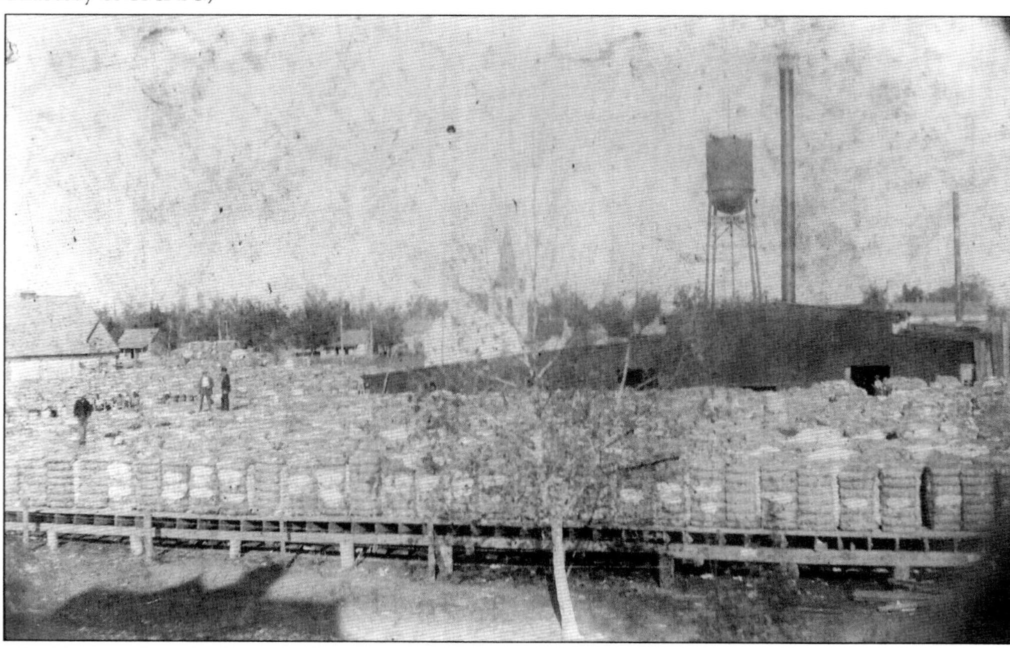

S. J. Jamison was a business leader in Hope. In 1908, the *Arkansas Gazette* of Little Rock did caricatures of leading businessmen around the state titled, "Men of Affairs." For Hope, the paper picked S. J. Jamison, who ran the Hope Lumber Company and the Hope Ice and Coal Company. (Courtesy of AHC.)

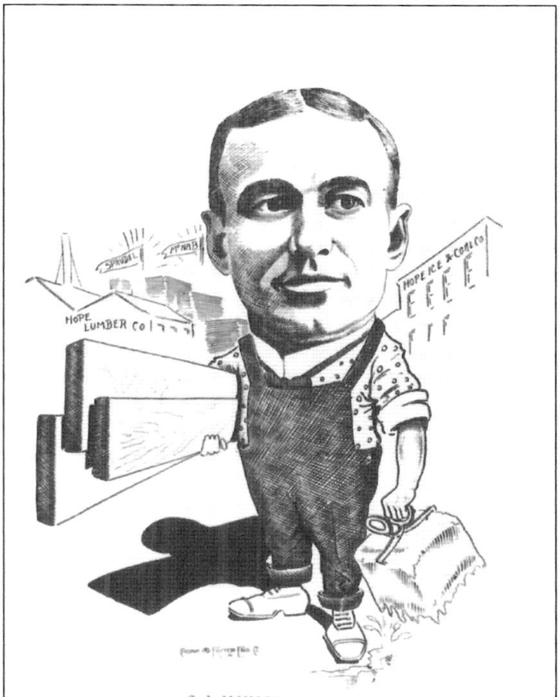

S. J. JAMISON, Hope

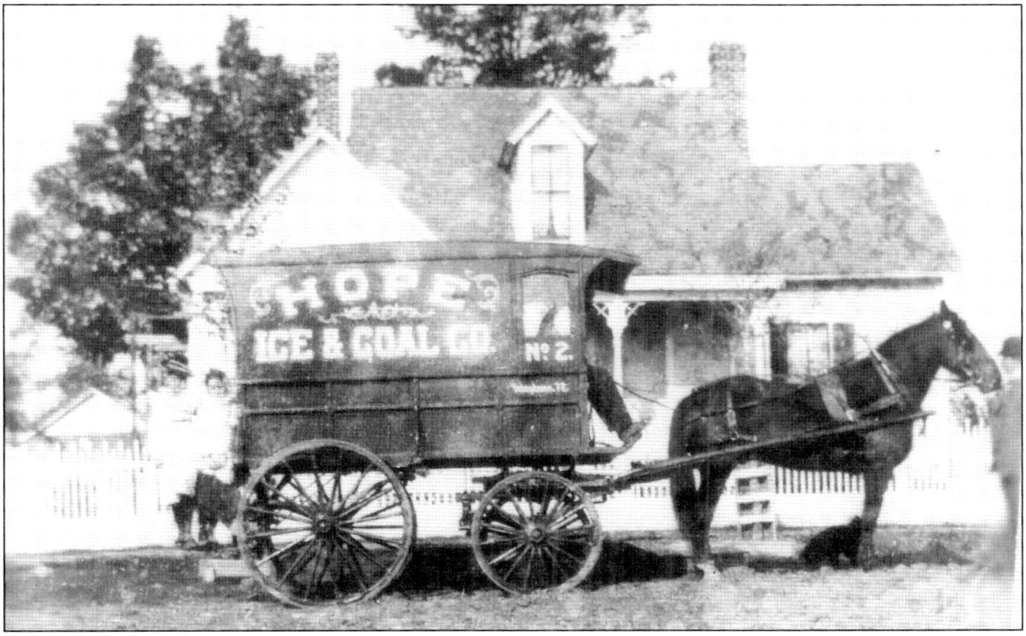

The Hope Ice and Coal Company was originally organized by Capt. Judson T. West. West later pushed for the town to form a municipally owned company, the Hope Water and Light Plant, to provide electricity and water to the community. In the photograph is one of the early Hope Ice and Coal Company wagons around 1900. (Courtesy of HVCM.)

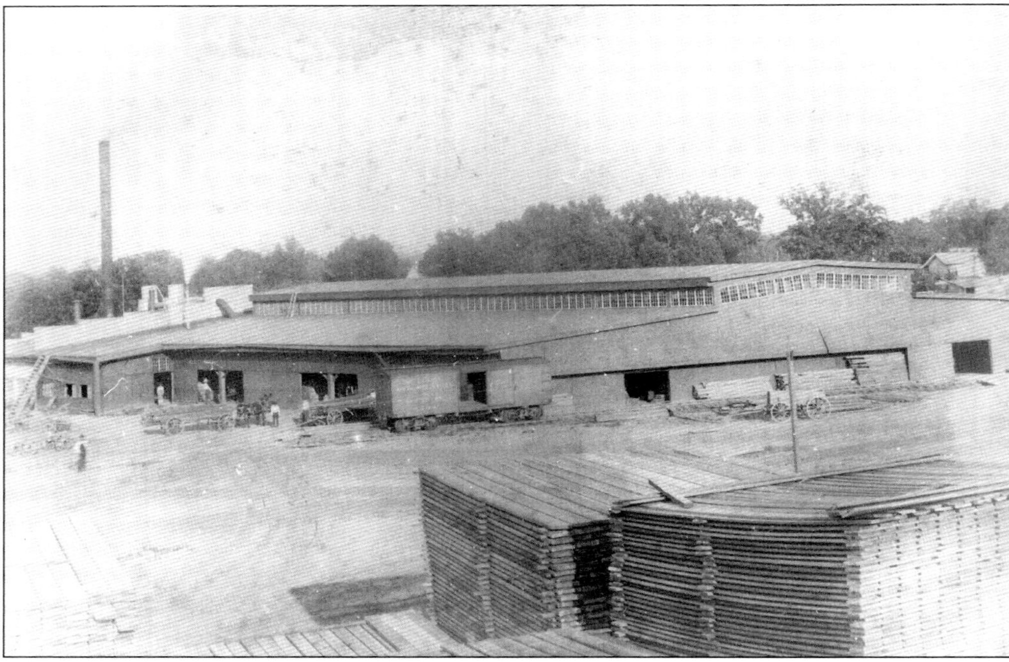

The *c.* 1910 photograph is of the Hope Lumber Company at 500 East Avenue A, looking southeast. The company was started in the 1890s and provided lumber to various parts of the United States, particularly the North and Northeast. (Courtesy of SARA.)

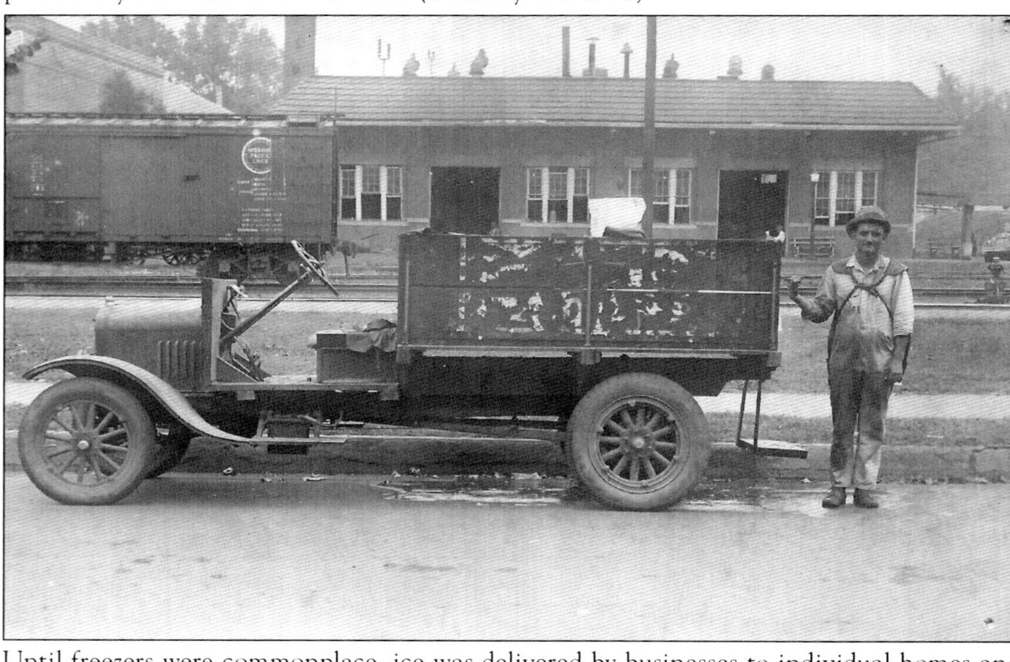

Until freezers were commonplace, ice was delivered by businesses to individual homes and establishments. It would be placed in an icehouse behind the home or in an icebox inside. In this photograph is salesman Pat Simpson, representing the Southern Ice Company in 1928. (Courtesy of Mary Nell Turner.)

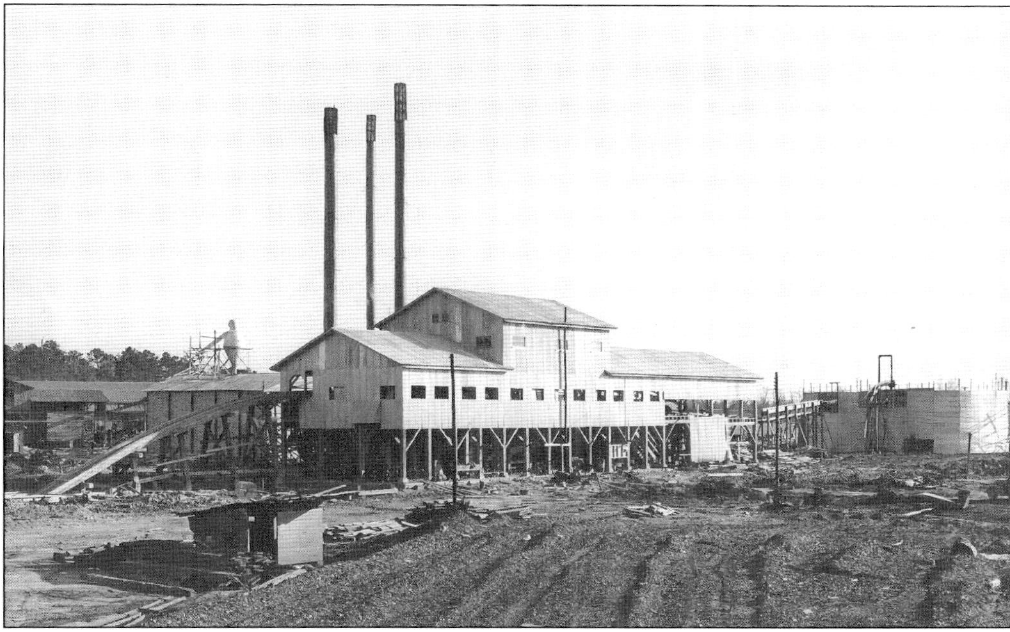

Hope continued to grow and prosper with other industries. Graydon Anthony Lumber Company was a contributor to the local lumber industry. The company and mill were located on the Lewisville Road, on the south side of town just off Arkansas Highway 29. The photograph shows the mill around 1950. (Courtesy of Graydon Anthony.)

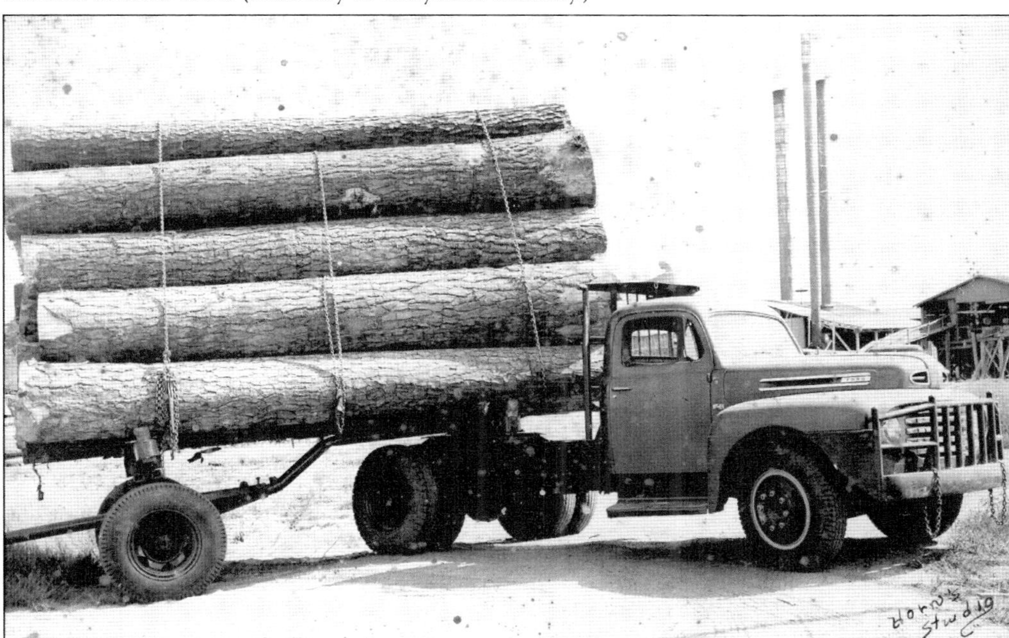

Old growth across south Arkansas was harvested in the early 20th century for the quality wood. Huge logs were brought in and made into good lumber. Taken around 1950, this photograph shows the types of logs used by the Anthony Lumber Company. (Courtesy of Graydon Anthony.)

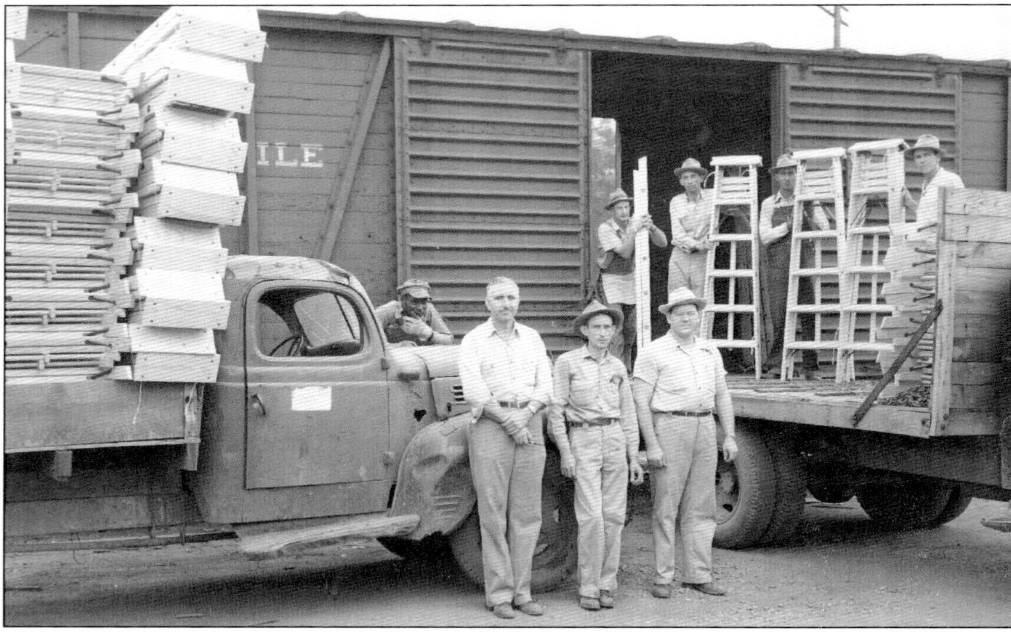

One industry in Hope was famous for making ladders. Here, employees of Southwest Wood Products of Hope are loading ladders onto a boxcar in 1949. The gentlemen standing in front of the truck are owners of the company. They are Frank King (left), James A. Gunter Jr. (center), and Homer Beyerley. (Courtesy of Don and Mary Parker.)

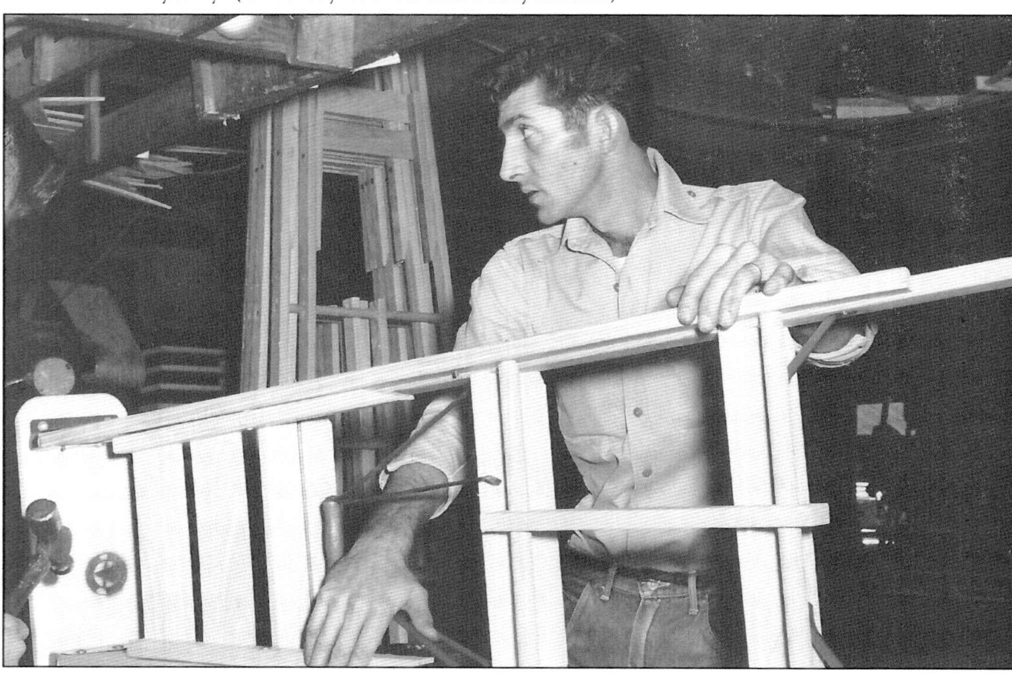

In this c. 1960 photograph, Southwestern Wood Products employee Darwin Smith makes one of the ladders at the factory in Hope. Ladders were shipped out via truck or rail to different buyers. (Courtesy of AHC.)

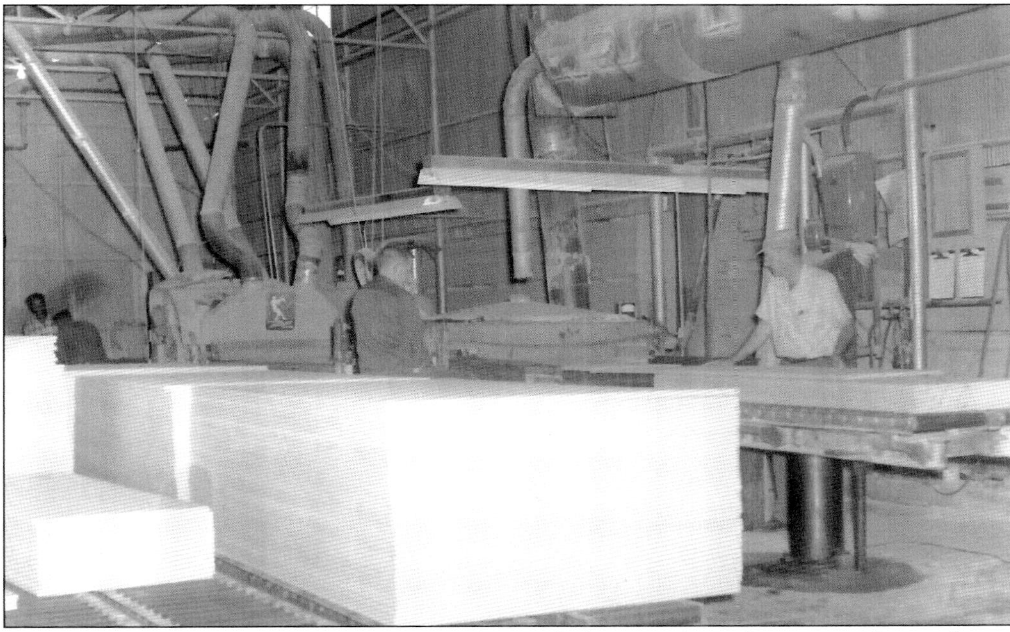

After World War II, the Forestry Southern Plaswood Plant was formed in Hope. Plaswood was a forerunner of modern particleboard consisting of wood chips, sawdust, and glue. The material was used to help with the building of houses and other structures. It was thought to last longer and be more durable. The photograph was taken in August 1961 inside the factory. (Courtesy of AHC.)

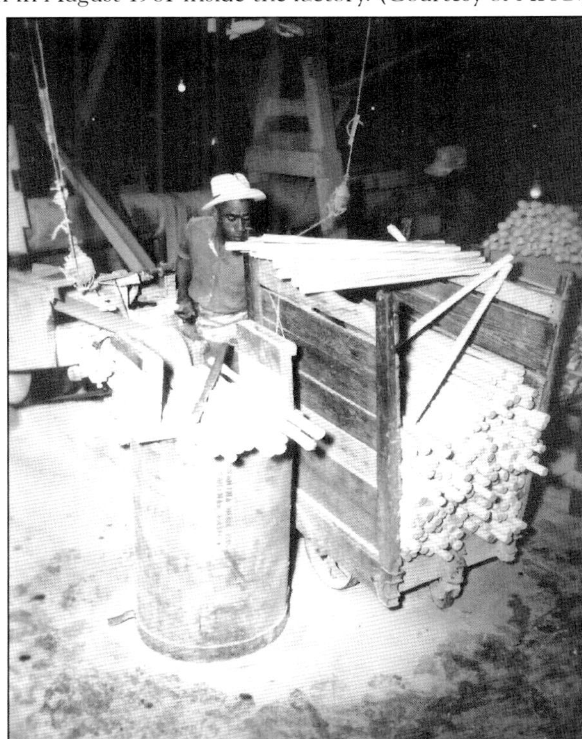

There was never an end to the variety of factories and materials made in Hope. In the 1920s, P. N. Blagg, who formerly worked for the Ivory Handle Company, decided to make walking canes out of hickory. These became very popular and fueled a successful business, later known as the Split Hickory Company, which made an assortment of canes for various purposes. The photograph shows an unidentified worker inside the factory in 1961. (Courtesy of AHC.)

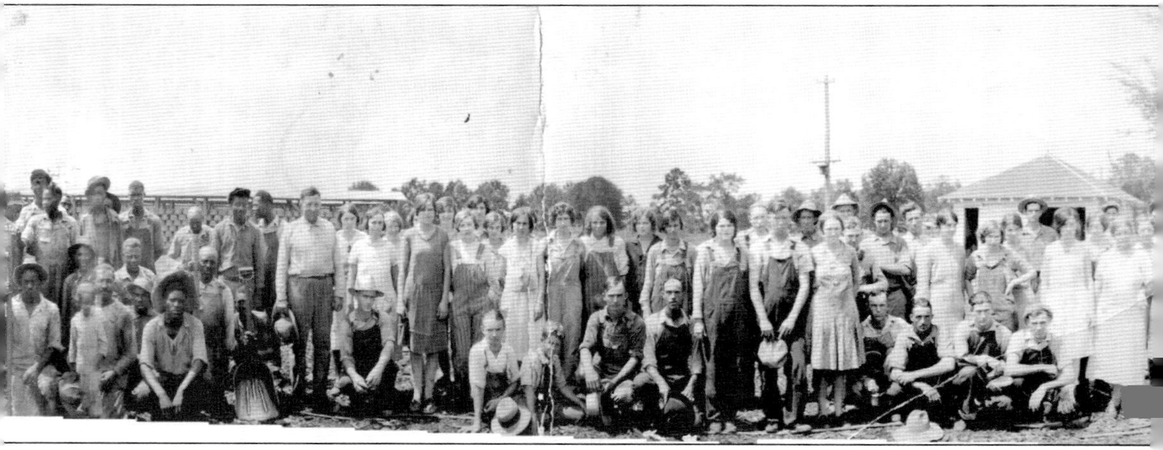

The Hope Basket Factory was established in the first decade of the 20th century and made wooden baskets. Located in the southwest section of town off Grady Street and connected by a spur to the Frisco and Louisiana and Arkansas Railroad, the factory provided jobs to many area

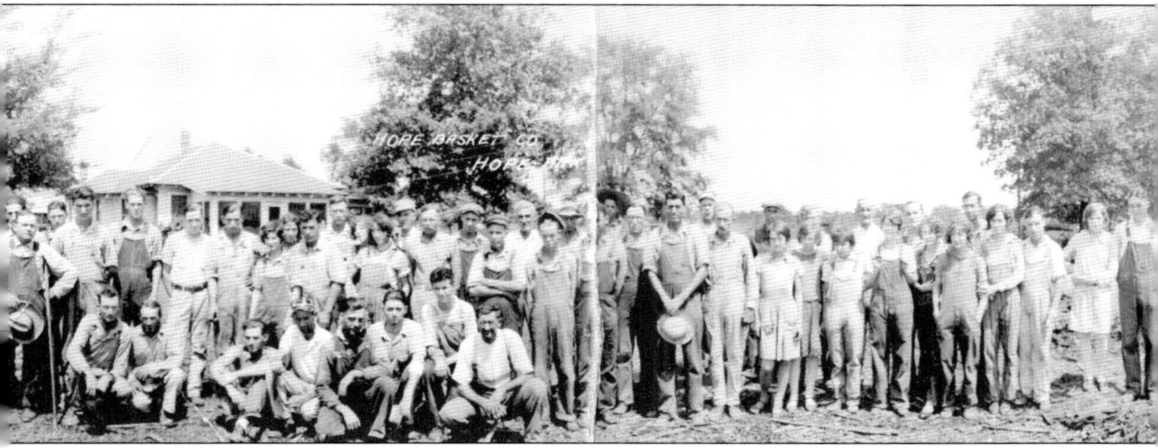

residents. This panoramic photograph shows a majority of employees wearing overalls. They are an equal mixture of men and women. The photograph was taken just before the beginning of the Great Depression. (Courtesy of Jesse Duckett.)

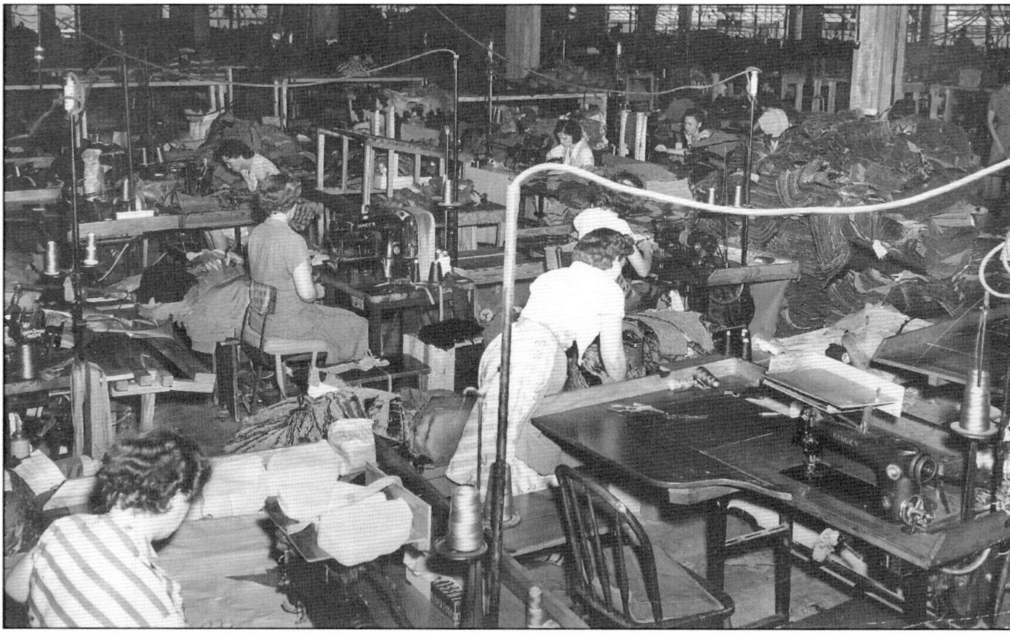

The manufacture of clothing became another industry in Hope during the World War II era and afterward. Located on the corner of Division and Hazel Streets, Shanhouse and Sons Company designed and tailored apparel. The *c.* 1950 photograph shows the inside of one of the workrooms at Shanhouse and Sons Company. (Courtesy of Mary Nell Turner.)

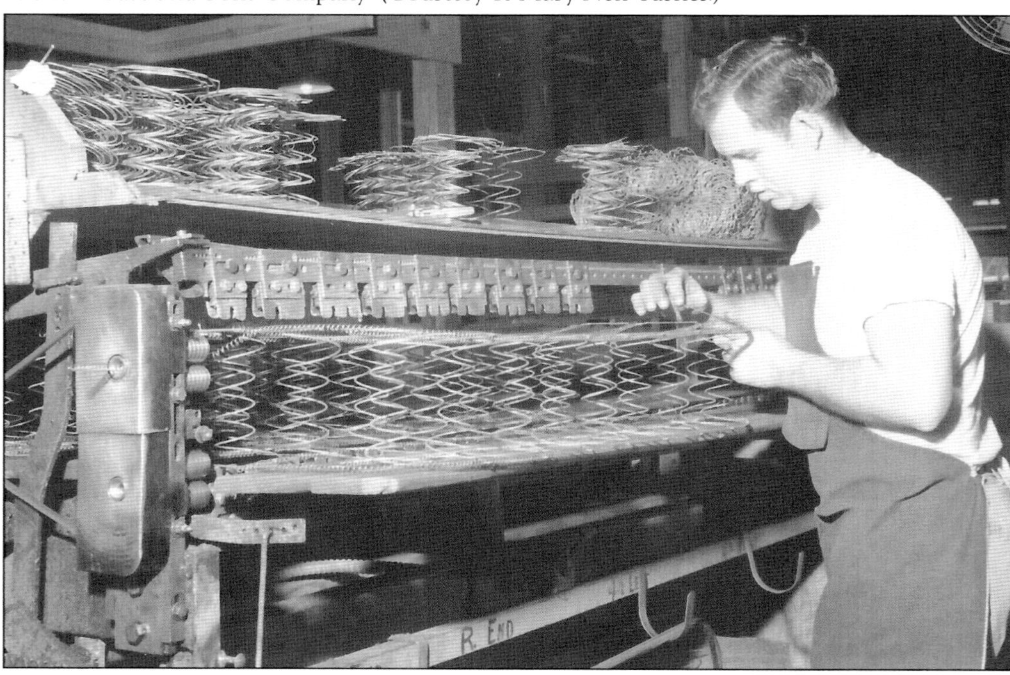

The Hope Wire Products Plant made bedsprings and bed frames along with other wire products. In a photograph taken by Ernest Deane for an *Arkansas Gazette* article on January 3, 1964, documenting Hope industries, employee Thomas Theis assembles a bed of springs. (Courtesy of AHC.)

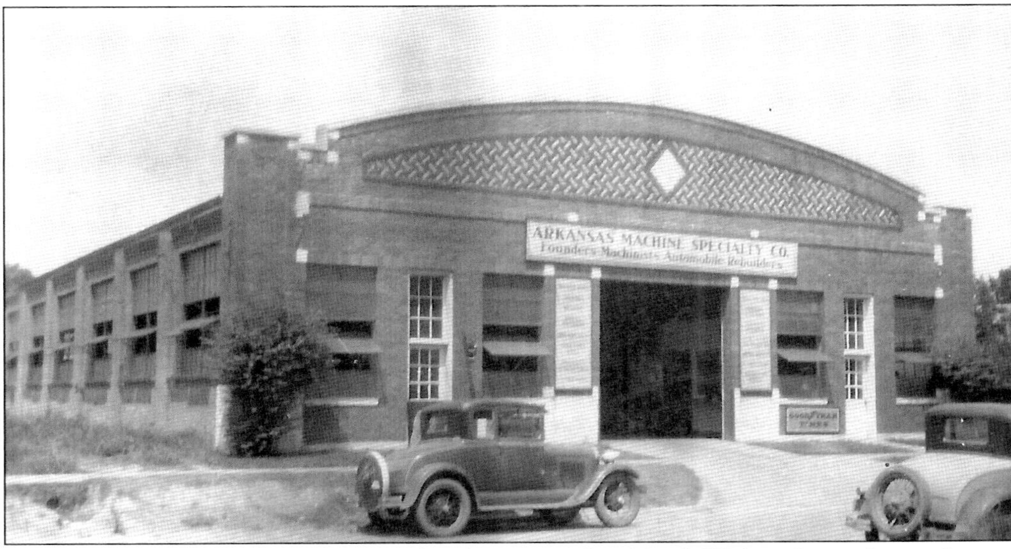

In 1928, the Arkansas Machine Specialty Shop opened on North Walnut Street. It was directed by Ernest Paul O'Neal, whose father was Nathaniel Paul O'Neal of the Hope Brick Works. In 1976, the building caught fire and burned to the ground. The shop moved to another location on South Walnut Street, where it continued to design and produce a variety of different machines for the state and region until closing in 1986. (Courtesy of Lloyd Paul Powell.)

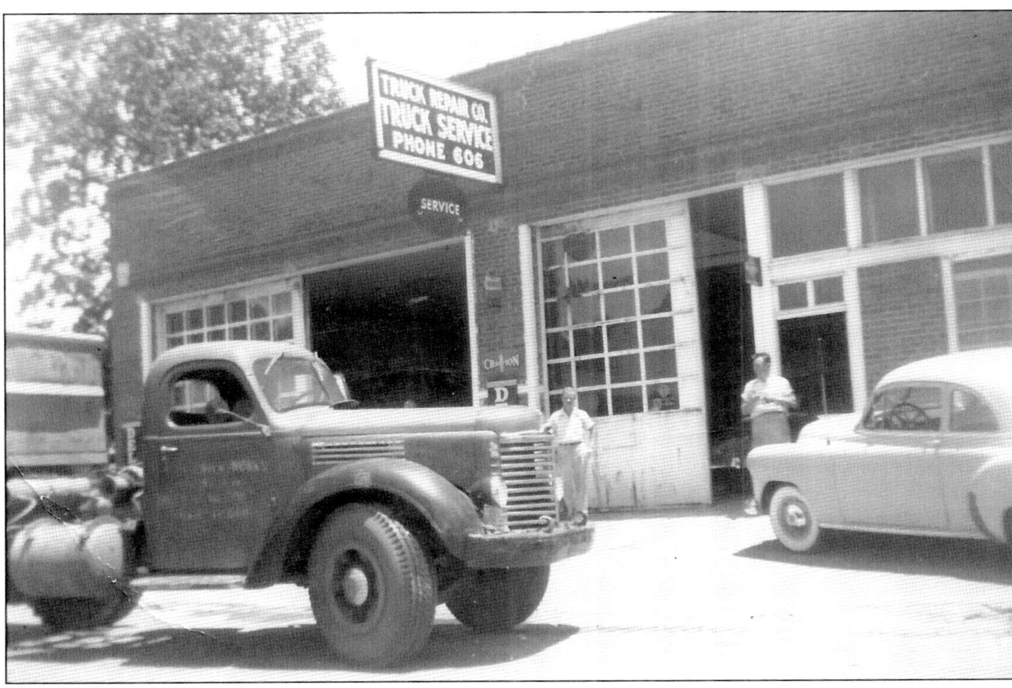

The Truck Repair Company, shown in this 1954 photograph, was at 419 South Walnut Street. Also owned by the O'Neal family and purchased to become a truck repair business in 1948, the company worked on a variety of truck parts and vehicles. (Courtesy of Lloyd Paul Powell.)

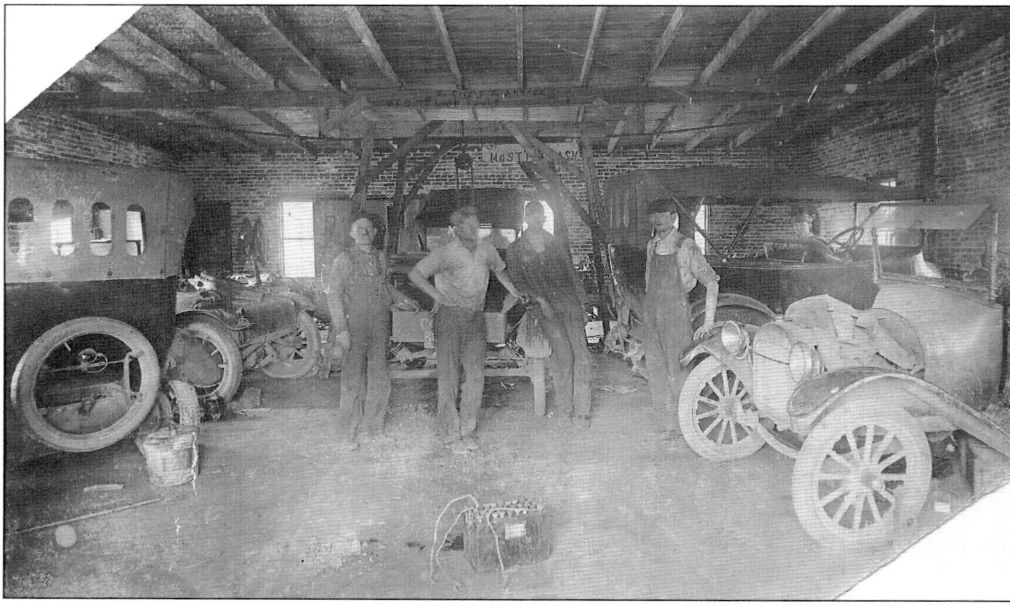

Service industries are common to any town. With the rise of the automobile, garages were needed for repairs. This photograph was taken of Gib Lewis's Garage at 319 South Walnut Street around 1920. The four men are, from left to right, Dewey Camp, Alonzo Camp, Williad Laseter, and Gib Lewis. The Chevrolet in the back right-hand corner belonged to Dr. G. H. Martindale. (Courtesy of SARA.)

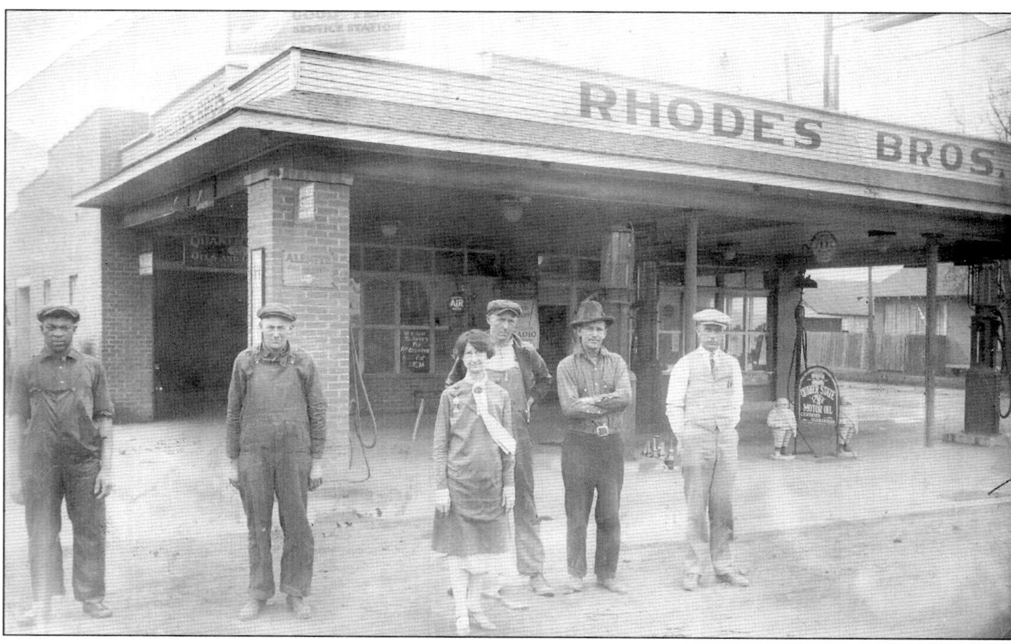

Seen in this c. 1925 photograph, Rhodes Brothers gas station was another spot known locally for automobile care. The employees are, from left to right, Batch, Early McIver, Ethel Rose, Herbert Lewellan, John C. Turner, and Thurman L. Rhodes. The building was located on Avenue A near the Snyker Hotel. (Courtesy of Mary Nell Turner.)

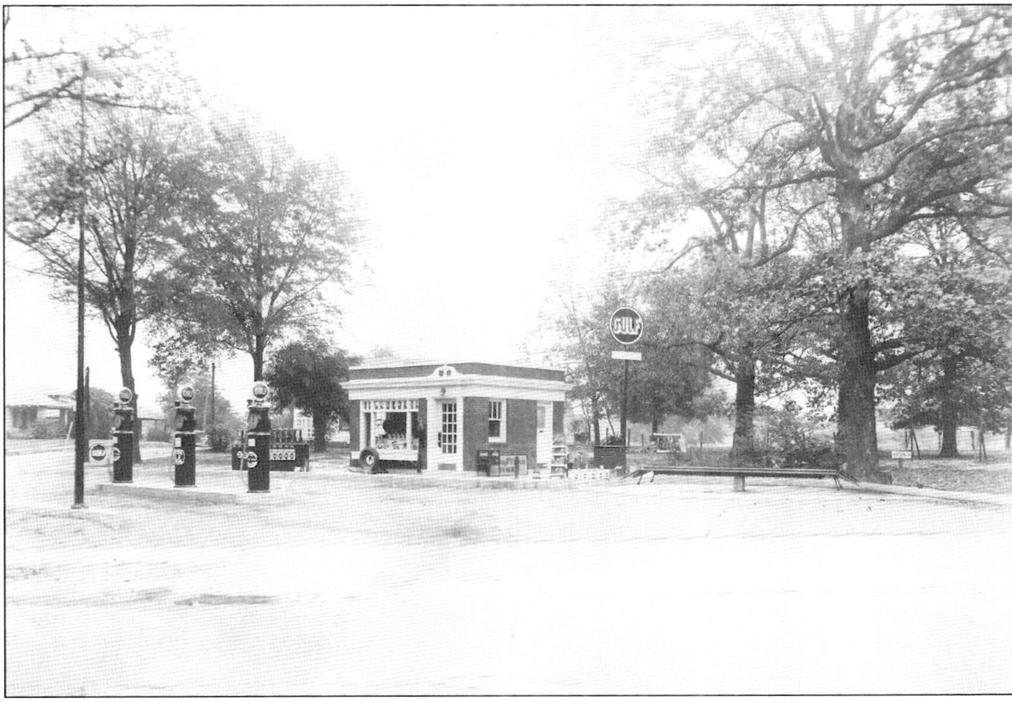

As travel increased, more gas stations were required to supply the fuel demand in Hope. In the 1930s, U.S. Highway 67, which came directly through town on Third Street, was completed and paved. This highway ran across the state of Arkansas from the northeast corner to the southwest corner. Around that same time, the Bundy family established the Gulf station shown in the photograph above at the intersection of Third and Shover Streets. In 1942, Bundy's daughter Leonice worked in the station. The photograph below was taken of her at work and was published in *Gulf News* magazine. (Both, courtesy of Janice Harrison.)

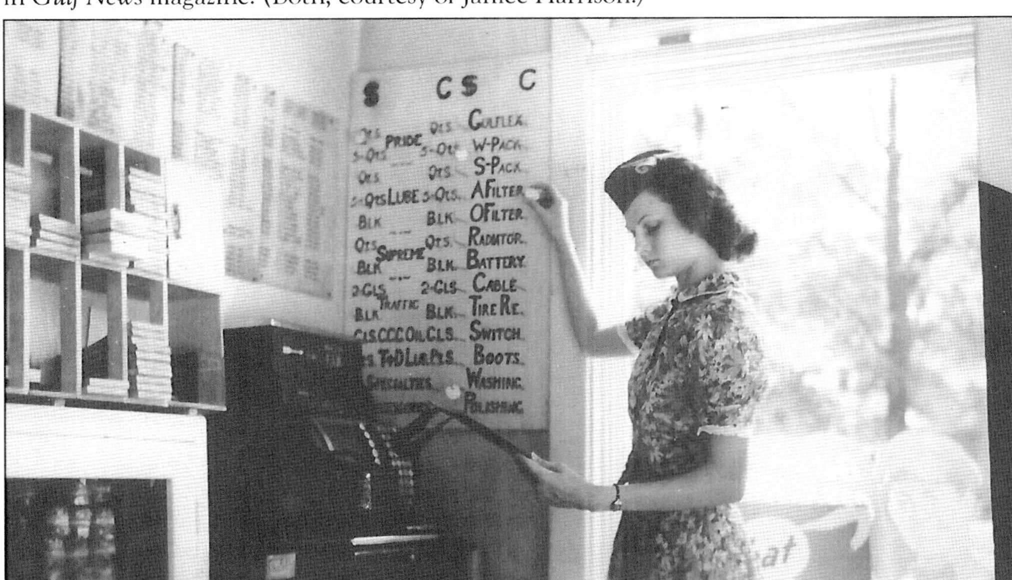

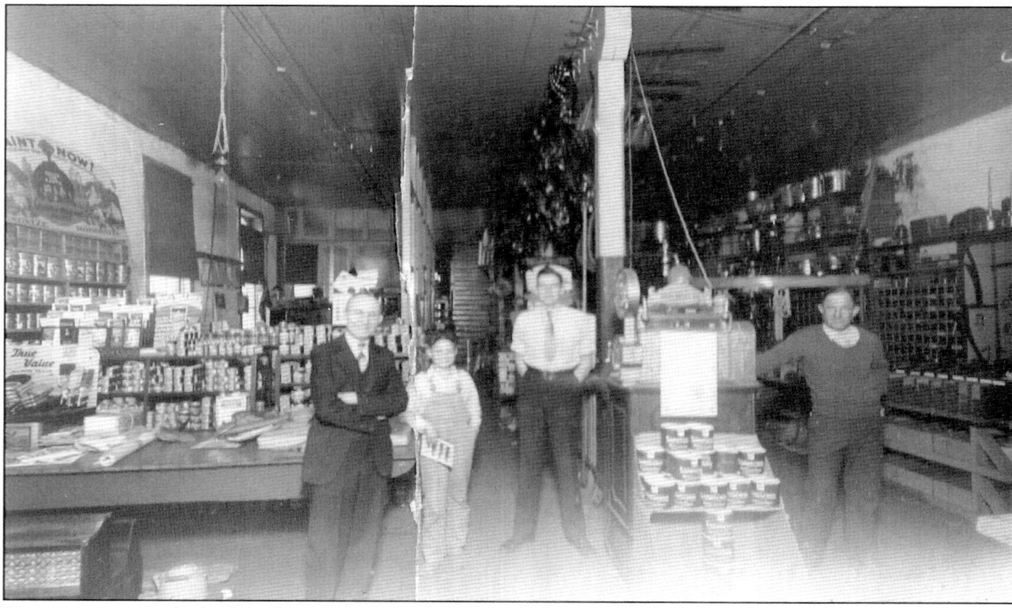

Every town needed a hardware store to supply general goods for home maintenance and repairs. This photograph was taken around 1936 of the interior of Hope Hardware, located on the corner of Elm and Second Streets. Around 1900, this same hardware had a third-floor showroom that sold coffins and wagons. The employees are, from left to right, Jim Atchinson, J. B. Ellen Jr., LaGrone Williams, and J. B. Ellen. (Courtesy of Keenan and Peggy Williams.)

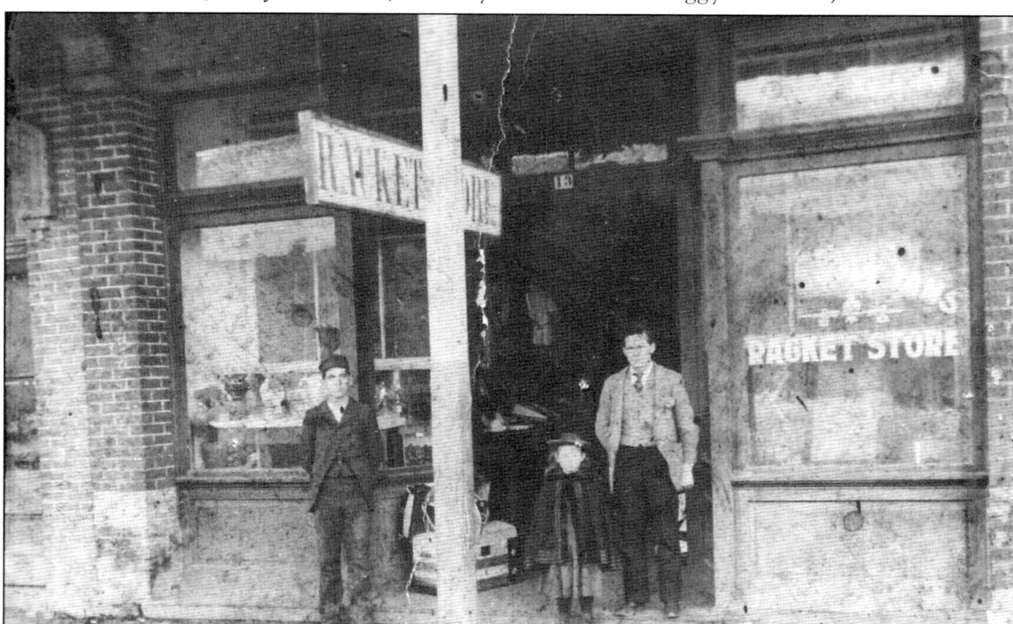

This *c.* 1890 photograph was taken of Leon S. Williams's Racket Store at 13 Second Street in downtown Hope. A racket store was an early version of a five-and-dime. Leon S. Williams stands at the entrance of the store. The boy and girl on the left are unidentified. (Courtesy of Keenan and Peggy Williams.)

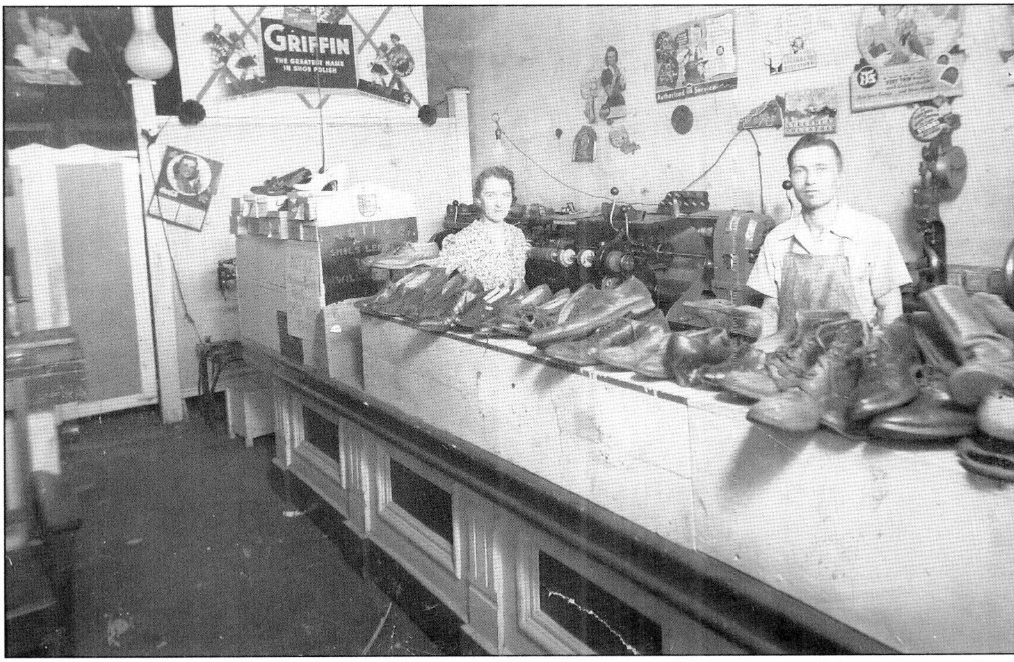

Shoes were once not expendable as they are today. They would be repaired for continued use and reuse. Around 1948, Essie Keen (left) and Virgil Fant were working in Keen's Shoe Repair on West Front (Division) Street. (Courtesy of Butch Fant.)

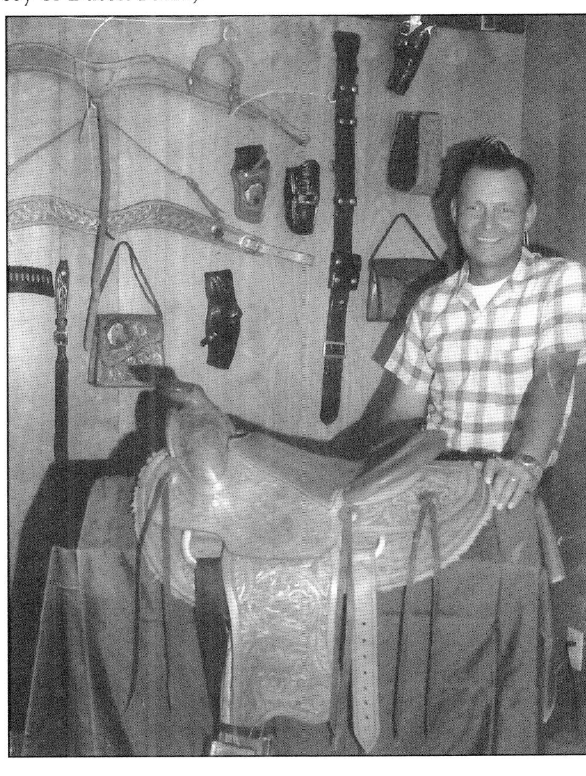

Some service businesses required skill and creativity. Such was the case with James W. Rowe, who crafted items from leather. Shown here in his leather shop at 216 Pritchard Street in 1953, Rowe displays a completed saddle featuring his hand decoration. (Courtesy of Kenny Rowe.)

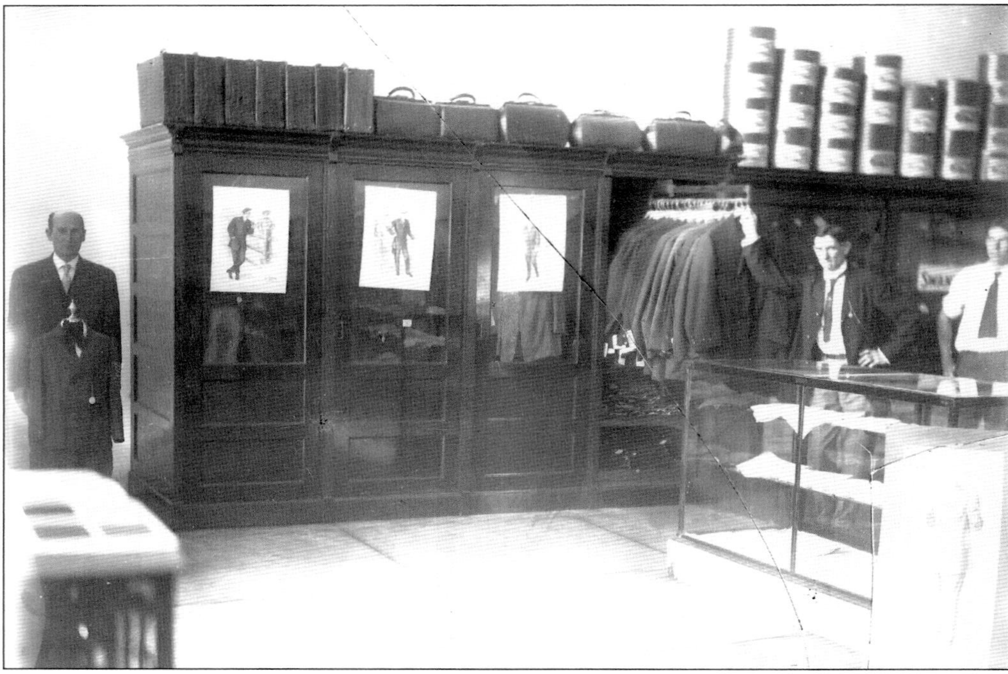

This photograph shows the interior of a men's clothing store in Hope around 1910. The location is unidentified, but the store demonstrates why Hope was viewed as a modern town supplying the latest goods. The display case has a pullout rack for different jackets, and suitcases can be seen along the top shelf. (Courtesy of Mary Nell Turner.)

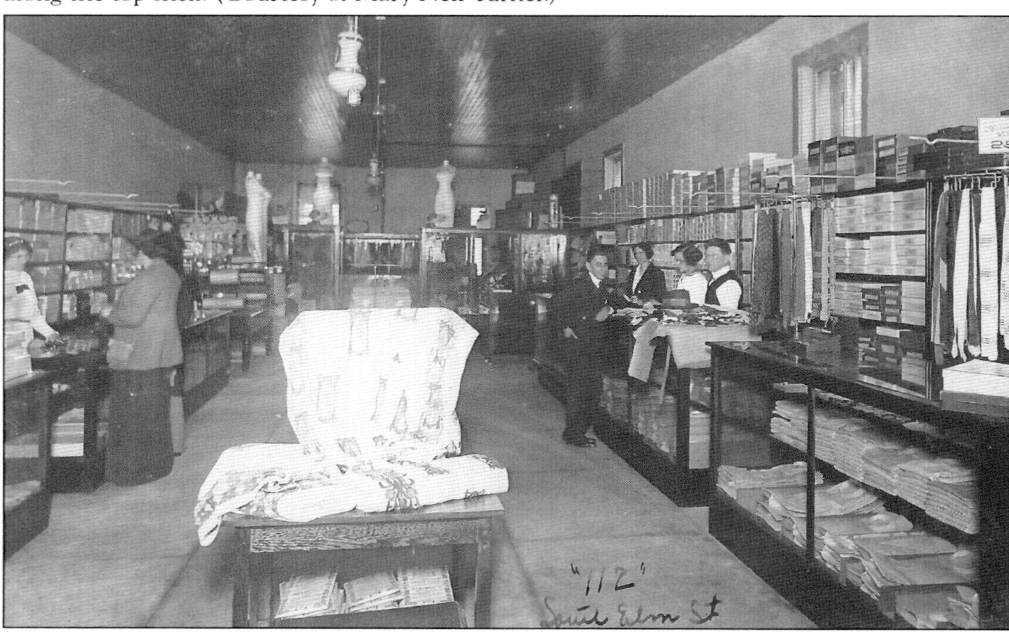

The store in this 1914 image at 112 South Elm Street was next to Haynes Brothers Department Store. Like other shops of its kind, it sold both material for making clothing and also completed dresses and other accessories. (Courtesy of SARA.)

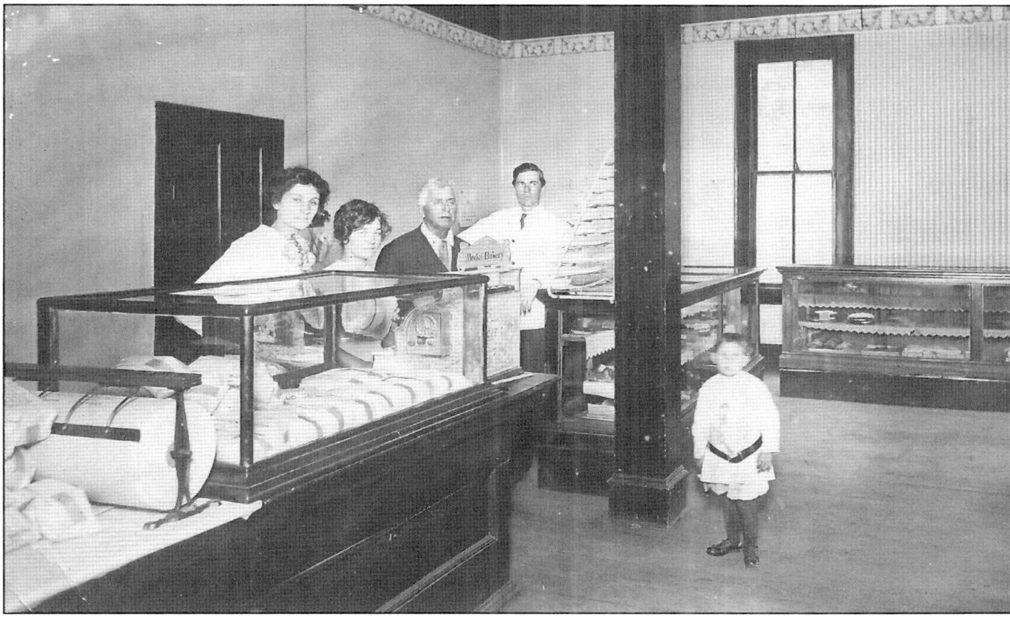

Other services provided in Hope were food-related. Hope had different bakeries around town, including the City Bakery run by the Bundy family. In this *c.* 1915 photograph are, from left to right, Jett, Ollie, Tommy, Leon, and Newt (Jett and Leon's son). (Courtesy of Janice Harrison.)

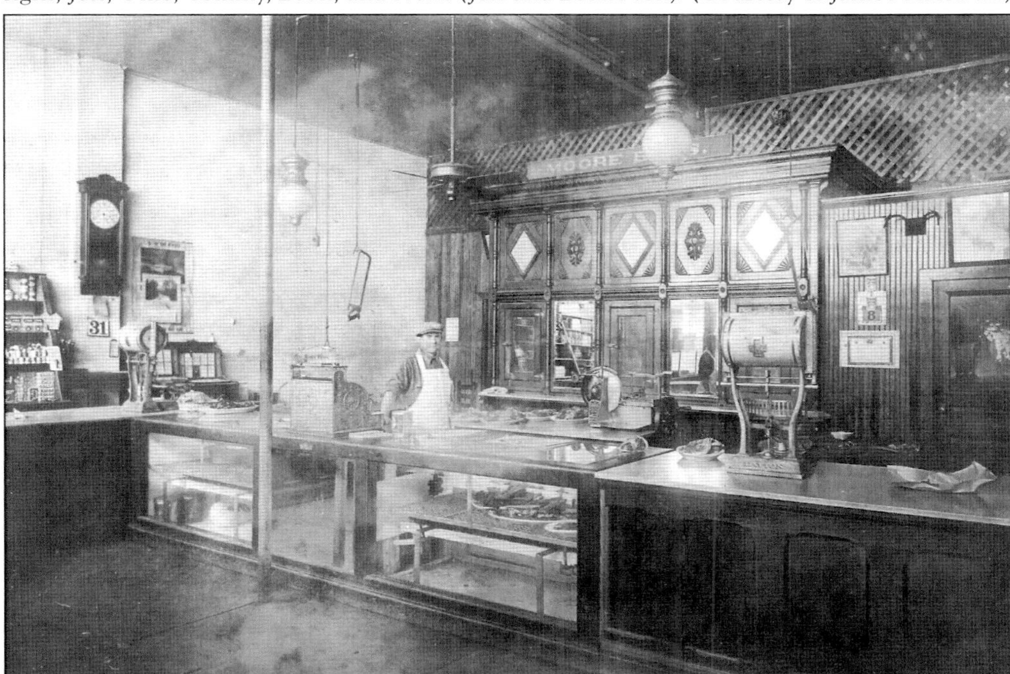

The Moore Brothers Meat Market provided its services to the town of Hope. The photograph was taken of the interior of the store around 1920. The gentleman is unidentified. A butcher saw hangs from the chain. (Courtesy of HVCM.)

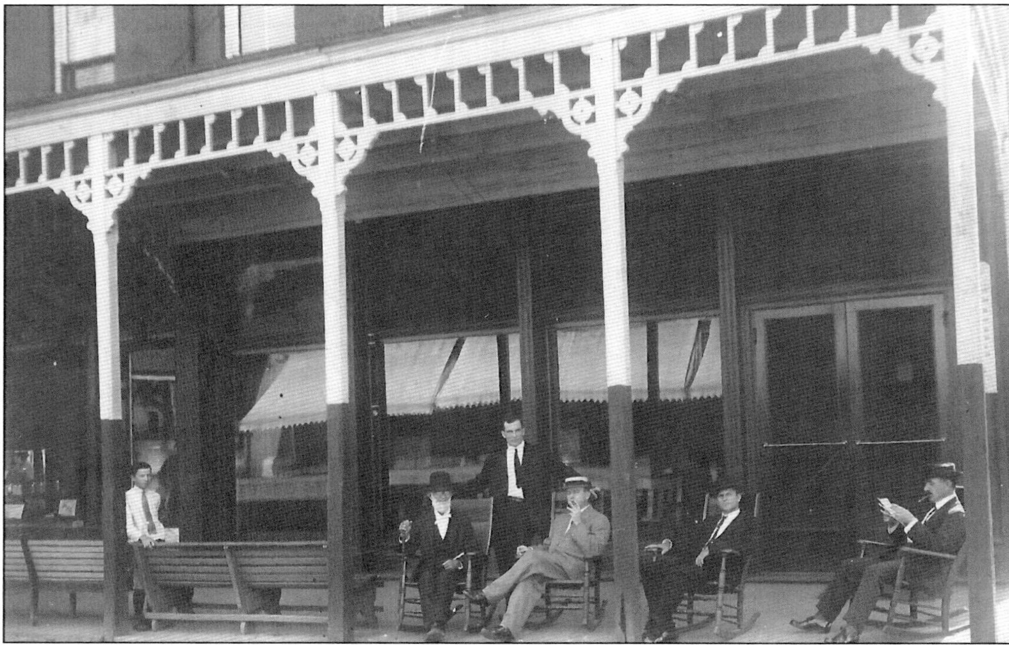

With the bustling nature of the railroad and different people traveling through Hope, hotels were needed to provide places for people to stay overnight. Downtown Hope had three major hotels. The Capitol Hotel was located across the street from the Missouri Pacific Passenger Depot on the corner of Main and Front (Division) Streets. The Barlow Hotel, at 102 Elm Street, was considered one of the best dining rooms in town and provided banquet space for events and civic club meetings. Among the gentlemen relaxing on the front porch of the Barlow around 1910 (above) is Rev. Horace Jewell (second from left). The Snyker Hotel (shown below around 1930) was across the Missouri Pacific Line on Avenue A. (Above, courtesy of SARA; below, courtesy of Mark Keith.)

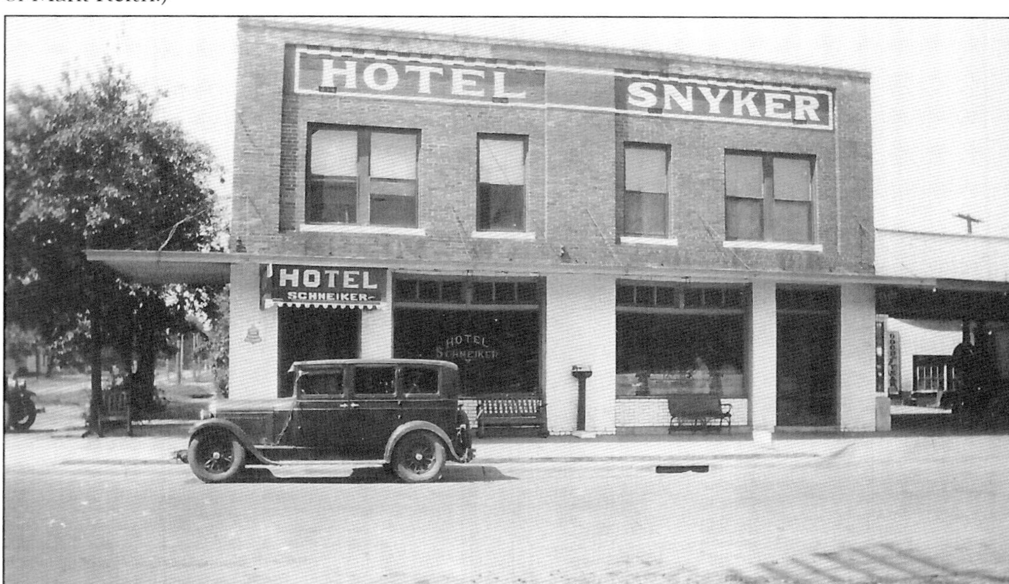

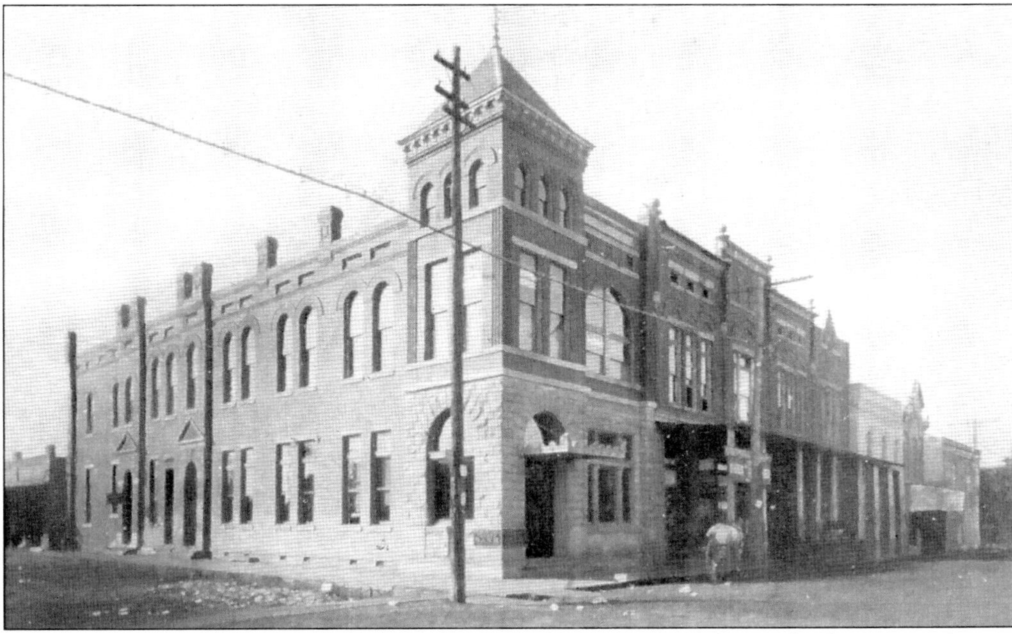

Three banks were formed in Hope during the early 20th century. The Bank of Hope was located on the corner of Second and Main Streets and later became First National Bank of Hope. The Hempstead County Bank (shown above around 1915) was located at 103 West Second Street on the corner opposite the Bank of Hope. This bank closed its doors during the Great Depression and never reopened. The third bank was Citizens National Bank, on the corner of Second and Elm Streets. It opened for business on August 11, 1912, with two employees, survived the Great Depression, and declared $1,300,000 in total resources in 1935, around the time of the photograph below. The Saenger Theater next door is playing *The Homecoming*, starring Clark Gable and Lana Turner. (Above, courtesy of SARA; below, courtesy of HVCM.)

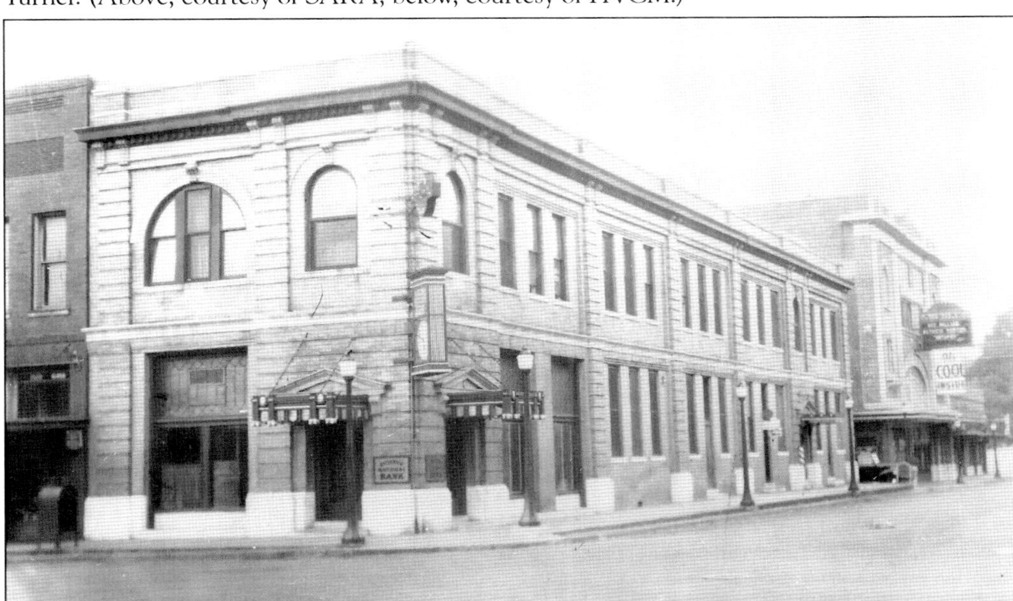

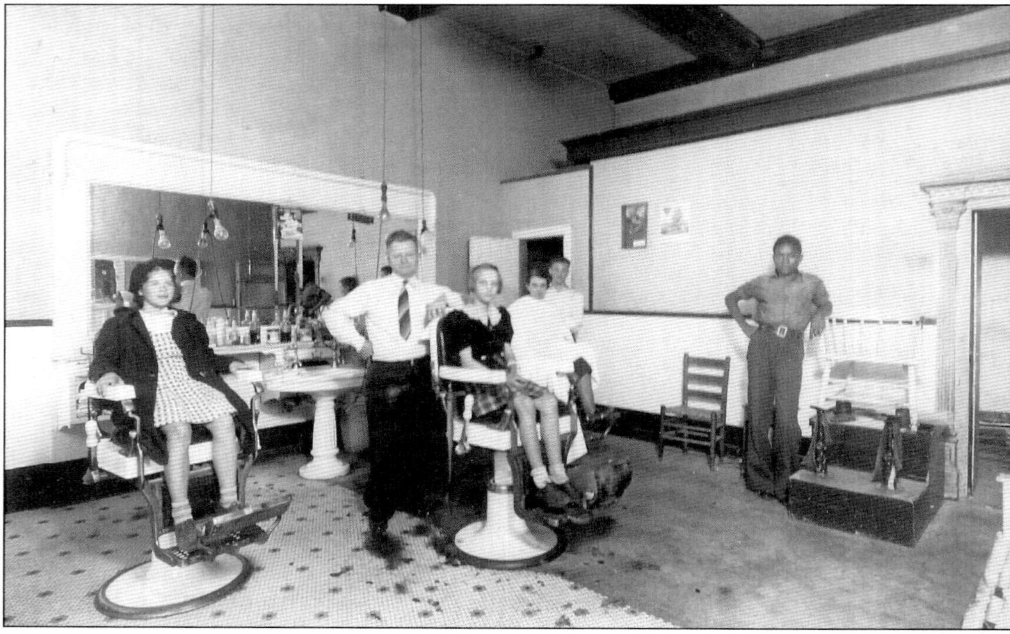

Keith's Barber Shop was located in the Citizens National Bank Building on the corner of Elm and Second Streets, across from Hope Hardware around 1935. From left to right are Virginia Keith Holmes, George Keith (owner), Emma Pearl Brotherton, unidentified, Phil Keith, and an unidentified shoe shiner. (Courtesy of Sterling Keith.)

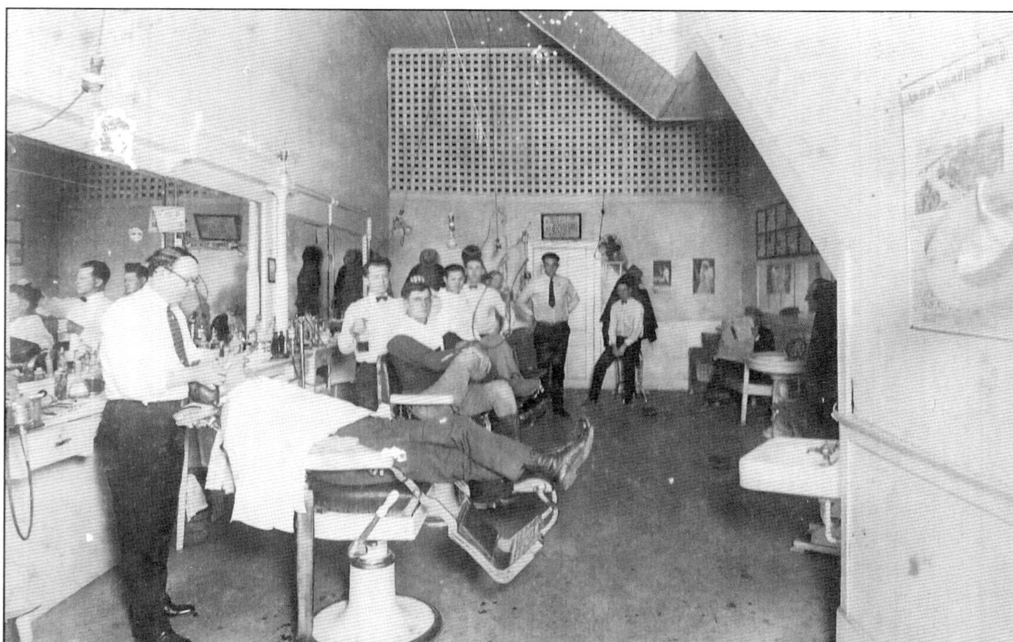

Other barbershops were located around town. At the Dixie Barber Shop in March 1926, a man is given a shave as other customers look toward the camera. The shop was located on Second Street between Main and Elm Streets. (Courtesy of Sterling Keith.)

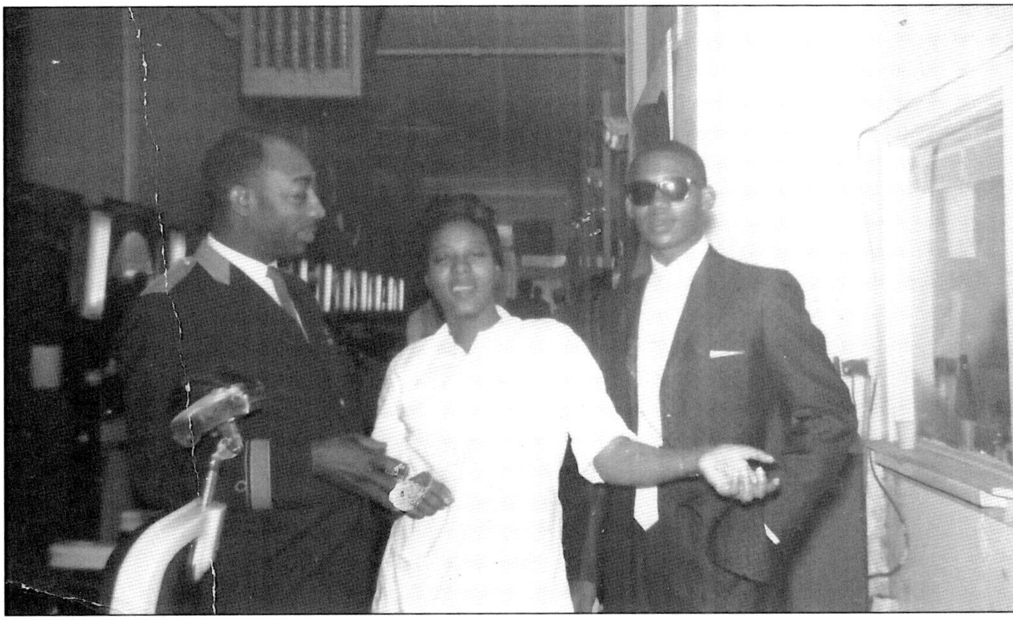

African Americans in Hope had their own barber and hair shops. Hazel Simpson was one of the hair designers in this community. After graduating from H. C. Yerger High School, she attended hair design school in Texas, shown in this photograph taken in the 1960s. Simpson later came back home and set up her own shop in Hope. (Courtesy of Hazel Simpson.)

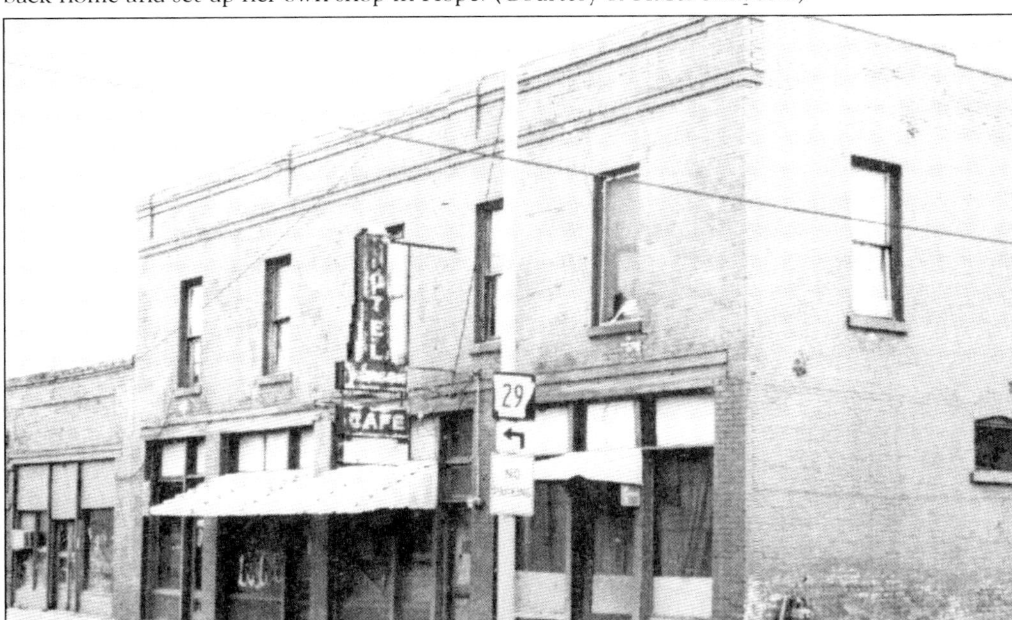

The Nelson Hotel was located on Third Street and was the local African American hotel from the 1930s to the 1960s. Hazel Simpson's hair shop was in this building for a period of time. The building served the African American community in Hope for several years. (Courtesy of Hazel Simpson.)

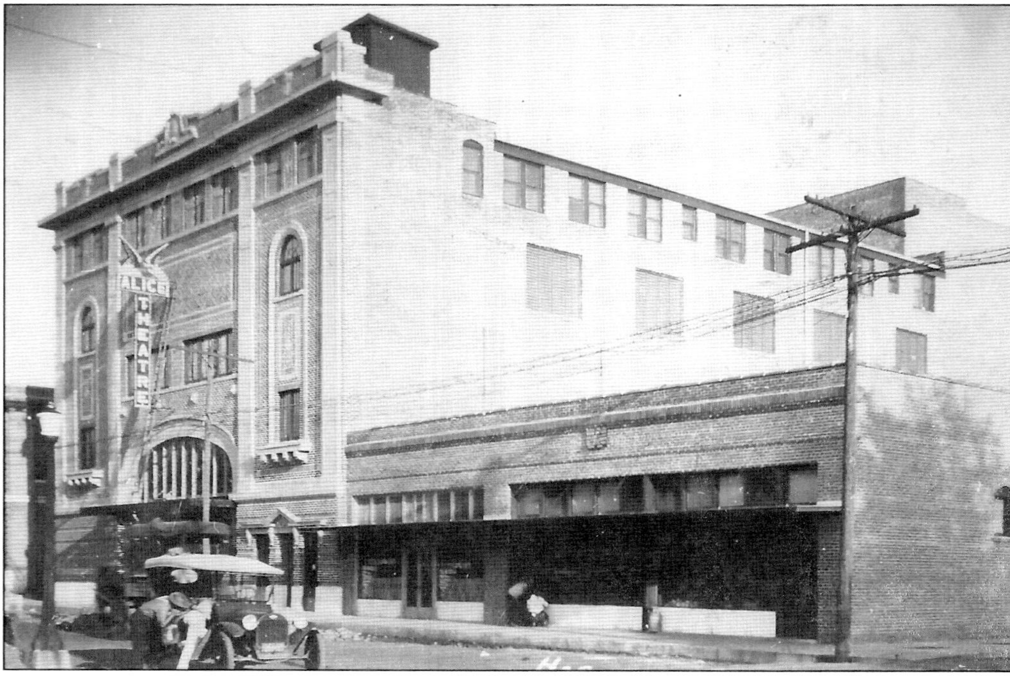

From its inception, Hope offered various forms of entertainment and theaters for its residents. The town originally had an opera house that provided a venue for traveling shows and vaudeville acts. Around 1920, the Alice Theatre (above) was built on Second Street. It was three stories high and contained a large stage with an orchestra pit, pipe organ, and room for scenery onstage. In 1922, the Alice Theatre burned and was replaced by the first Saenger Theatre in 1927. On Easter Sunday in 1944, the theater burned and was followed by a smaller theater with the same name (below). Both Saenger theaters echoed portions of the Alice Theatre's ornate facade. (Both, courtesy of SARA.)

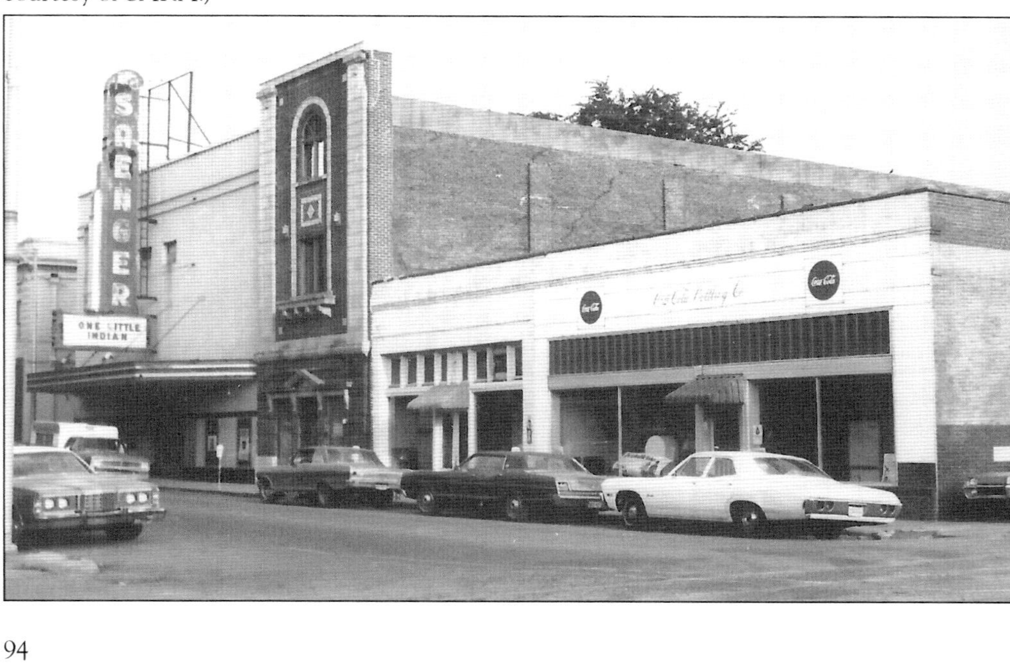

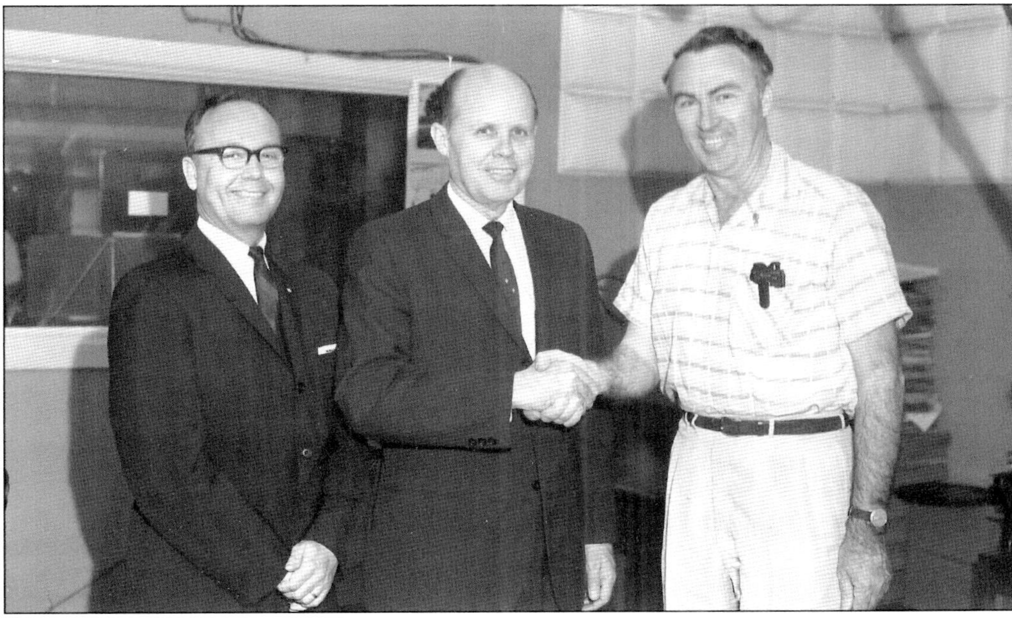

On May 20, 1964, KXAR, the local radio station, switched to 1,000 kilowatts, which expanded its outreach to southwest Arkansas. In the photograph are, from left to right, George Frazier (ex-mayor of Hope and a member of the radio commission), Frank Douglas (mayor of Hope), and Haskel Jones (manager of KXAR). In 1948, the station won a Peabody Award for emergency assistance to Cotton Valley, Louisiana, after the town was hit by a tornado. (Courtesy of Mark Keith.)

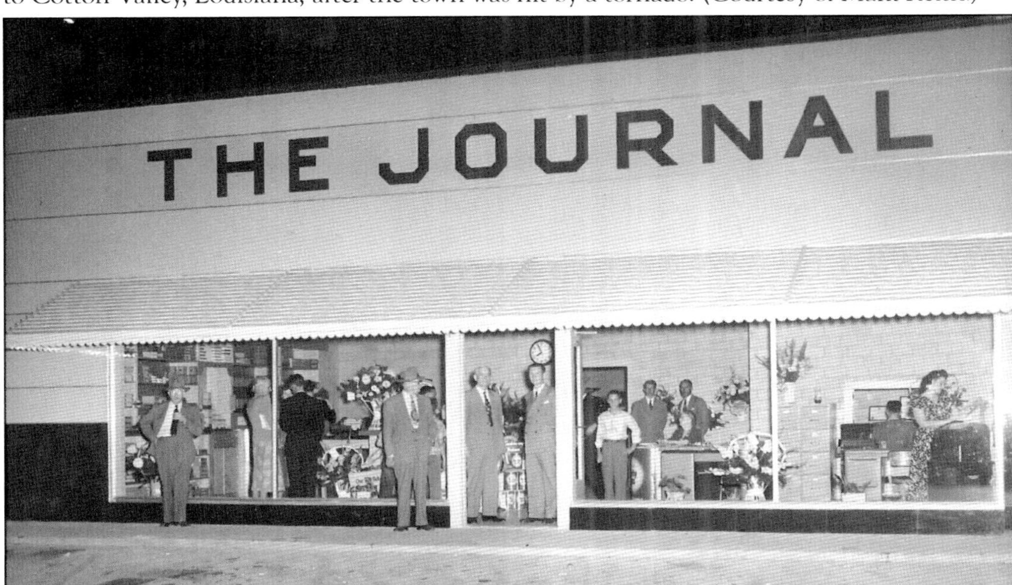

On May 15, 1940, a new newspaper, the *Hope Journal*, came on the scene. The *Journal* continued for a brief time and later closed after 1951, leaving only the *Hope Star*. The photograph was taken on Saturday, October 1, 1949, during an open house for the *Journal*'s new office at 218 East Second Street. The paper's editor, Kelly Briant, who later became Arkansas secretary of state, stands in the right-hand side of the doorway. (Courtesy of Don and Mary Parker.)

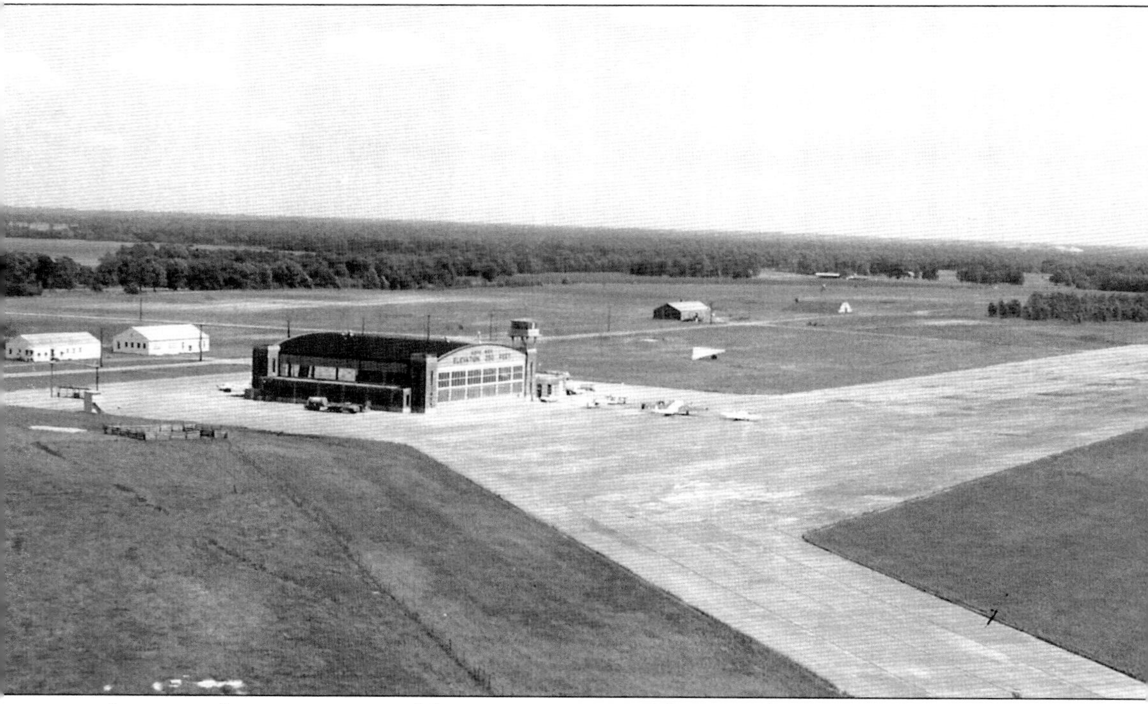

In terms of commerce, one of the major impacts on Hempstead County and Hope was Southwest Proving Ground. In July 1941, it was announced that Hope would become the site of a 15-million-dollar facility for testing aerial and ground munitions for the armed forces. The airport shown in the photograph was one of the few in the nation to have concrete runways when it was built to accommodate bombers and other aircraft. The proving ground encompassed over 37,000 acres and was 5 miles wide and 15 miles long. Some of the best farmland in Hempstead County was included in this tract. After World War II, previous owners were allowed to purchase their lands back from the federal government. (Courtesy of Mary Nell Turner.)

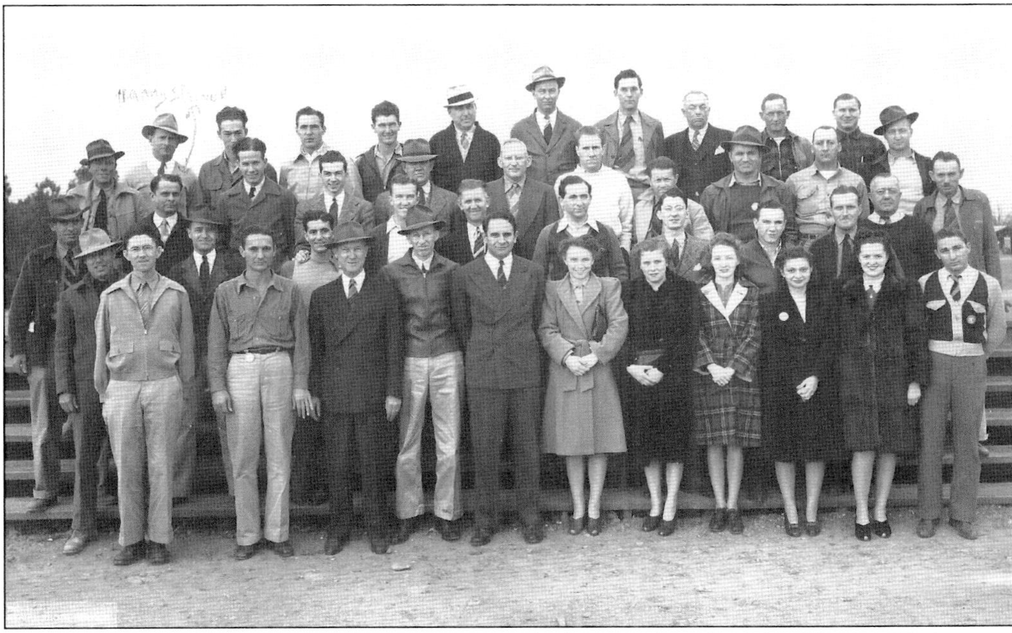

Residents of Hope and Hempstead County received jobs to work at the federal facility. Each person was assigned to different areas, such as security, clerical work, the electrical department, and others. Hope plumber Harry Shiver (third row, second from left) poses in an employee photograph on December 10, 1941. (Courtesy of SARA.)

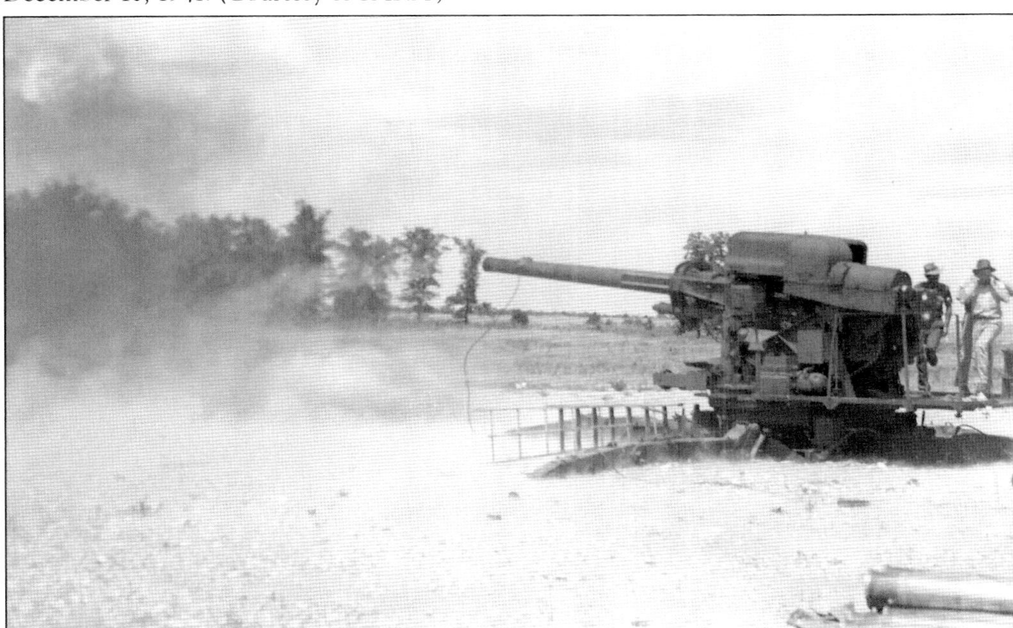

Ammunition that was to be used for the armed forces during World War II was tested in the area. In the photograph, an army artillery gun test fires a shell. Much of the ammunition fired into the area can still be found and is still being cleaned up by professional explosives experts who dispose of the materials. (Courtesy of HVCM.)

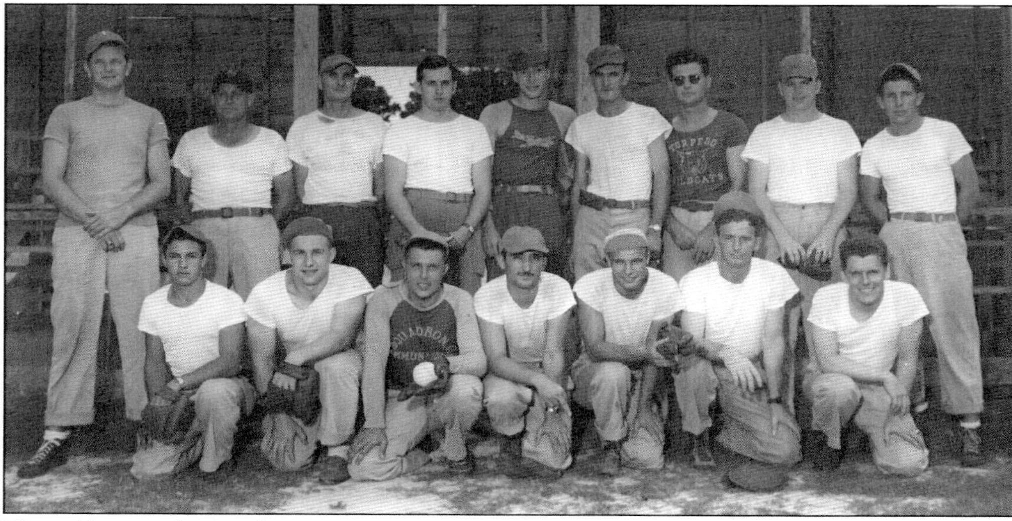

The soldiers at the Southwest Proving Ground formed a baseball team during the war. They are identified, from left to right, as (first row) Pvt. Ernest F. Bocquin, Sgt. John R. Allan (Weather), Pvt. Ernest L. Hoot, Sgt. John S. Allopenna (Weather), Pvt. Kenneth K. Pixley, T.Sgt. Raymond M. Swafford Jr., Capt. Francis S. Johnson; (second row) 1st Lt. Clarence D. Mitchell Jr., T.Sgt. Leslie E. Clark, M.Sgt. Vernon W. Christie, Pvt. Malcolm B. Allen (Ordnance), Cpl. Robert J. Lewis, Sgt. Aloysius A. Feldman, T.Sgt. Robert W. Minamyern, Cpl. Raymond J. McIntyre, and Pvt. Edward B. Price. (Courtesy of Mary Nell Turner.)

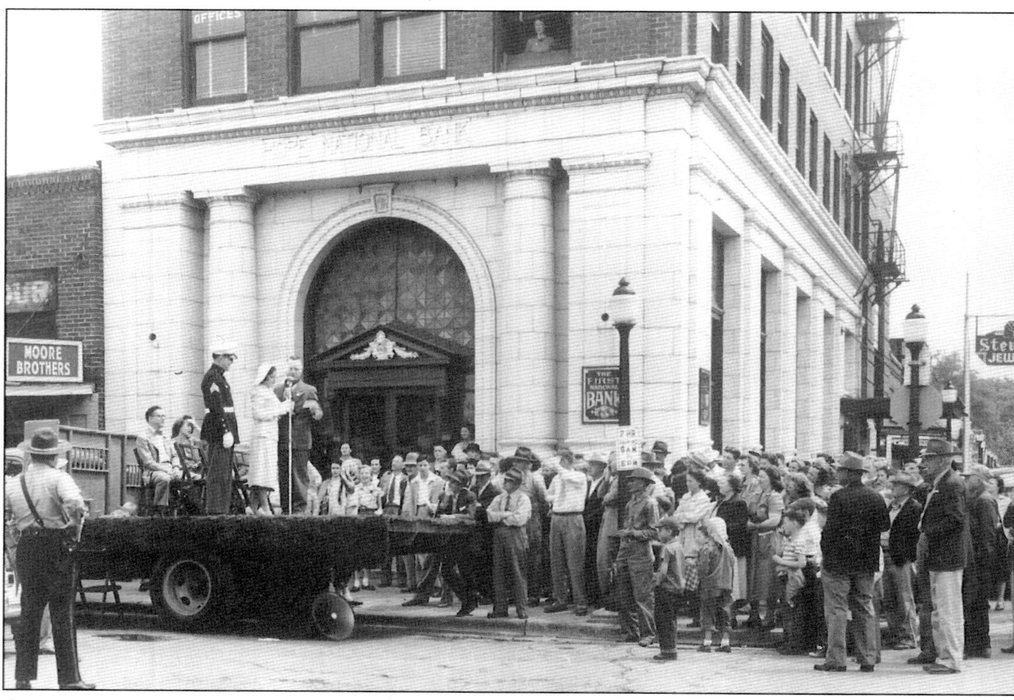

As in many towns across America during World War II, war bonds were sold in Hope. In front of the Hope First National Bank building on Main Street in 1943, residents listen to the reasons why war bonds could help pay combat costs. (Courtesy of Mary Nell Turner.)

Four

Celebrations

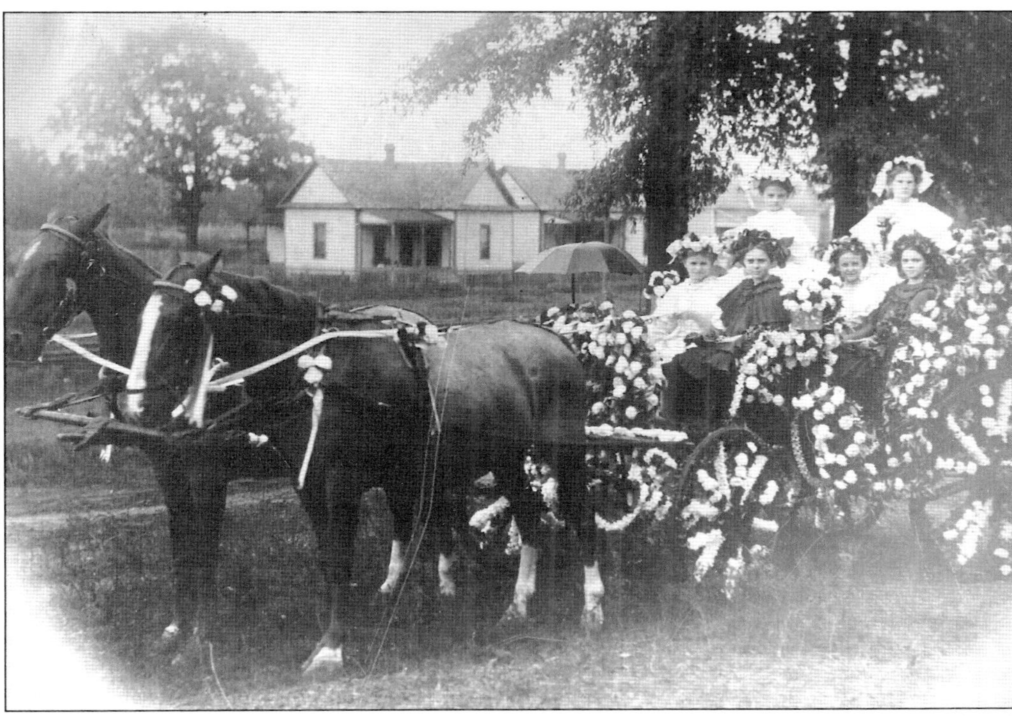

Parades and celebrations were a common occurrence in Hope. In this photograph, local girls ride a float trimmed with flowers, which won second prize in a 1910 parade. They are, from left to right, Floride Greening , Chester Andrews, Jean Lasetere, Effie Mae Bridewell, Cornelia Betts, and Evelyn von Jagersfield. (Courtesy of SARA.)

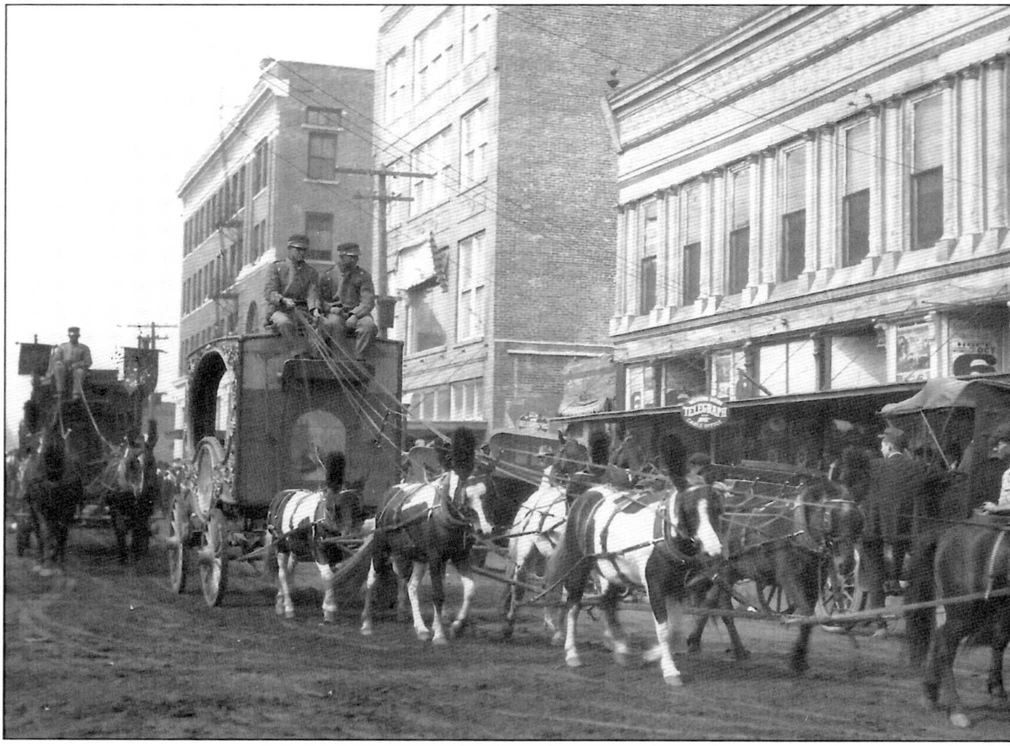

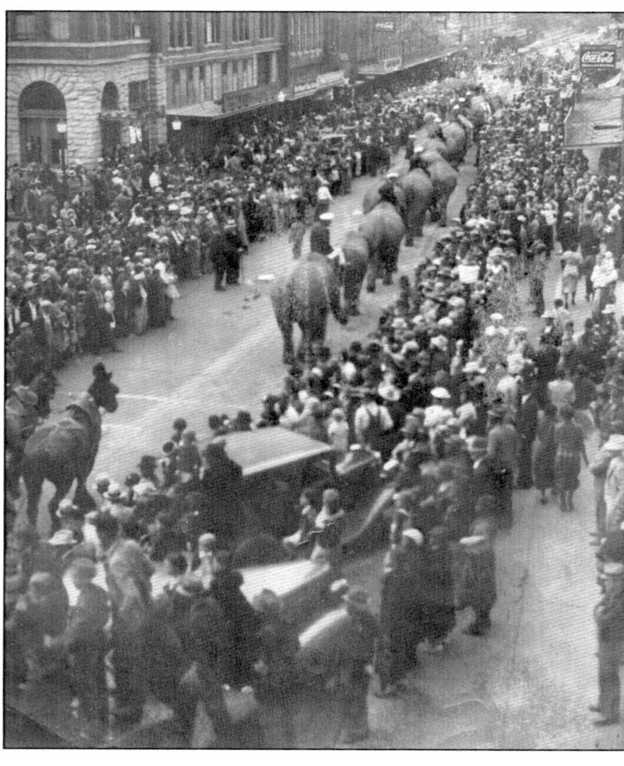

Above, a 1920 parade celebrates the Ringling Brothers and Barnum and Bailey Circus. The "Greatest Show on Earth" came to town by railroad and unloaded animals from specialized cars. A parade took place on Second Street and was described as being almost 1 mile long. Spectators followed the route to the circus grounds off West Avenue B to see the first show for 75¢. Around 1930, the circus returned to Hope and paraded elephants down Second Street heading west (left). (Above, courtesy of SARA; left, courtesy of Don and Mark Parker.)

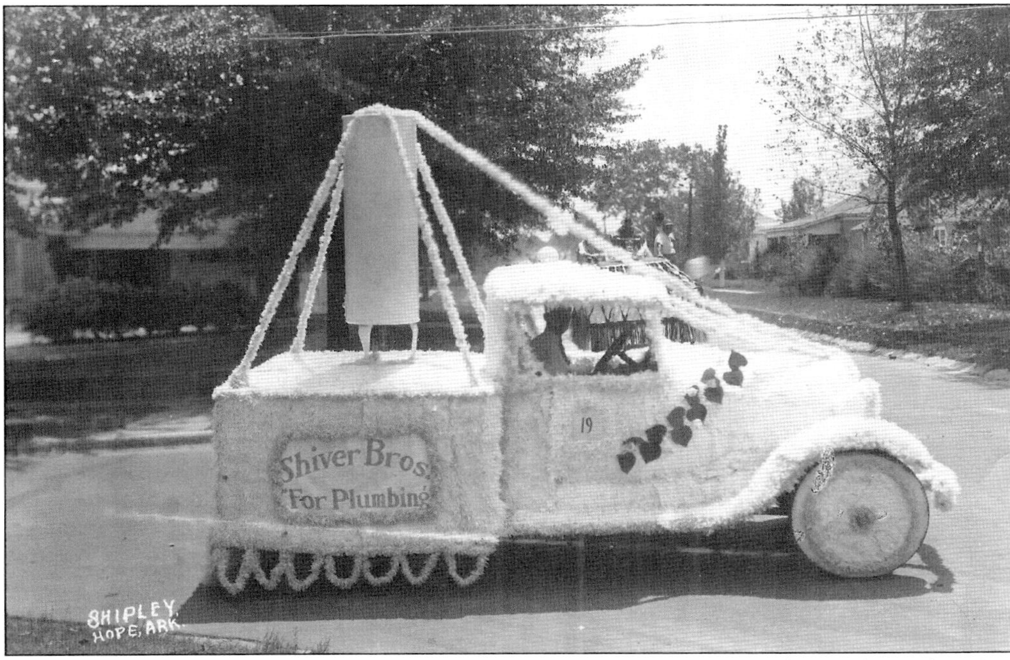

Businesses in town would sponsor different floats to advertise in local parades. In the mid-1920s, a Shiver Brothers Plumbing float showcases a hot water heater. The entire truck, including wheels, is completely covered with material. (Courtesy of SARA.)

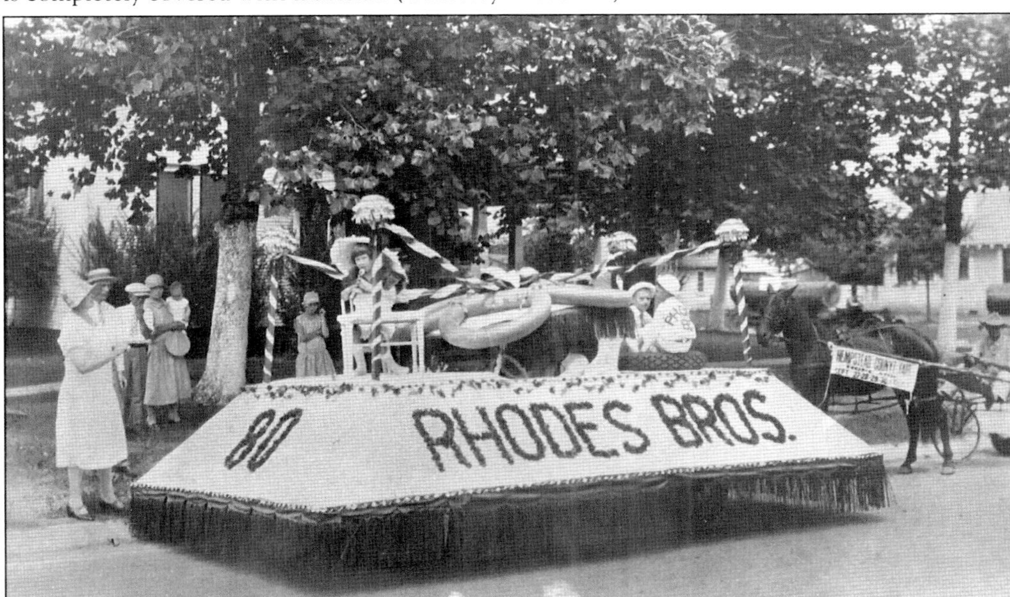

A Rhodes Brothers Service Station float travels the first Watermelon Festival parade route in 1926. Emma Jean Hays is the little girl riding in front, playing the part of a secretary at her table. On the back, McDowell (Mac) Turner and Vasco Bright, wearing white sailor hats, throw balloons from the big spare tire. Herbert Lewallen, a Rhodes Brothers employee, drives the vehicle. Other businesses in town sponsored different floats. (Courtesy of SARA.)

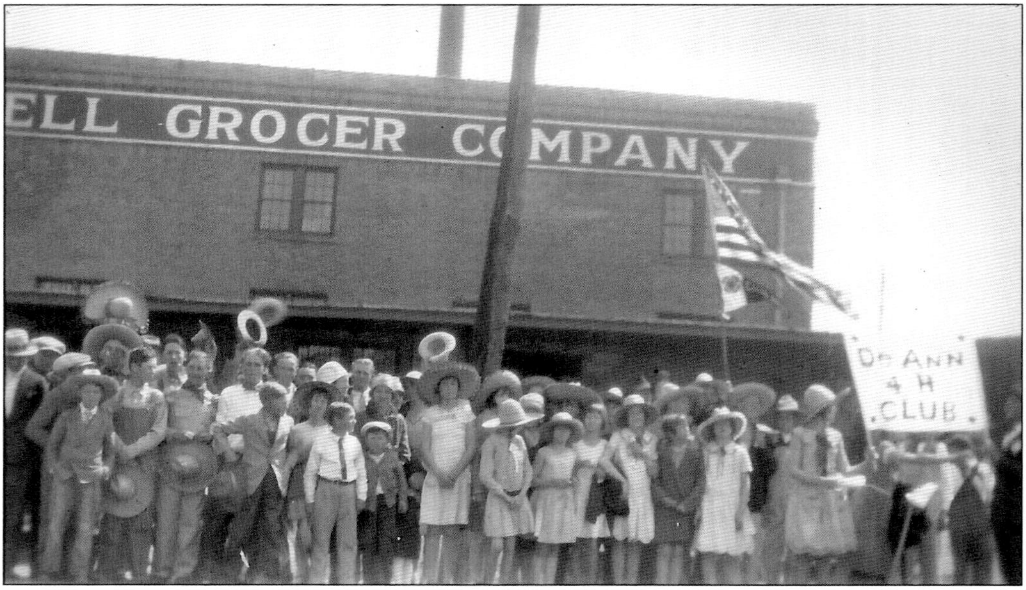

Parades in Hope were usually held around the time of the county fair and rodeo in late September. Groups from throughout the county would come to Hope to be a part of the festivities. These photographs were taken around 1925. Above, the 4-H Club from DeAnn, which is located a few miles northeast of Hope, stands in front of the Plunkett-Jarrell Grocery Company on the corner of Avenue A and North Elm Street. In the photograph below is a group from Center Point, located in adjacent Howard County. (Both, courtesy of SARA.)

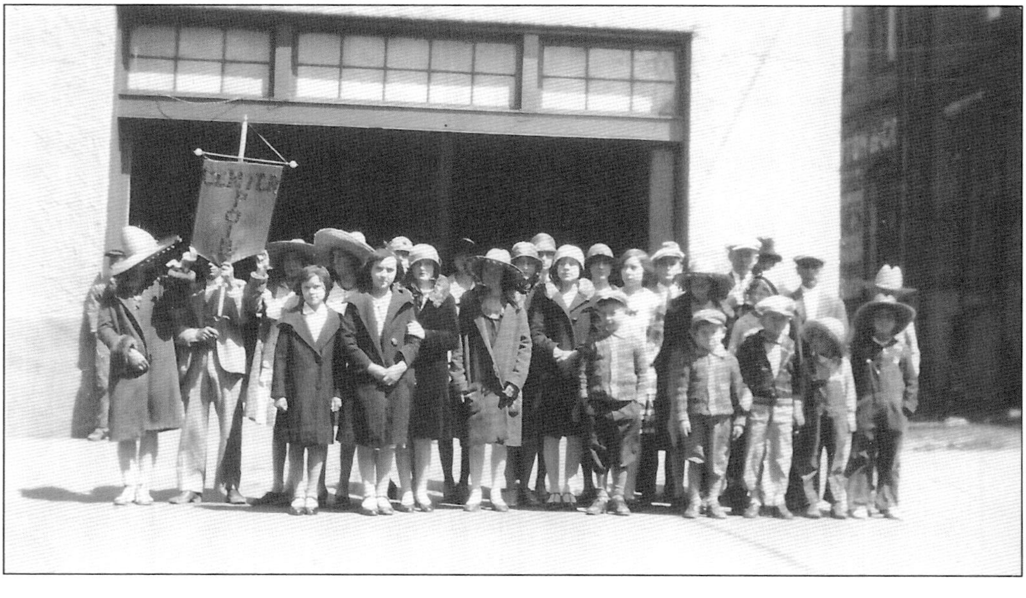

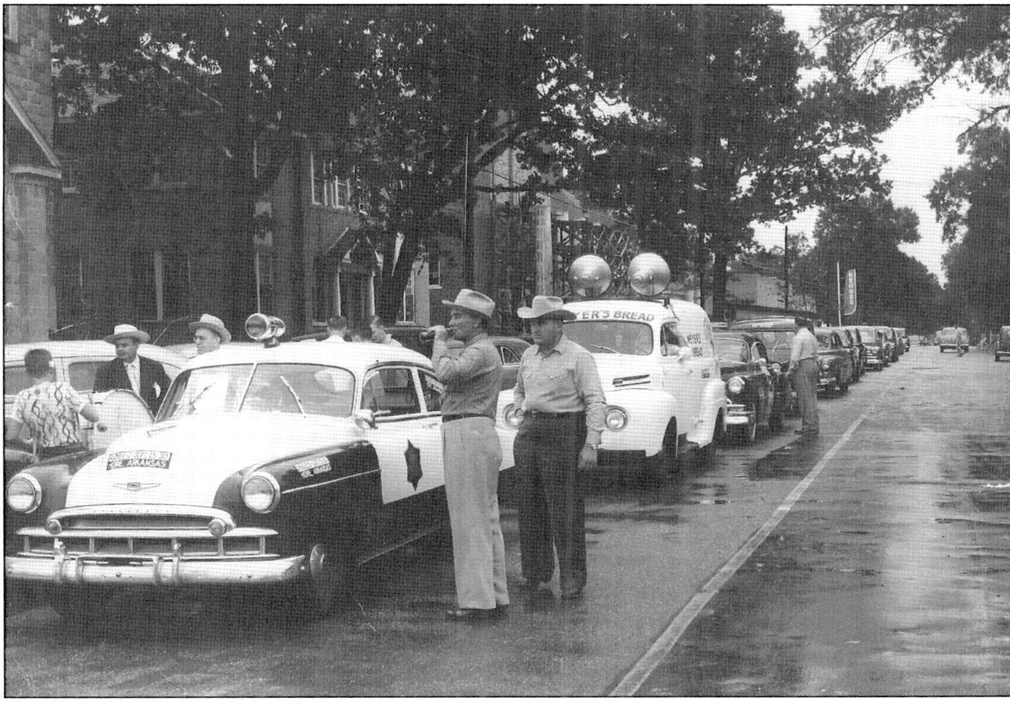

In 1949, Norman Moore (left center) and Milton Mossier are among the city and county officials setting up for the Third District Fair Rodeo parade on Main Street. The new First Baptist Church sanctuary is under construction in the background. (Courtesy of Mary Nell Turner.)

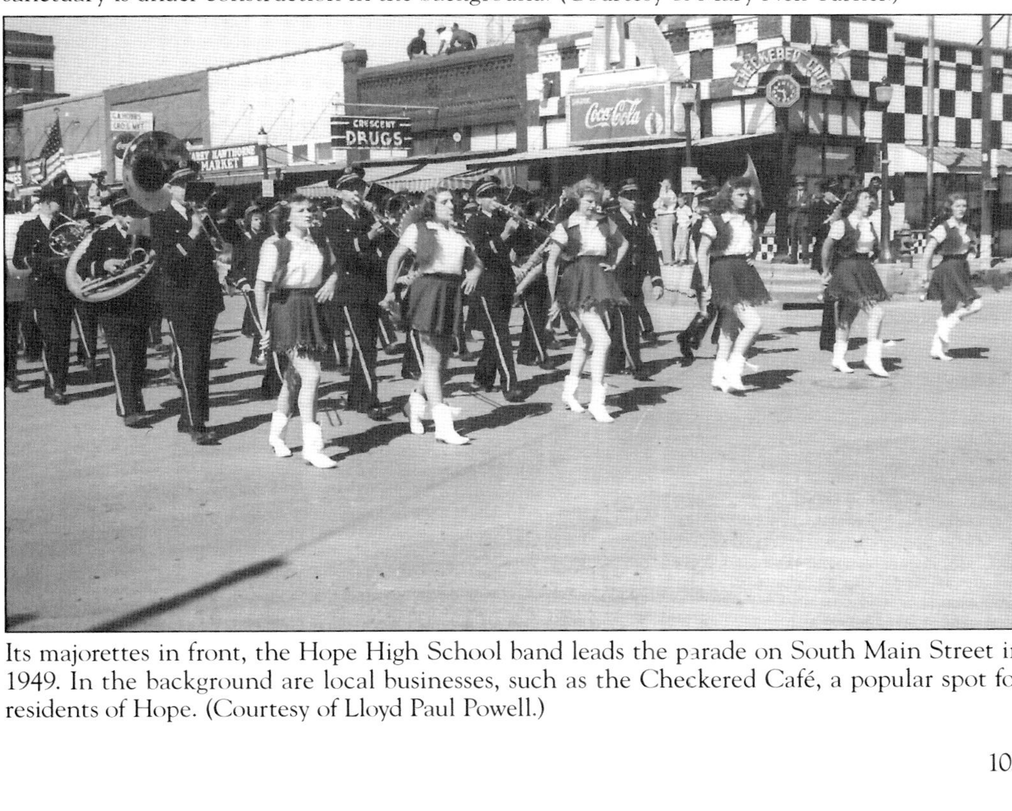

Its majorettes in front, the Hope High School band leads the parade on South Main Street in 1949. In the background are local businesses, such as the Checkered Café, a popular spot for residents of Hope. (Courtesy of Lloyd Paul Powell.)

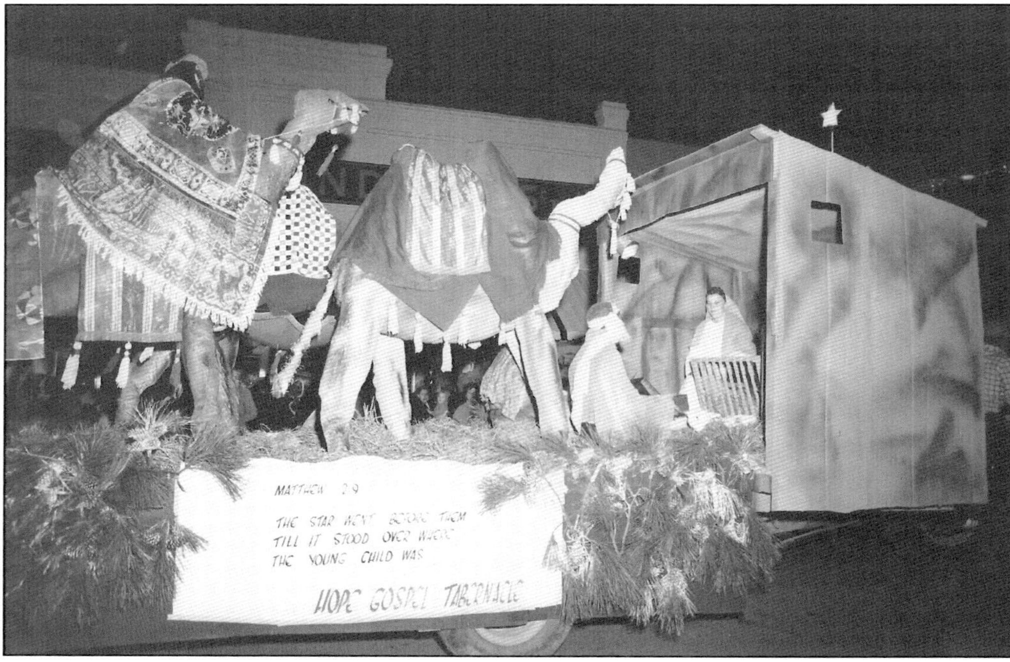

Businesses, civic groups, and churches would put together floats for a parade to celebrate the Christmas season. In this 1955 image, members of Hope Gospel Tabernacle portray the Nativity scene. (Courtesy of First Assembly of God of Hope.)

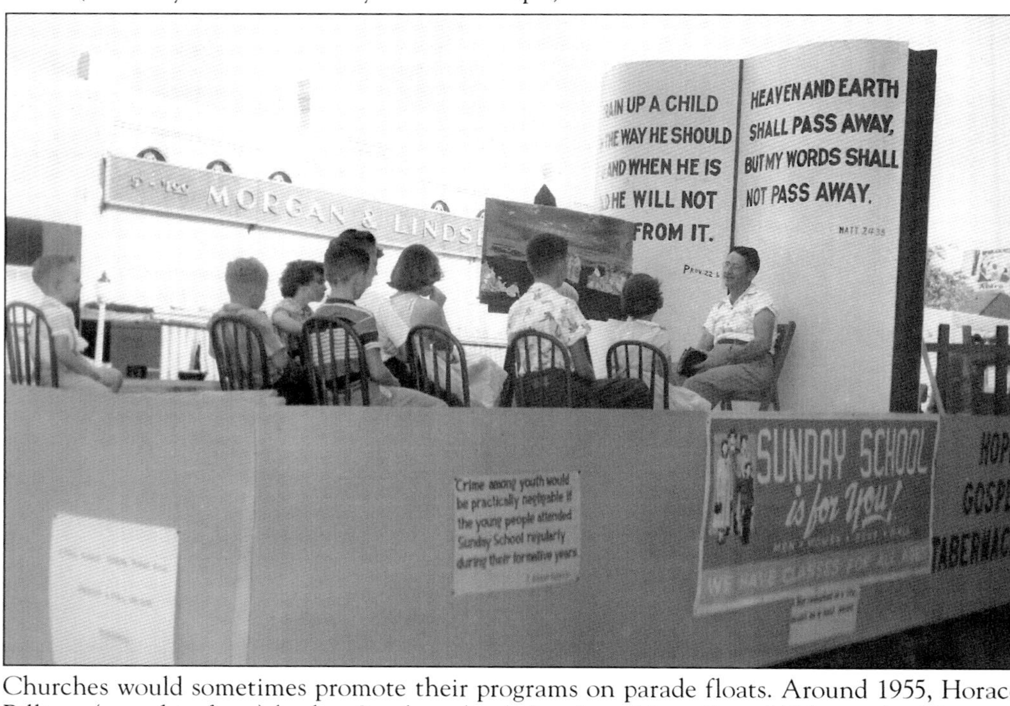

Churches would sometimes promote their programs on parade floats. Around 1955, Horace Billings (seated in front) leads a Sunday school class from Hope Gospel Tabernacle. (Courtesy of First Assembly of God of Hope.)

As far back as 1895, Hope and Hempstead were known for large watermelons grown in the area's sandy soil. This postcard, titled "Way Down in Dixie," shows a man about to cut into a 149.75-pound Black Diamond watermelon, a common variety at the time. (Courtesy of Keenan and Peggy Williams.)

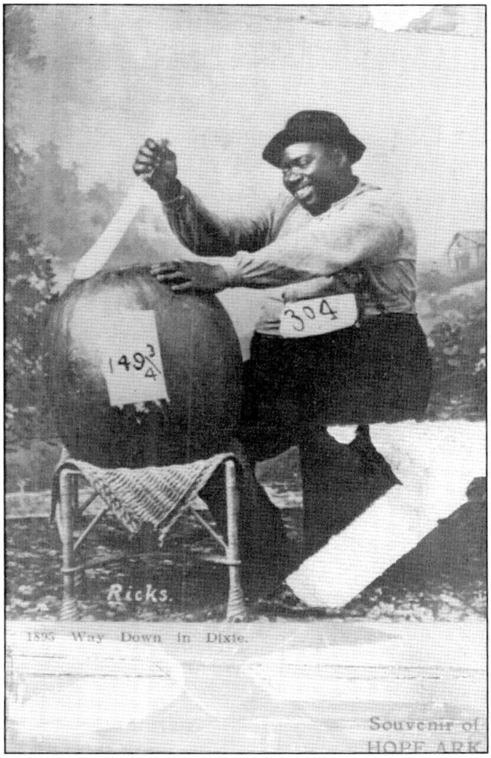

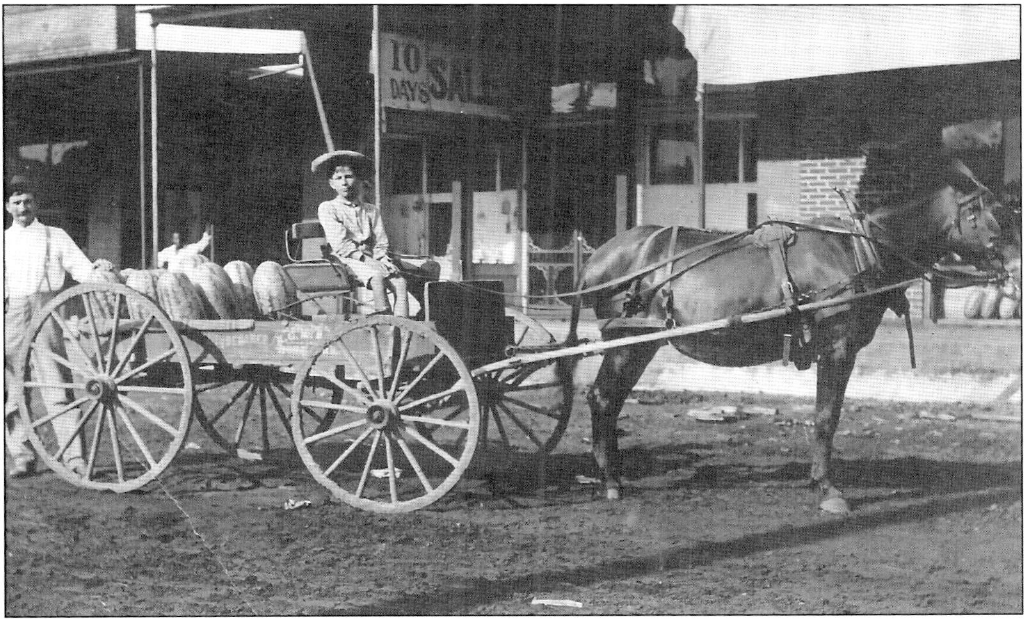

Farmers would bring their products to town to sell. Around 1905, John Kelly Briggs stands next to a wagon loaded with watermelons in downtown Hope. His son, Fred, sits on the wagon. In 1916, John S. Gibson of Gibson Drug Store at 107 West Division Street began to offer prizes for the largest watermelon grown. (Courtesy of Mary Nell Turner.)

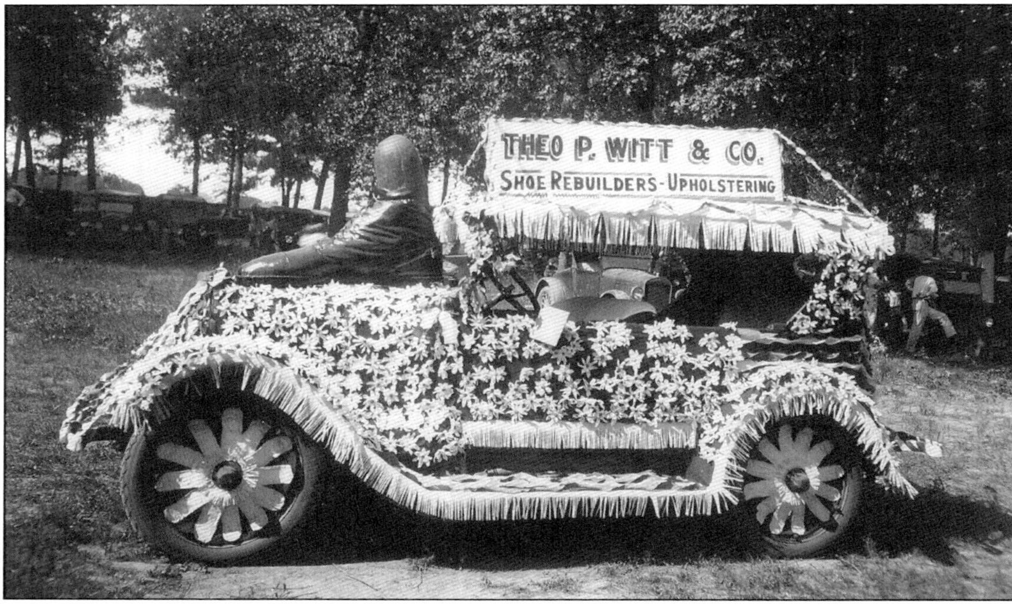

In the 1920s, W. Y. Foster, head of the chamber of commerce, noticed the large size of watermelons being grown and pushed for a watermelon festival to advertise the county. The first festival and parade took place on August 12, 1925. Business owners and civic clubs decorated elaborate floats like the one shown above, put together by Theo P. Witt and Company shoe store. A Watermelon Queen was part of the festival activities. In the photograph below, Arkansas National Guardsmen escort the Watermelon Queen and her court in one of the early festivals. (Both, courtesy of SARA.)

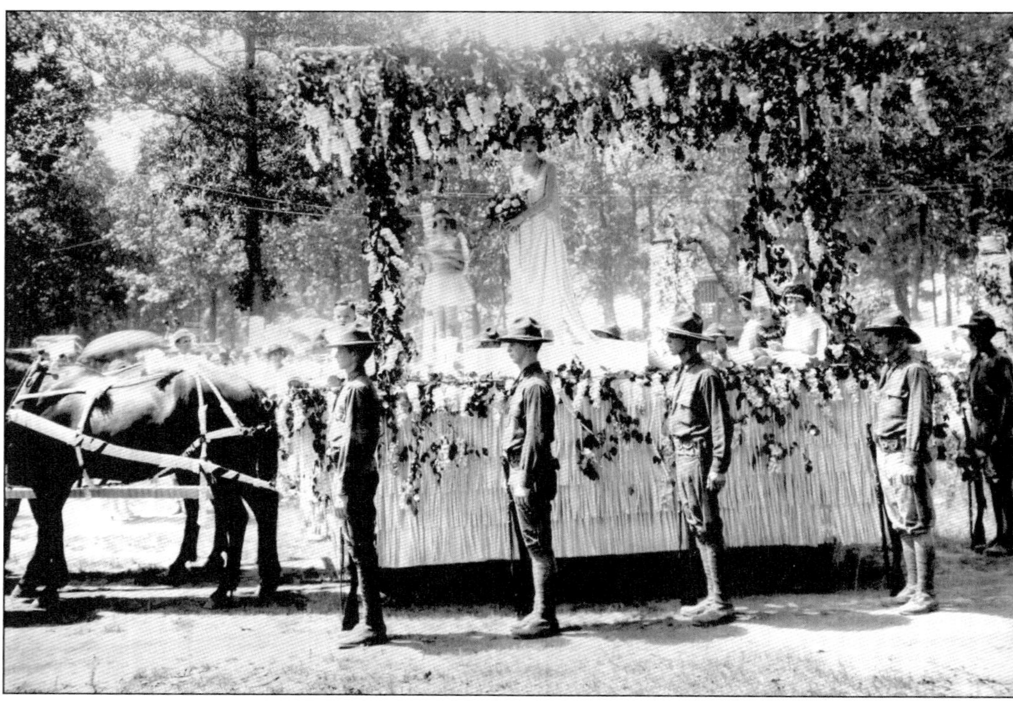

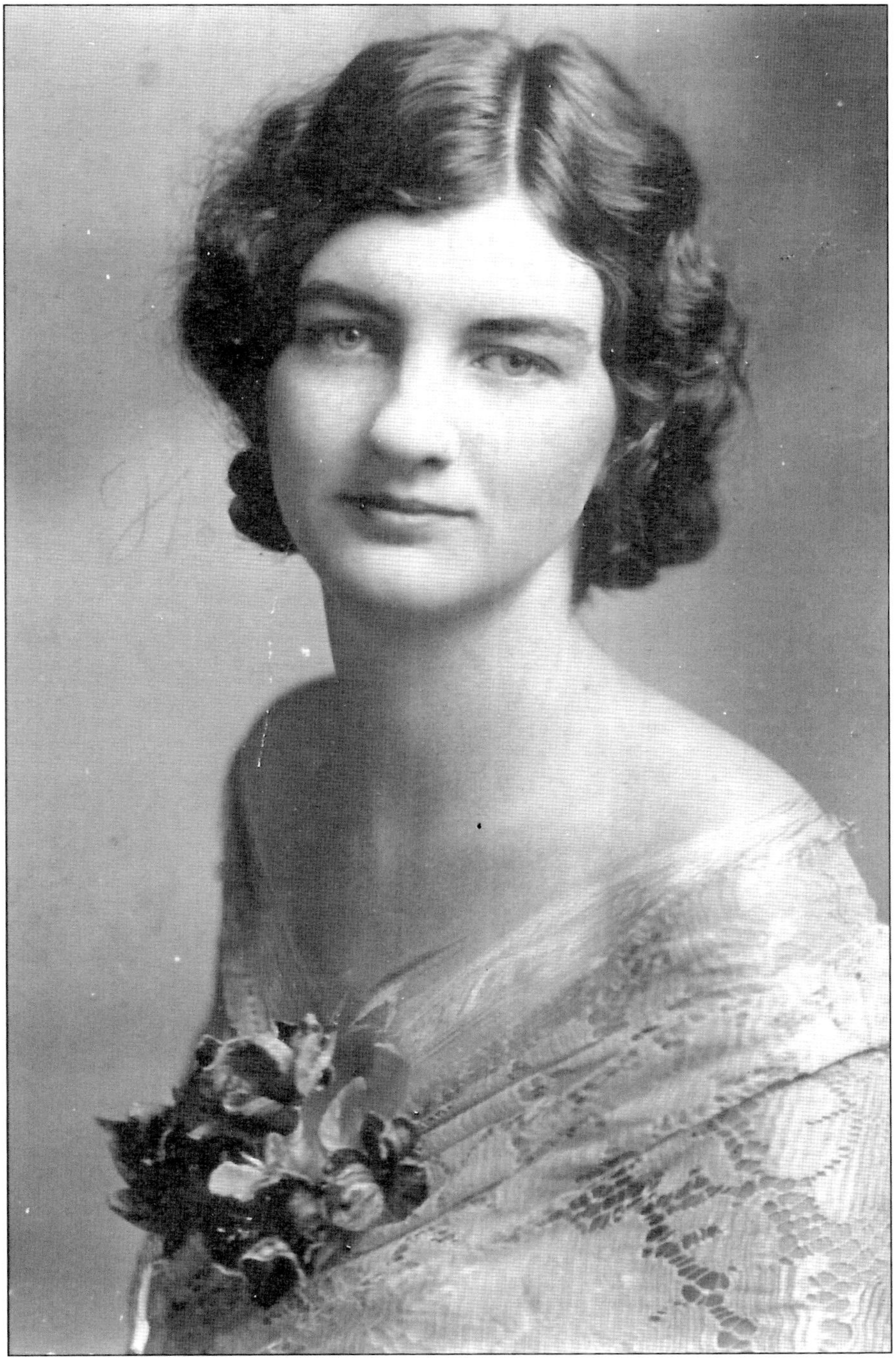

The watermelon festivals of the 1920s continued the tradition of the Watermelon Queen and Court. This 1929 image shows Watermelon Maid Connie Clenderon. Other maids in Watermelon Queen Geraldine Busby's court were Margaret Porter, Mattie Mae Kent, Swan Garner, Vera Houston, Annabelle Philbrick, Audrey Cox, Margaret Simmons, Margaret Hicks, Frances Monts, and Fern Martin. (Courtesy of Barbara Ann Burke.)

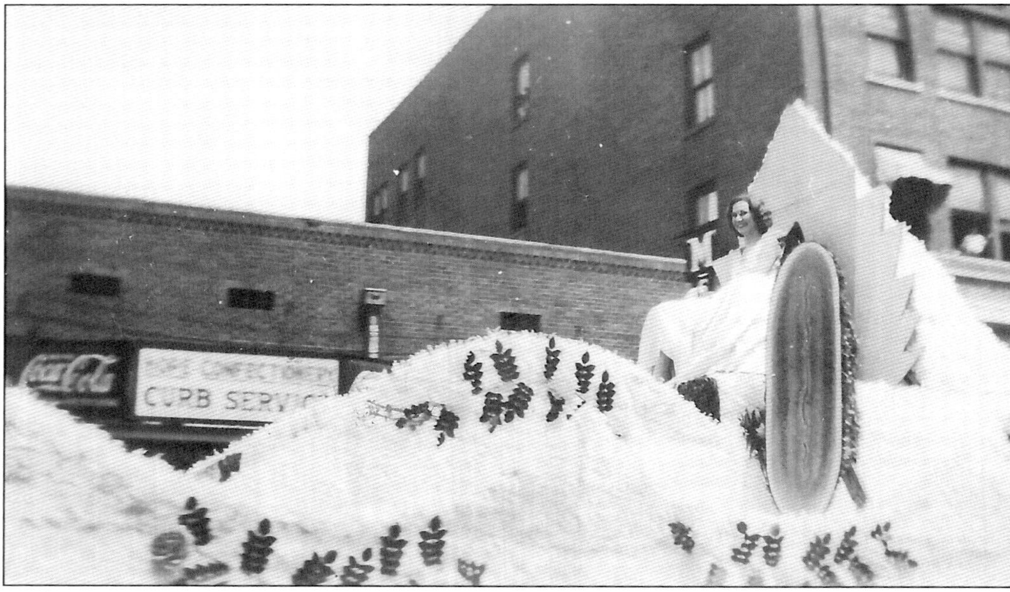

In the 1927 Watermelon Festival parade, Queen Sarah Louise Gentry sits on her throne atop a large float. (Courtesy of SARA.)

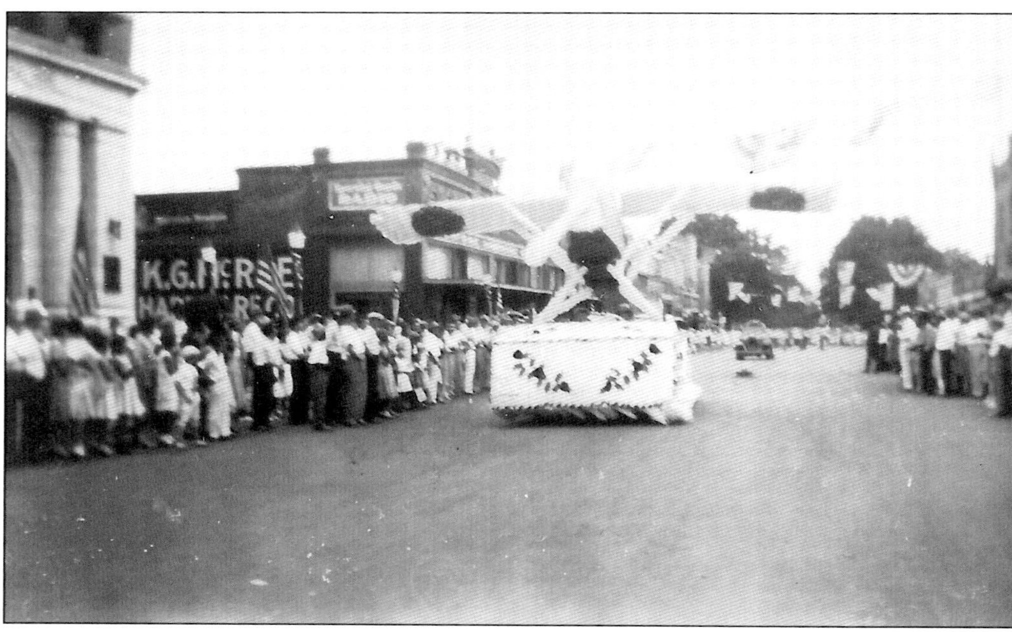

In 1927, an elaborate float in the shape of an airplane was part of the celebration of the Hope Watermelon Festival. People attended from all over the county to see the different parade floats. (Courtesy of SARA.)

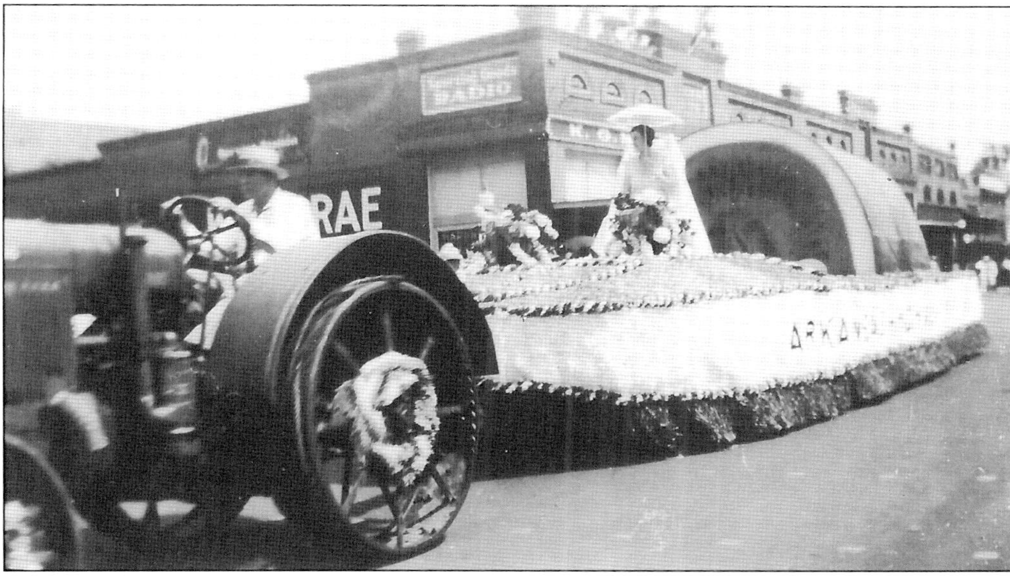

Various designs were always a part of the parade. In this 1927 entry, an unidentified woman sits in front of a gigantic slice of watermelon. (Courtesy of SARA.)

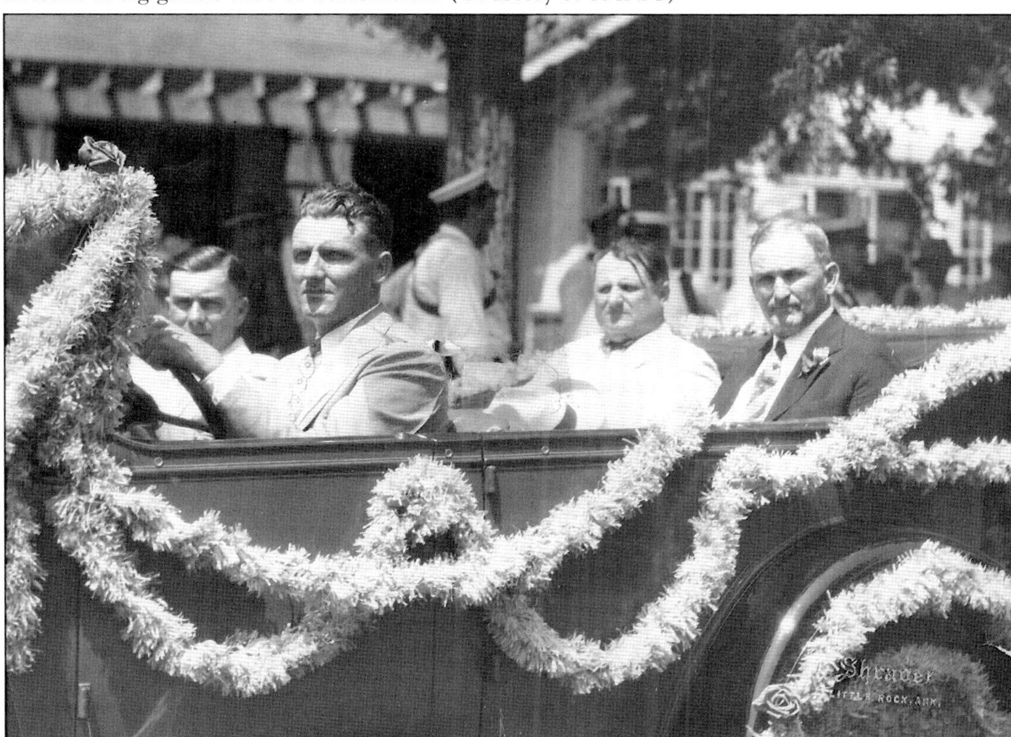
A special guest attended the third annual Watermelon Festival in 1928. Sen. Joe T. Robinson of Arkansas (far right), the 1928 Democratic nominee for vice president, rides in a car with, from left to right, Roy Anderson (president of the Hope Chamber of Commerce), Steve Carrigan, and Barney Hamm. (Courtesy of SARA.)

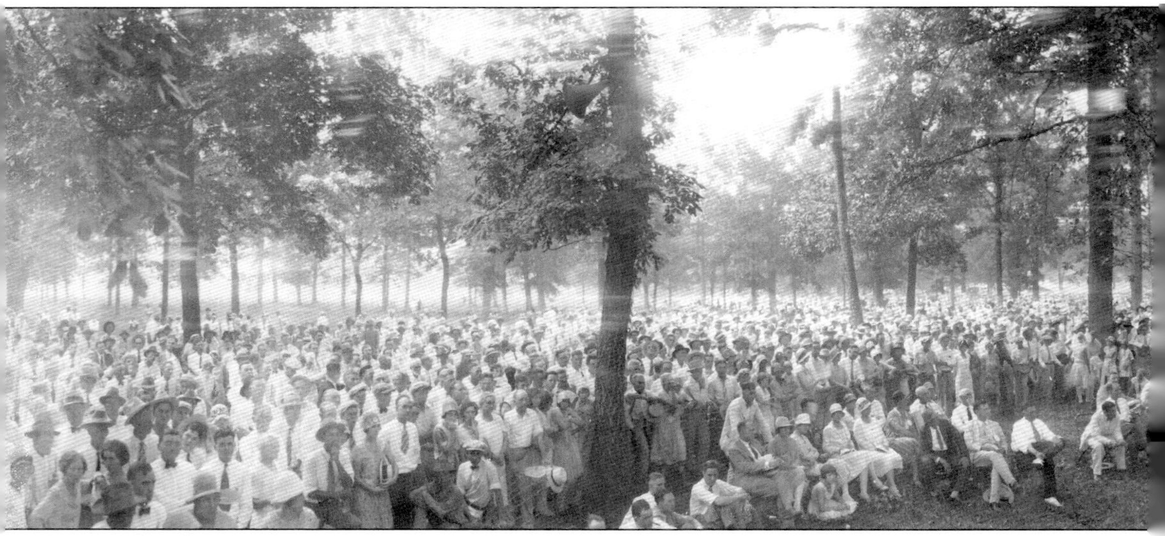

After the parade, residents of Hope and guests went down to the Hope Fair Park to hear Senator Robinson speak. The event took place on August 9, 1928. Robinson was the running mate for Democratic presidential candidate and New York governor Alfred Smith in the elections of 1928 against Republican candidates Herbert Hoover and Charles Curtis. In the crowd near the front,

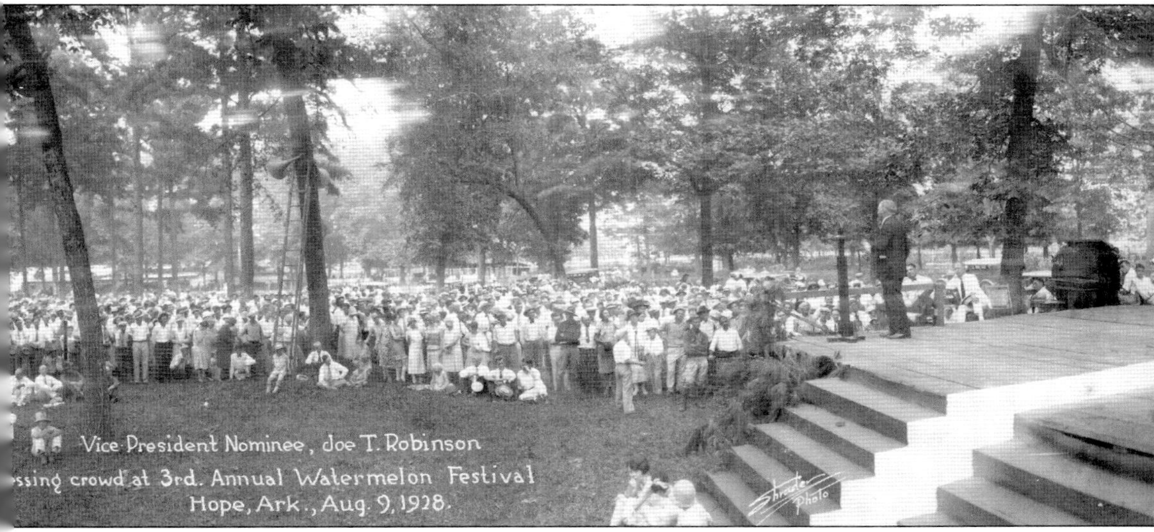

the young girl sitting with her legs crossed is Mary Sue Evans, the daughter of local leader Roy Anderson. She died on December 27, 2009, at age of 95 and was the last person known to be alive who attended Robison's speech. (Courtesy of SARA.)

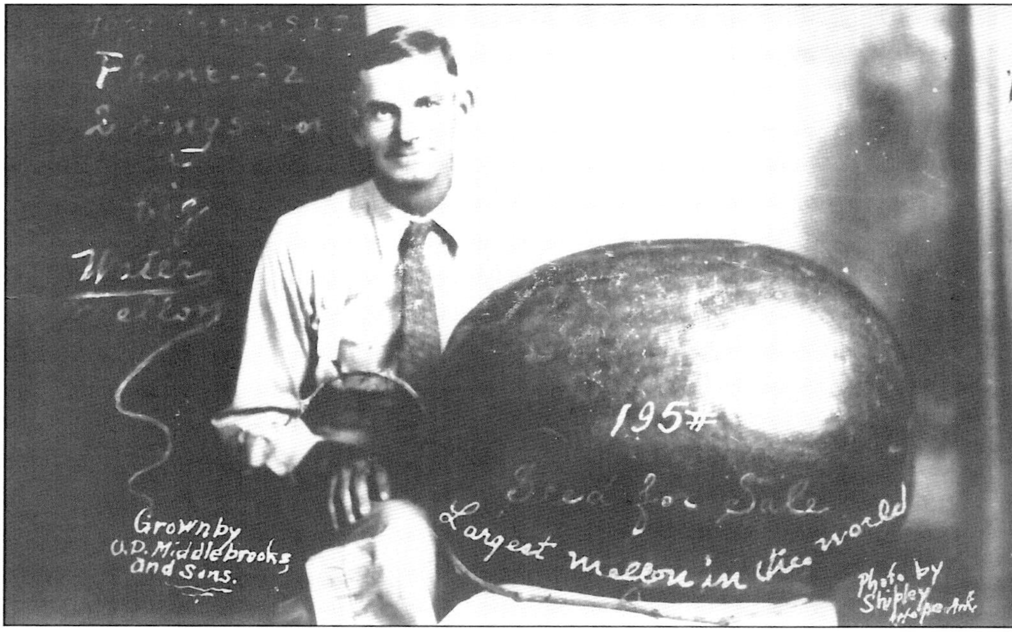

In September 1935, Oscar D. Middlebrooks and his sons, Arnold and Melvin, grew a 195-pound watermelon. The watermelon beat the world record holder at the time and brought the title back to a resident of Hope and Hempstead County with the last record being made by the Middlebrooks family in 1930 for a melon weighing 164.75 pounds. The title lasted for 45 years. (Courtesy of Brad and Annette Rogers.)

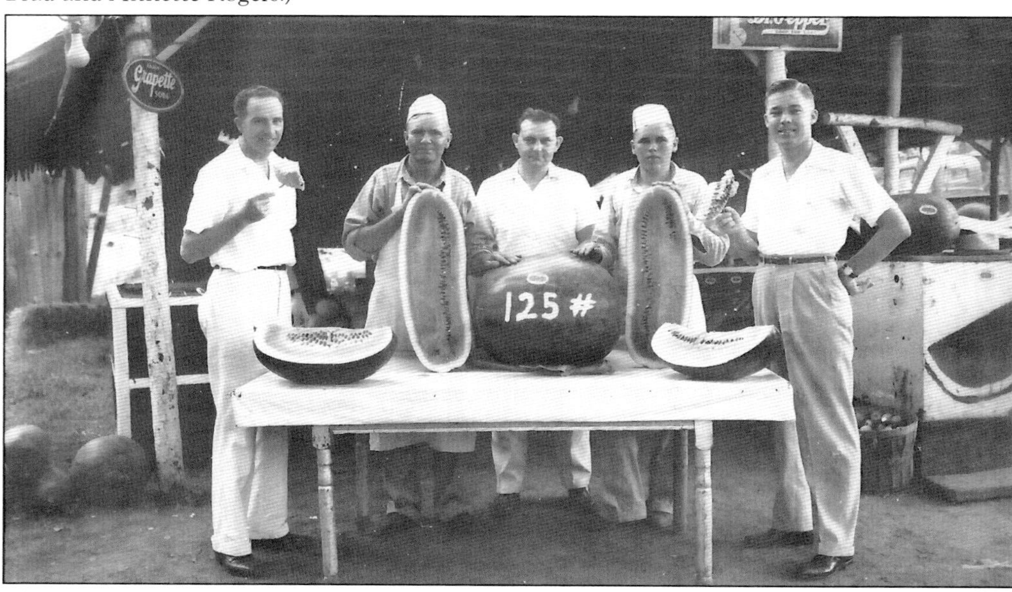

The watermelon became famous and a signature for Hope. By 1948, watermelon stands were popular tourist stops in Hope. At the Smith family stand, from left to right, are Harry Hawthorne, A. A. Smith (owner), Joe Jones, Elmer Smith (A. A.'s son), and Syvelle Burke. The watermelons were grown by Arnold Middlebrooks, son of Oscar D. Middelbrooks. The melon in the center weighs 125 pounds. (Courtesy of HVCM.)

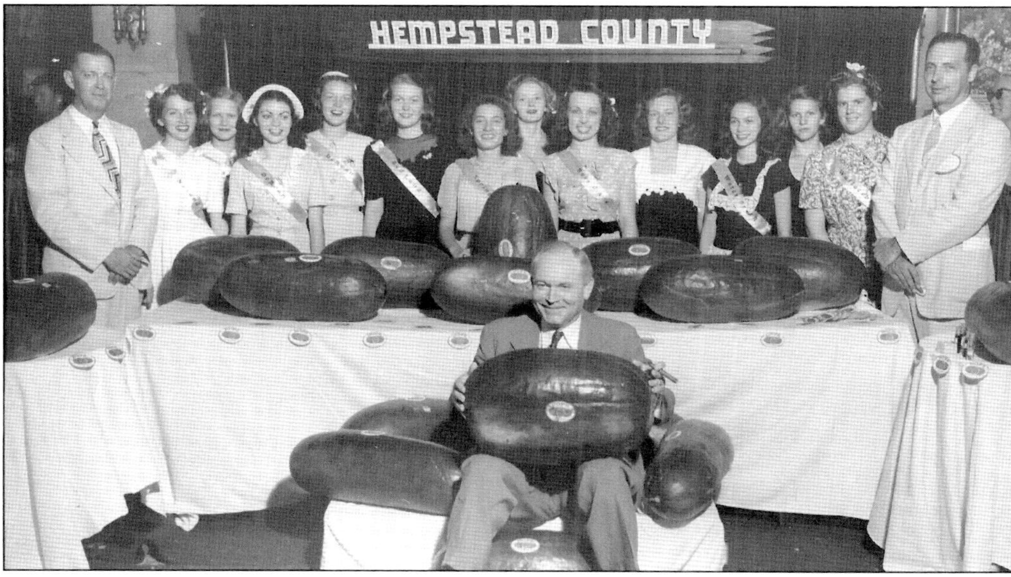

In August 1945, Gov. Ben Laney of Arkansas visited Hope to celebrate the home of the world's largest watermelons. He had Hope watermelons placed on a train and shipped to governors across the country. After a speech to the local Rotary Club at the Barlow Hotel, Laney holds a giant Hope watermelon. Standing behind the governor, from left to right, are Lile Brown (president of the chamber of commerce), Hazel Spillers, Elizabeth Wilson, Mary Carolyn Andrews, Matilda McFaddin, Polly Ann Williams, Betty Ann Benson, Vivianna Beauchamp, Jessica Clarice Brown, Barbara LaGrone, Laura Ann Garanflo, Bonnie Anthony, unidentified, and Mayor Albert Graves. (Courtesy of SARA.)

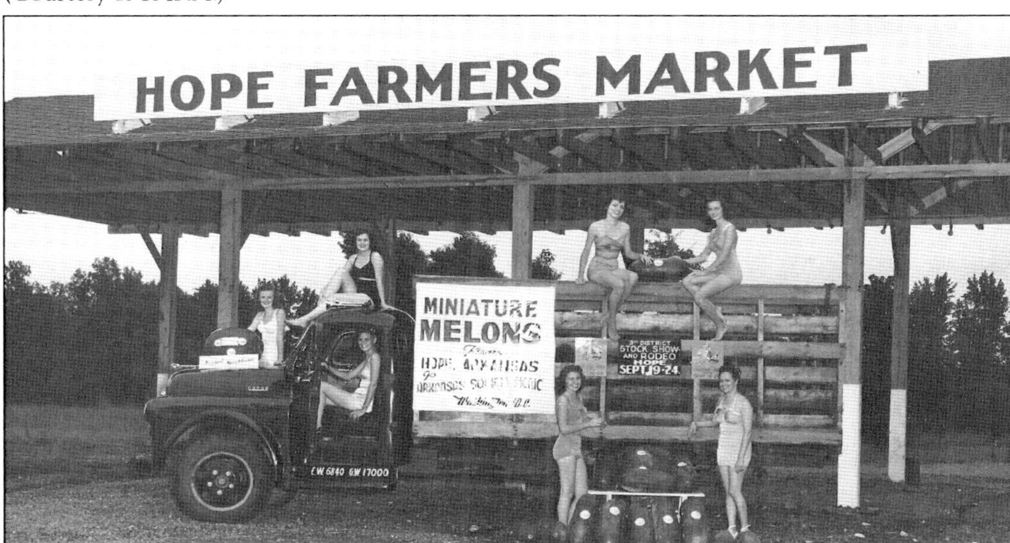

Hope continued to be advertised around the country as the home of the world's largest watermelon. In 1949, a total of 3,000 melons were shipped to Washington, D.C., for the annual picnic of the Arkansas Society on August 28. The ladies are identified, from left to right, as (first row) Rose Tueseth (in truck), Maxine Bowden and Marian Head; (second row) Prudence Parker, Patsy McPherson, Mary Carolyn Andrews, and Laura Ann Garanflo. (Courtesy of HVCM.)

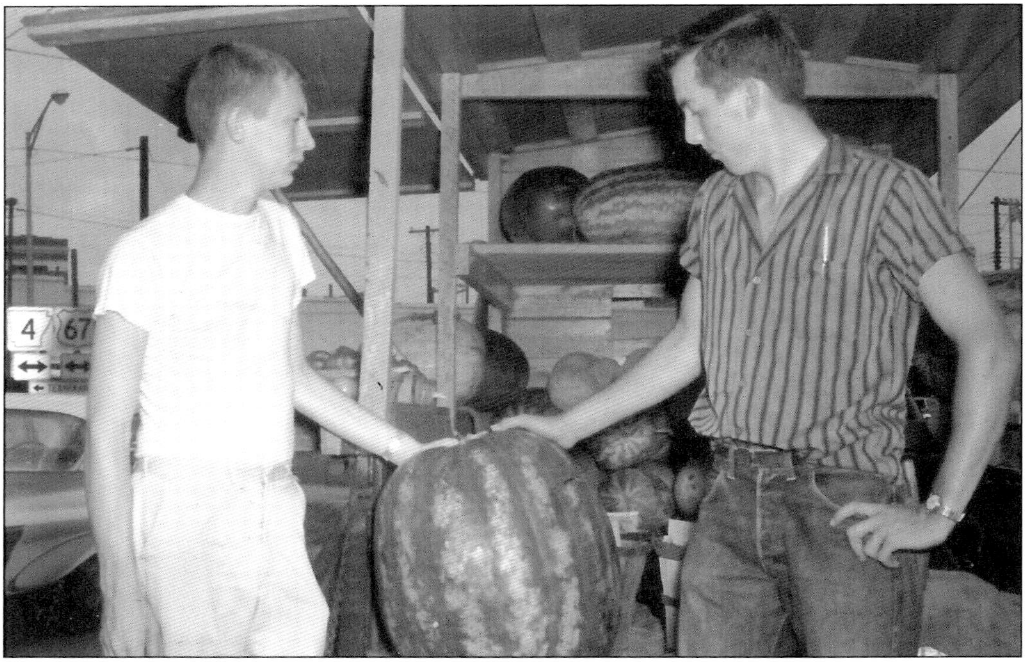

Watermelon stands were always common around Hope in August. Ernie Deane of the *Arkansas Gazette* in Little Rock photographed these two unidentified gentlemen selling 97-pound melons near Main Street in August 1961. They were parked in front of the First Baptist Church on South Main Street, a common site for watermelon stands. (Courtesy of AHC.)

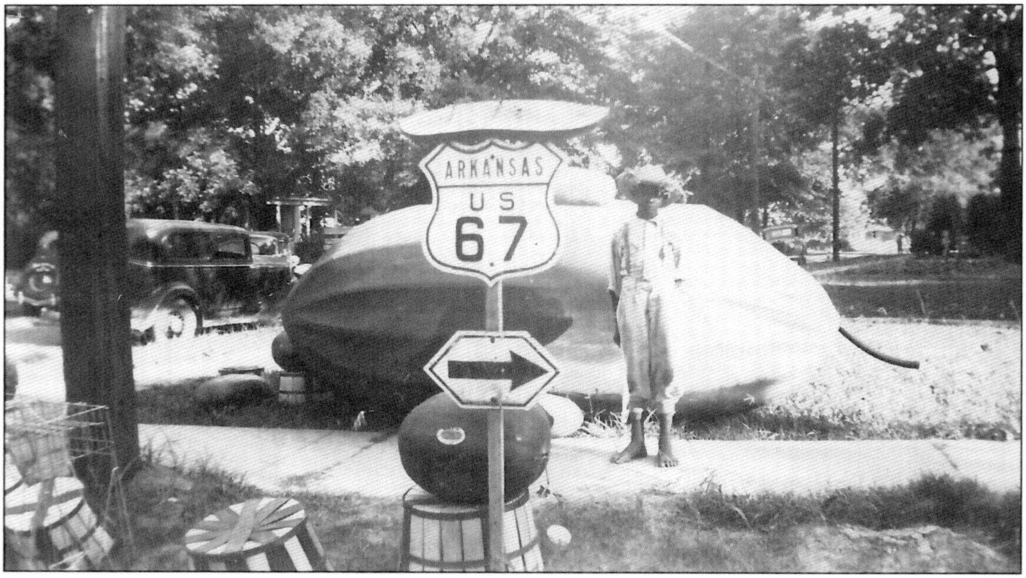

Roadside stands were also situated along U.S. Highway 67, which went directly through Hope. In this 1945 photograph, an unidentified man is selling Hope watermelons and baskets made at the Hope Basket Company. At this time, labels advertising Hope watermelons were printed and placed on all watermelons from Hope. Such a label can be seen on the watermelon in front. (Courtesy of SARA.)

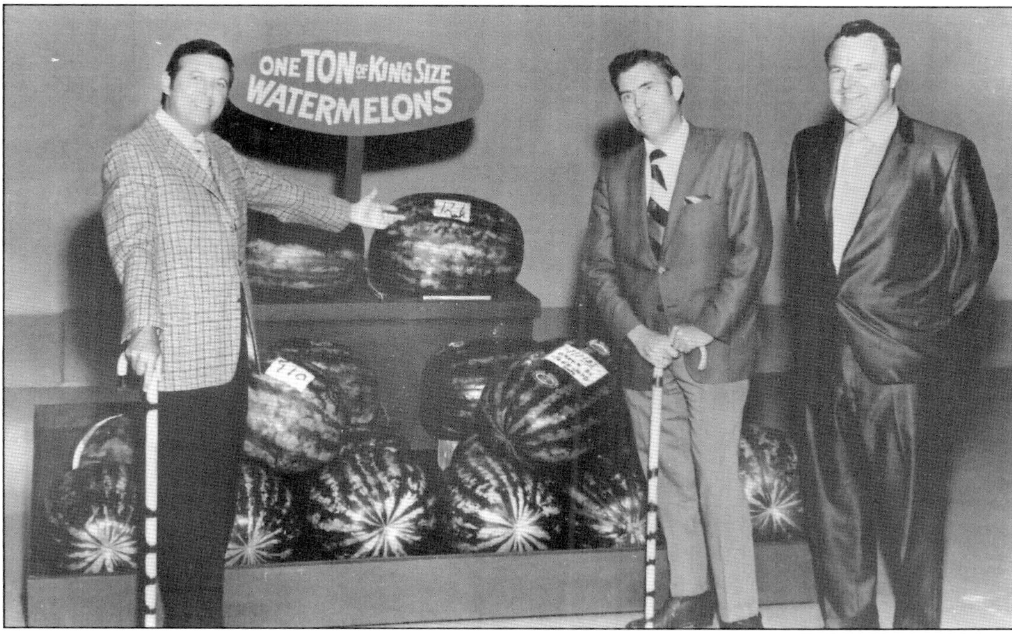

By the 1960s, the intrigue and fervor over Hope watermelons had decreased. The watermelon festivals were no longer celebrated in August. Local leader C. E. "Pod" Rogers Jr. decided to change that. In 1969, he went around the country advertising watermelons from Hope and is seen here (center) along with local businessman Carter Russell (far right) on *Let's Make a Deal*, with Monty Hall (far left). (Courtesy of Brad and Annette Rogers.)

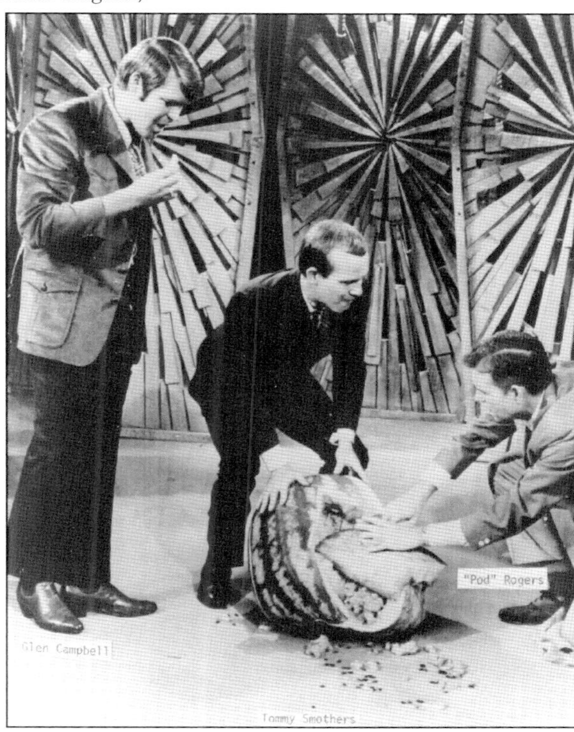

Pod Rogers continued his campaign to raise awareness once more about the home of the world's largest watermelon. In this image from a 1969 appearance Rogers made with Tommy Smothers and Glen Campbell on *The Glen Campbell Goodtime Hour*, the skit features a watermelon from Hope. (Courtesy of Brad and Annette Rogers.)

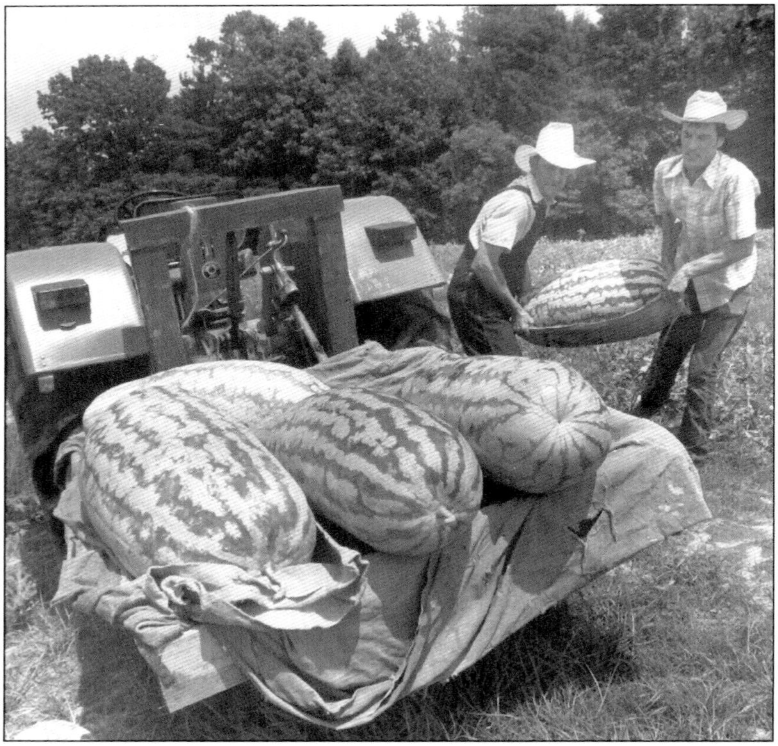

In 1979, the Ivan and Lloyd Bright family continued the Hempstead County tradition and grew a world record–sized watermelon weighing 200 pounds. In 1985, Ivan's grandson, Jason Bright, grew a 260-pound melon. And in 2005, his father, Lloyd, would grow a watermelon weighing 268.8 pounds. Once again, Hope was put back on the map as "Capital of the World's Largest Watermelon." (Courtesy of Brad and Annette Rogers.)

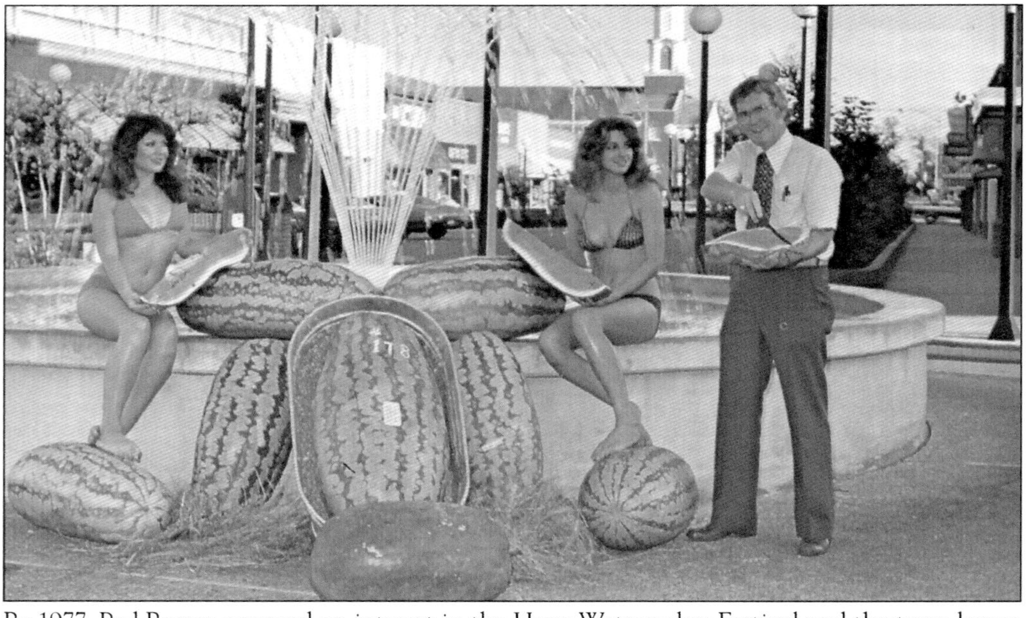

By 1977, Pod Rogers renewed an interest in the Hope Watermelon Festival and the town began hosting a festival every August in the Hope fair park. This photograph became a famous postcard advertising the Hope Watermelon Festival and the city of Hope. Identified, from left to right, are Relynn Little (Watermelon Queen), Kim Wright (Watermelon Queen), and Pod Rogers. (Courtesy of Brad and Annette Rogers.)

Five

Celebrities

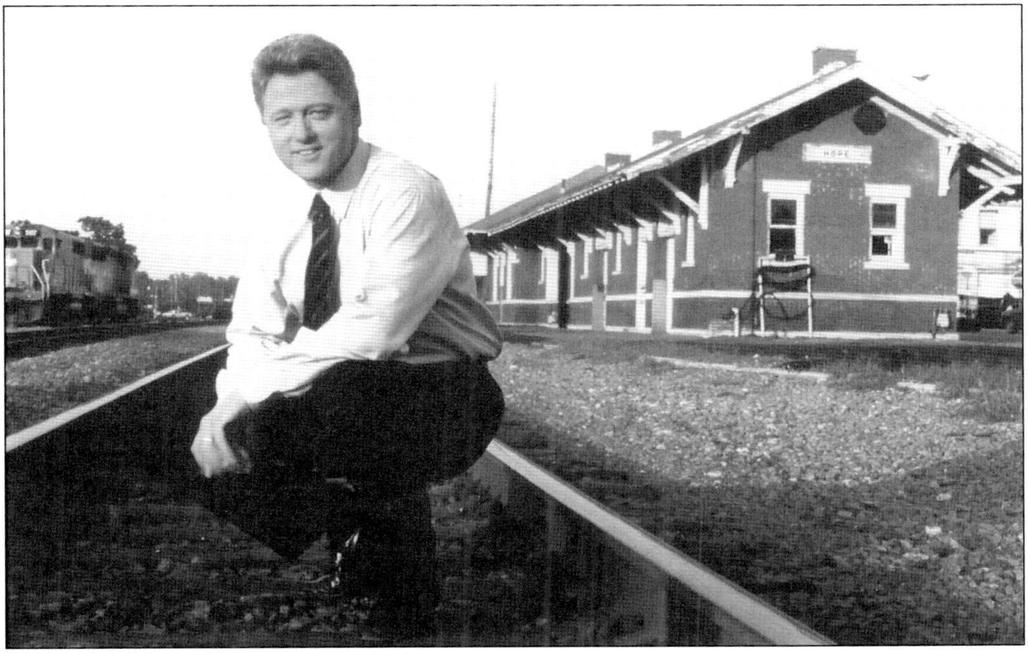

From its beginnings, Hope was a town that provided people with the means to a new life. From its early settlement, the town was known to be a place where someone could strike it rich and make dreams come true. That philosophy may have influenced certain people who lived in Hope. In the early days of his 1992 campaign and recalling his earlier years as a resident, future president Bill Clinton poses near the Hope depot. (Courtesy of the Clinton Presidential Library.)

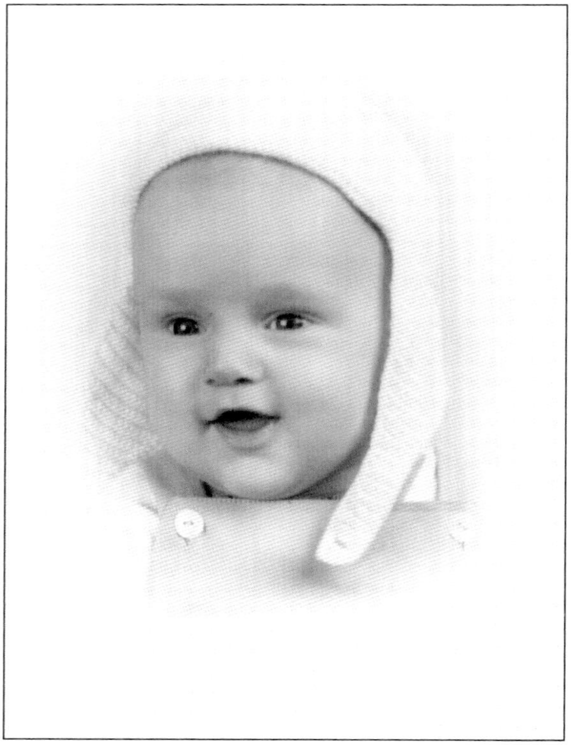

Bill Clinton was born on August 19, 1946, at the Julia Chester Hospital in Hope to Virginia Kelly and was named William Jefferson Blythe III, after his father. He did not take his stepfather's surname, Clinton, until he turned 14. (Courtesy of HVCM.)

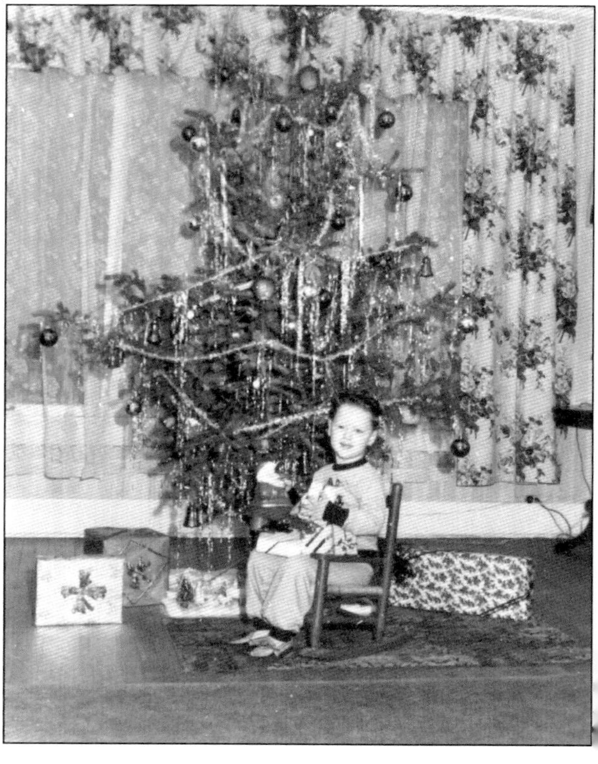

Bill Clinton enjoys a Christmas at the Hervey Street home of his grandparents, Eldridge and Edith Cassidy, where he and his mother lived for the first four years of his life. When he would play outside, he would sometimes play with next-door neighbor Vince Foster. (Courtesy of HVCM.)

At age five, Bill Clinton broke his left leg above the knee while playing jump rope at Marie Purkins's kindergarten. He had forgotten to take off his cowboy boots and the left boot got hung on the rope. He was placed in the hospital for a time, where his mother, Virginia Kelly, sits at his bedside. (Courtesy of HVCM.)

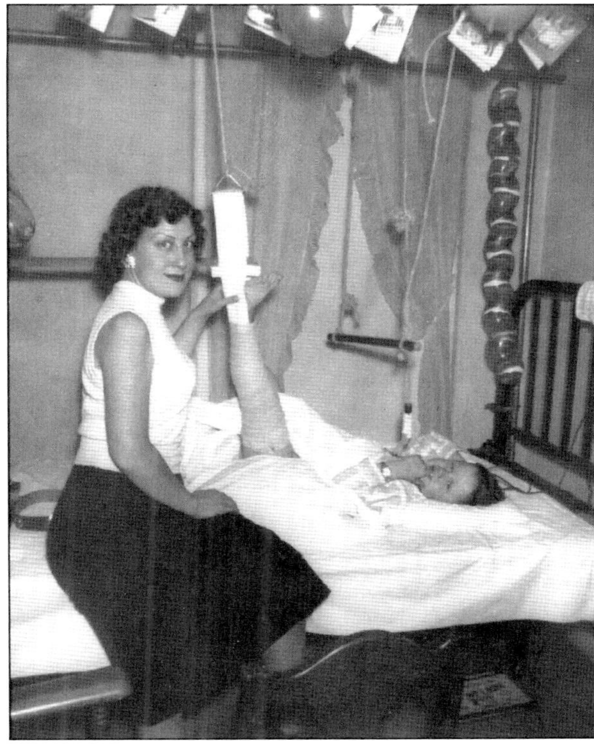

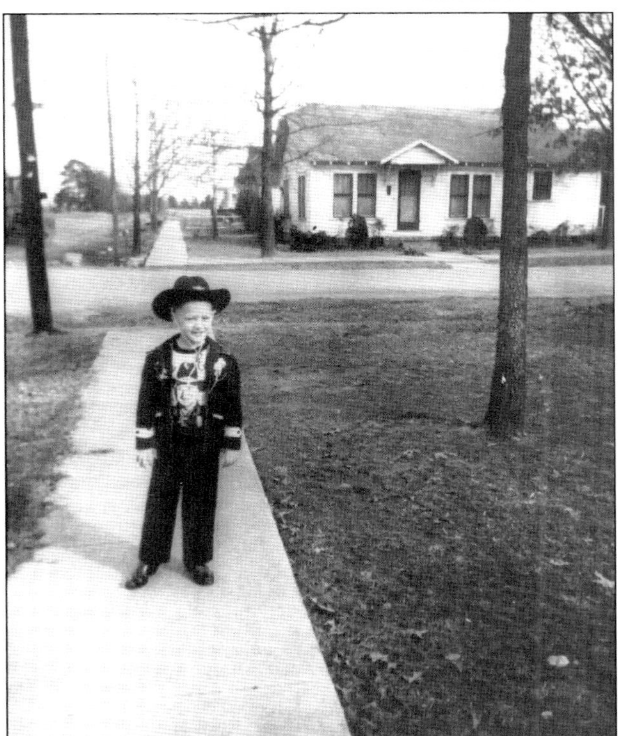

By 1950, cowboys were the heroes of the day. At age four, Bill Clinton, his mother, and new father, Roger Clinton, moved into a house in the expanding suburbs of Hope at 321 Thirteenth Street. Bill Clinton is seen here wearing his cowboy suit outside the house. (Courtesy of HVCM.)

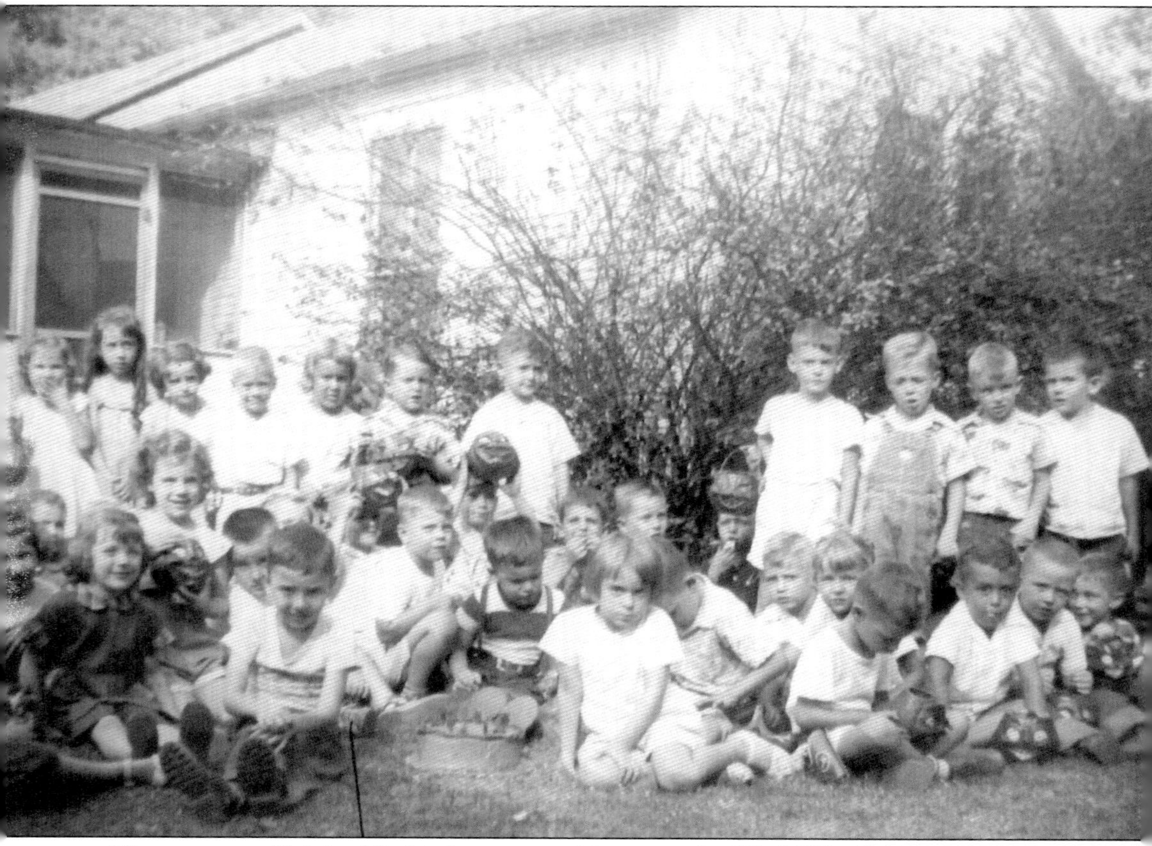

There was no official public kindergarten in Hope just after World War II. Many residents of town sent their children to a local private kindergarten run by Marie Purkins. In 1951, the children celebrating Larry Thrash's fifth birthday pose for a picture. They are, from left to right, (first row) Rose Ann Williams, unidentified, Diane Ellis, Phala Brown, Joe Purvis, Larry Thrash, unidentified, Mack McLarty, Richard McDowell, George Wright, four unidentified, Carter Hardage, Mary Beth Allen, Bob Trout, Tim Holt, Al Weisenberger, and Ricky Butler; (second row) Jan Ellis, Linda Thrash, unidentified, Johnny Anthony, Susan Cook, Jack Caldwell, Bill Clinton, Dan Jones, unidentified, Buddy Anthony, Charles Beyerley, and unidentified. (Courtesy of HVCM.)

The son of Dorsey W. and Mae Huckabee, Mike Huckabee was born August 24, 1955, in Hope. His father was in the Hope Fire Department, and his mother worked at Louisiana Transit Company. This is a photograph of Huckabee in eighth grade. (Courtesy of HVCM.)

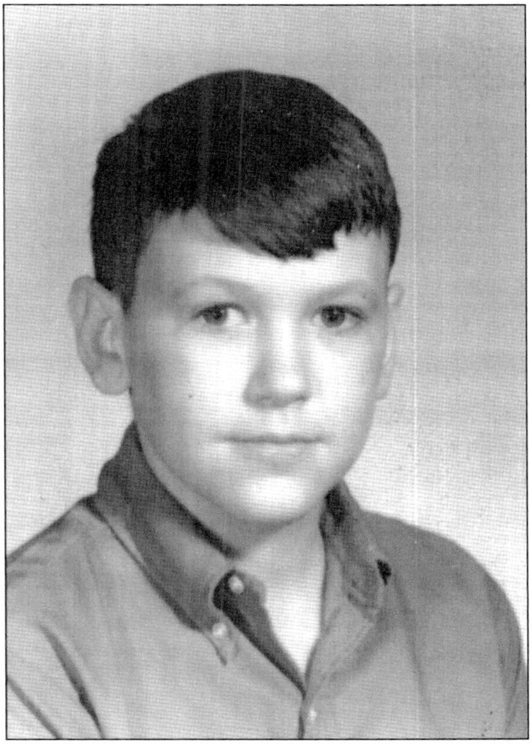

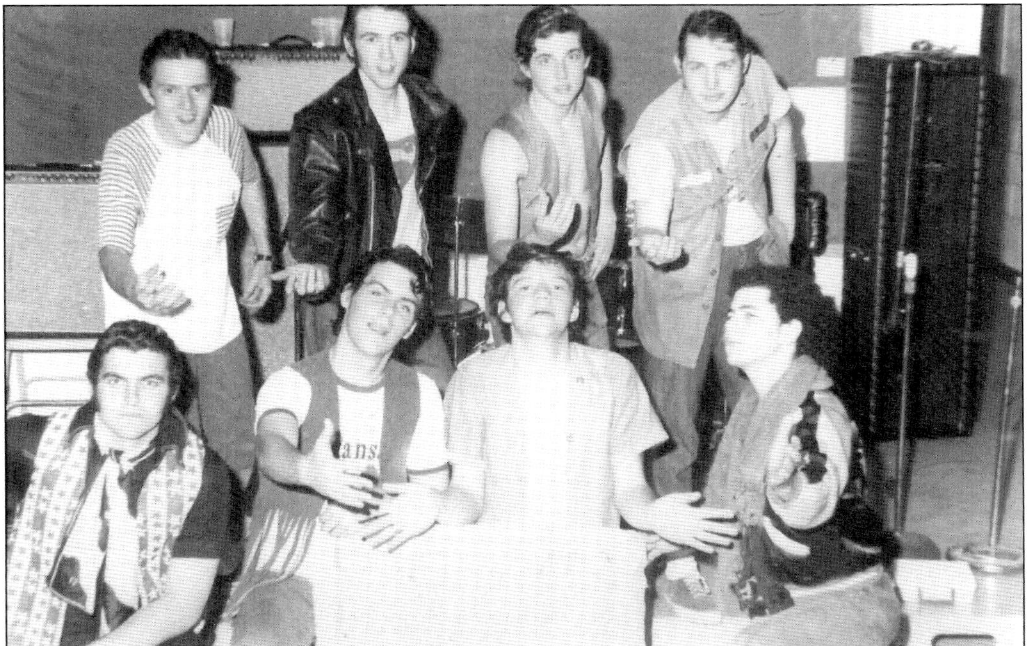

Mike Huckabee, from the very beginning of his life, enjoyed music and playing a guitar. While in high school, he and some friends formed the Bois D'Arc Boogie Band, named for a lake southwest of Hope. Huckabee is standing in the back row, second from left. (Courtesy of HVCM.)

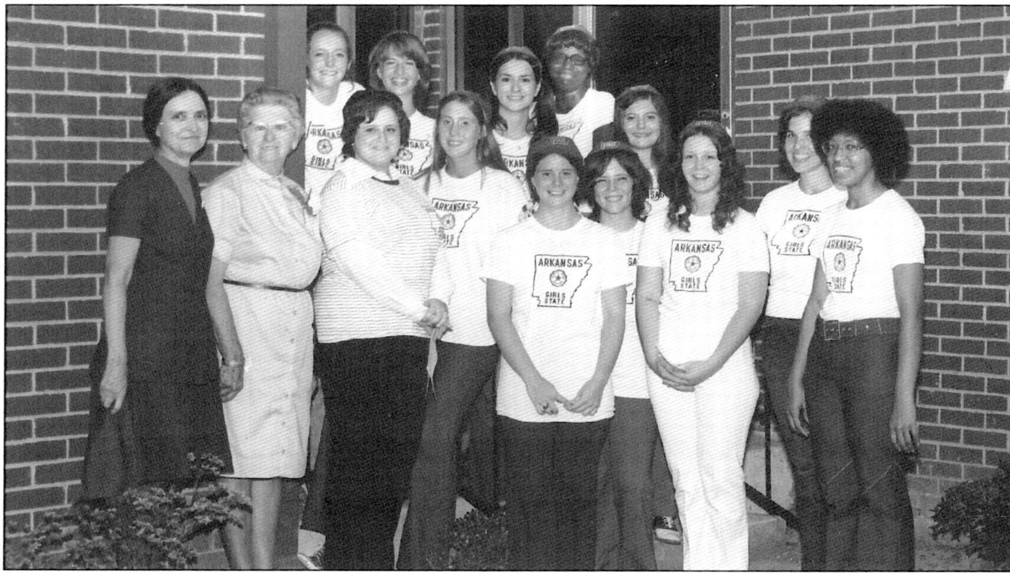

In the summer of 1972, Mike Huckabee attended Boys State, where he was elected governor. His future wife, Janet McCain, went to Girls State as part of the Hope High School delegation in this photograph. They are, from left to right, (first row) Mary Nell Turner (sponsor), Claudia Kuykendall (sponsor), Mary Jane Reynga (sponsor), Janet McCain (Huckabee), Mary Nell Branch, Debbie Impson, Patti Page, Catherine Stuart, and Kathy Graves; (second row) Judy Reynga, Debbie Crank, Sue Butler, Sharolette Hidles, and Betty Ruth Honeycutt. (Courtesy of HVCM.)

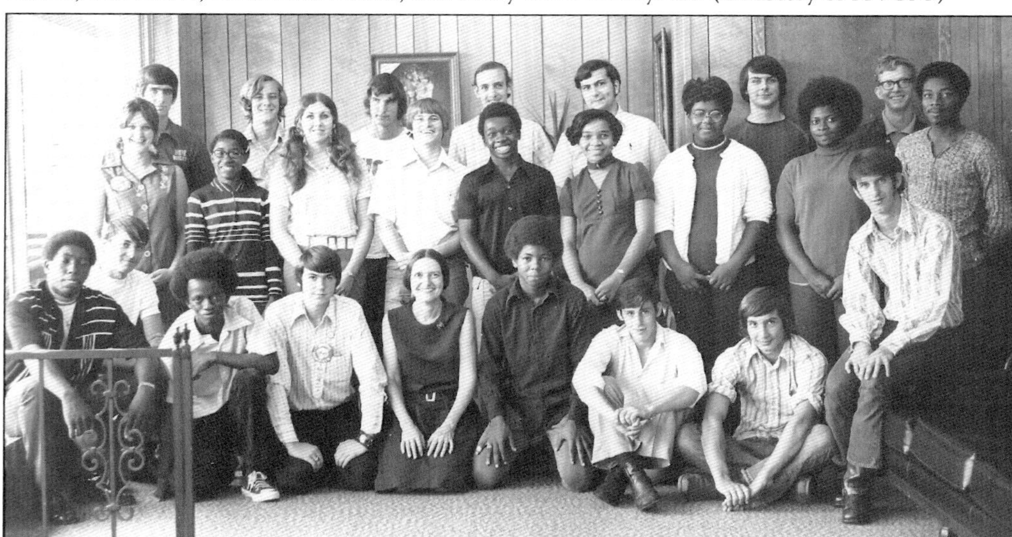

Because of their good conduct, Mike Huckabee's homeroom teacher, Mary Nell Turner, took the senior class to get a group photograph in 1973. Identified are, from left to right, (first row) Joe Stuart, Tony Pettit, Ronald Carter, Mike Huckabee, teacher Mary Nell Turner, James Stuart, Ray Gove, Mike Newton, and Don Lively; (second row) Debra Richardson, Darlene Dixon, Kathy Cox, David Baker, Eddie Ricky Brown, Nancy Palmer, Patricia English, Eunice Mays, and Sim Walker; (third row) Ricky Hart, Ray King, Randy Biddle, Russell Plumley, Verne Wickliffe, Tommy Russell, and Perry Henley. (Courtesy of HVCM.)

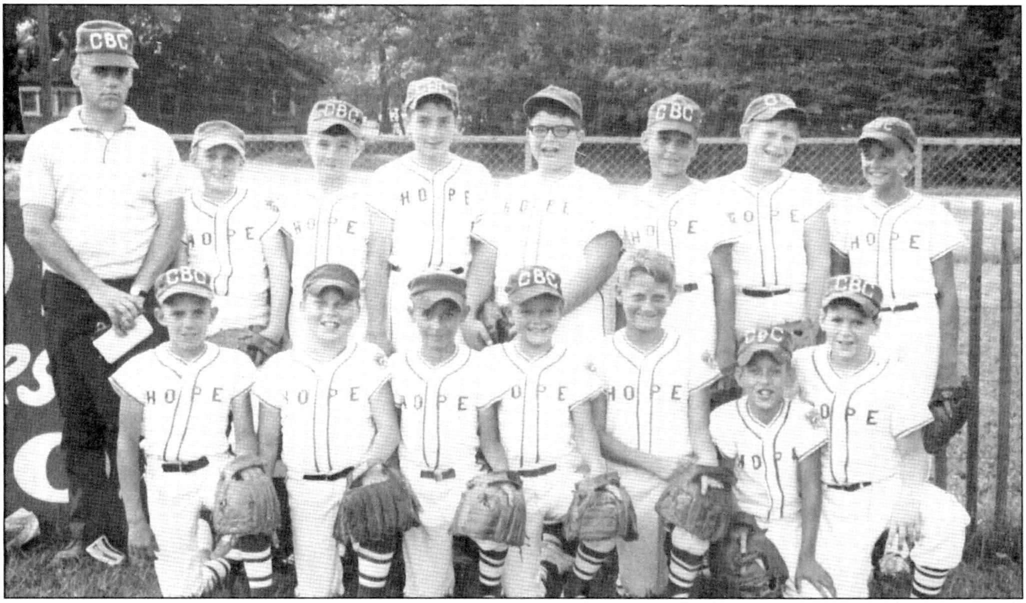

Mike Huckabee was involved in different community activities as a child, such as the Little League baseball team sponsored by the Century Bible Class in Hope around 1967. Team members are, from left to right, (first row) D. Hamilton, K. Rowe, T. Pettit, T. McCoy, R. McBay, C. Rhodes, and Mike Huckabee; (second row) Jim Gunter (coach), R. Smith, D. Sanders, R. Watterson, D. Williams, D. McCoy, M. Treat, and J. Barker. (Courtesy of Jim Gunter.)

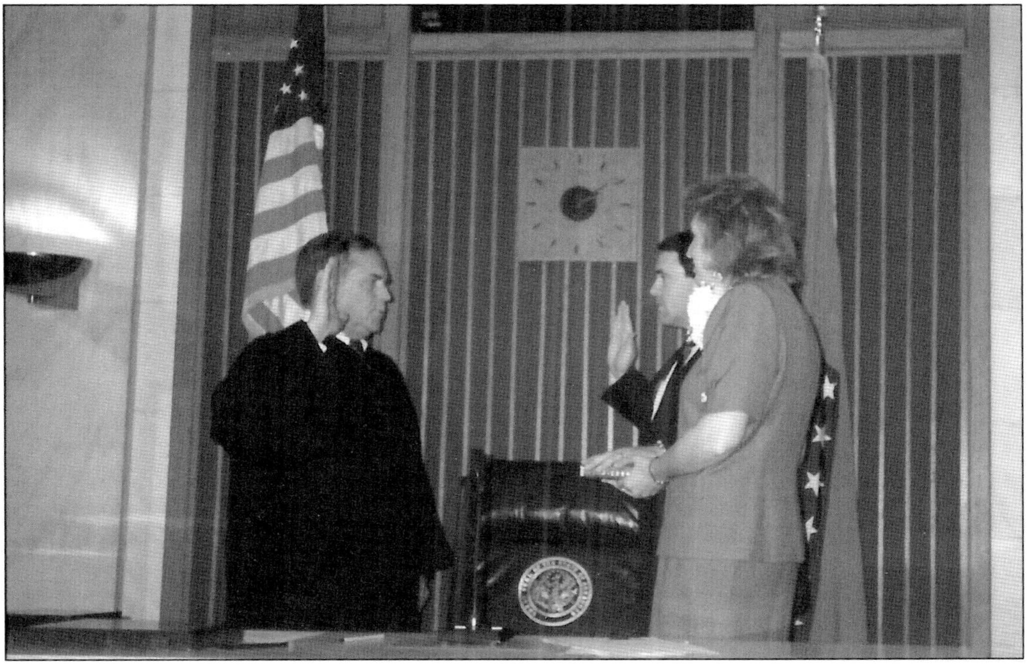

In 1993, Mike Huckabee is sworn in as lieutenant governor of Arkansas by his former Little League baseball coach, Chancery judge Jim Gunter of Arkansas' 8th Judicial District. His wife, Janet Huckabee, stands beside him at the state capitol in Little Rock. (Courtesy of Jim Gunter.)

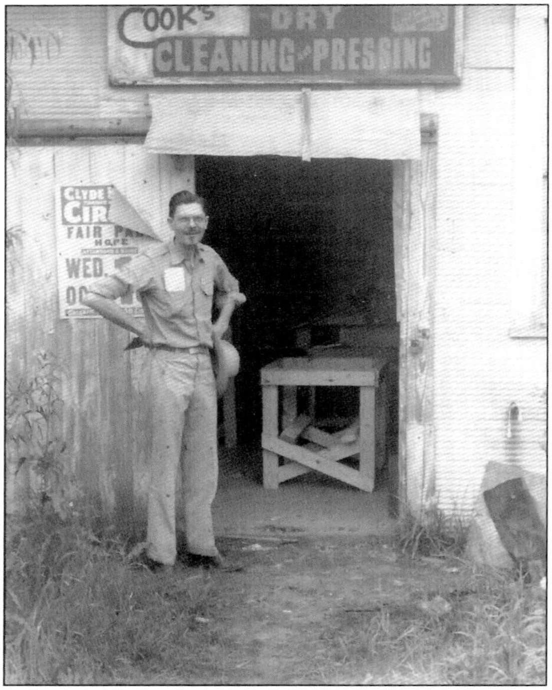

Paul Klipsch served as an ordnance officer at the Southwest Proving Ground during World War II, reaching the rank of lieutenant colonel. After leaving the service, he fulfilled his desire to make speakers. He started his factory, seen here in 1946, in a shed behind Cook's White Star Laundry in Hope. (Courtesy of SARA.)

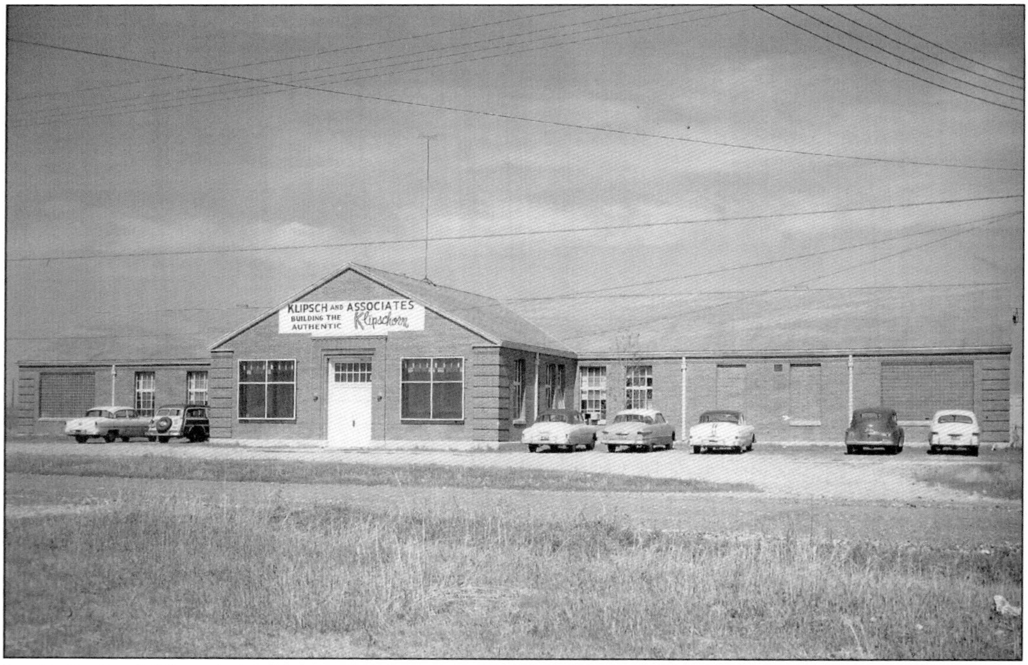

By 1950, Paul Klipsch had moved the factory back to the proving ground area north of Hope and used some of the old wartime buildings as his factory. During the 1950s, his company expanded into a leading manufacturer of quality speakers known worldwide. The Klipschorn speaker is considered by many to be the best loudspeakers in the world and has been in production for over 50 years. (Courtesy of SARA.)

Patsy Montana, originally Ruby Blevins, lived for most of her childhood in Hope, where her father worked for the post office. Ruby graduated from Hope High School in 1928. Here she is seen at age 16, already demonstrating her music skills. (Courtesy of Mark Keith.)

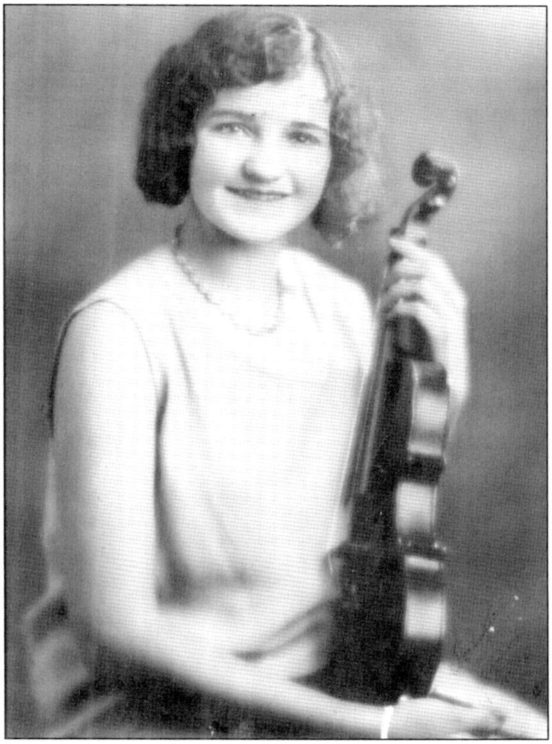

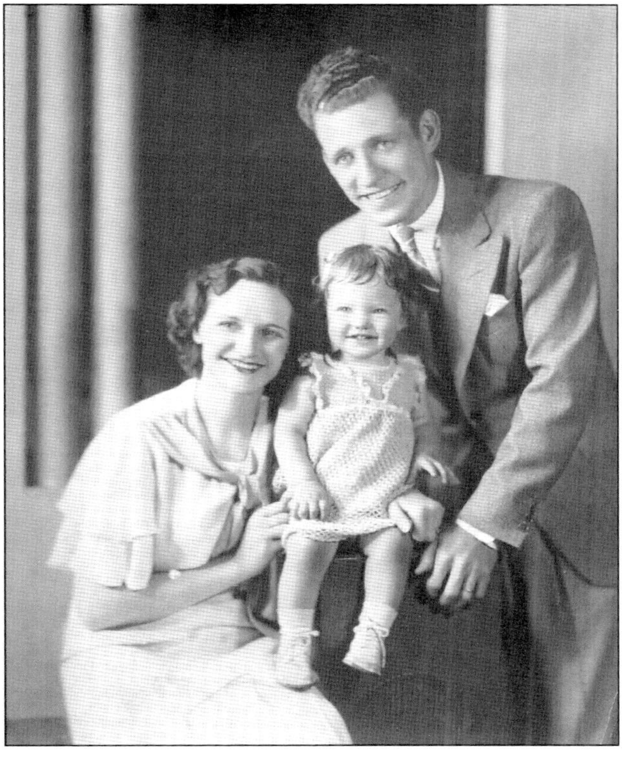

After graduation, Ruby Blevins went to work on a career in country music and took the stage name "Patsy Montana." In this 1935 photograph, she poses with her husband, Paul Rose, and their daughter, Beverly. (Courtesy of Mark Keith.)

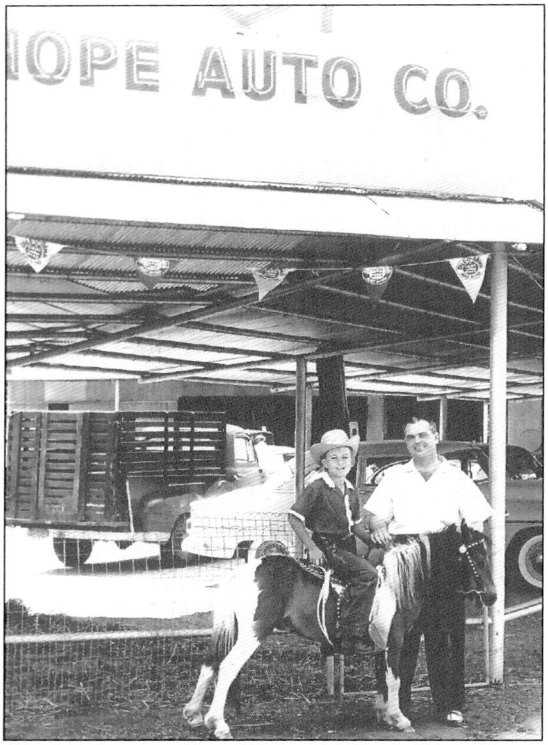

Thomas Franklin "Mack" McLarty III was born on June 14, 1946, to Thomas F. Jr. and Helen Hesterly McLarty. Thomas F. McLarty Jr. owned and operated the Hope Motor Company, a Ford dealership, and Helen became the first woman named to the Arkansas Industrial Development Commission. Mack is seen in this photograph in 1958 with his father at the family business. (Courtesy of Mack McLarty.)

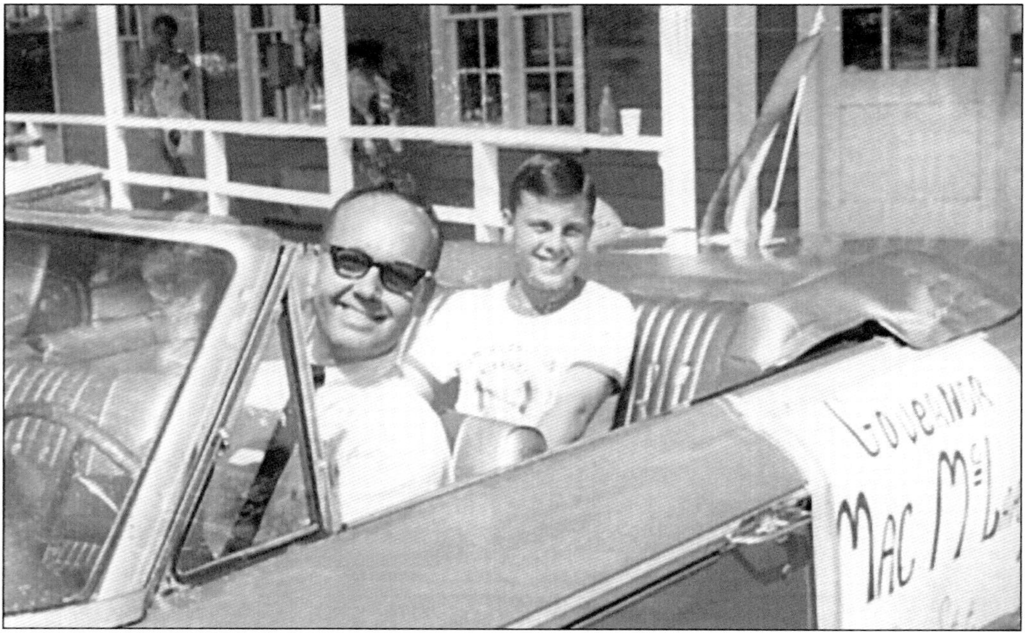

Mack McLarty graduated from Hope High School in 1964. In this 1963 photograph, he is escorted by local civic leader and businessman George Frazier after his election as governor of Arkansas Boys State. McLarty would go on to become the first Arkansan to serve as White House chief of staff, under Pres. Bill Clinton from 1993 to 1994. (Courtesy of Mack McLarty.)

INDEX